Curriculum and Imagination

The story of curriculum theory and development over the last fifty years is one of a lack of imagination, dominated by the results-driven "objectives model" of curriculum, judging effectiveness through exam results and league tables.

Curriculum and Imagination describes an alternative "process" model for designing, developing, implementing and evaluating curriculum, suggesting that curriculum may be designed by specifying an educational process which contains key principles of procedure.

This comprehensive and authoritative book:

- offers a practical and theoretical plan for curriculum-making without objectives;
- shows that a curriculum can be best planned and developed at school level by teachers adopting an action research role;
- complements the spirit and reality of much of the teaching profession today, embracing the fact that there is a degree of intuition and critical judgement in the work of educators;
- presents empirical evidence on teachers' human values.

Curriculum and Imagination provides a rational and logical alternative for all educators who plan curriculum but do not wish to be held captive by a mechanistic "ends-means" notion of educational planning. Anyone studying or teaching curriculum studies, or involved in education or educational planning, will find this important new book fascinating reading.

James McKernan is Professor of Education at East Carolina University, a constituent institution of the University of North Carolina. He has authored and edited several scholarly books and has several decades of educational experience in Europe and North America.

Curriculum and Imagination

Process theory, pedagogy and action research

James McKernan

Routledge
Taylor & Francis Group

LONDON AND NEW YORK

First published 2008
by Routledge
2 Park Square, Milton Park, Abingdon, Oxon OX14 4RN

Simultaneously published in the USA and Canada
by Routledge
270 Madison Ave, New York, NY 10016

*Routledge is an imprint of the Taylor & Francis Group, an informa
business*

© 2008 J. McKernan

Typeset in Garamond by
Book Now Ltd, London
Printed and bound in Great Britain by
TJ International Ltd, Padstow, Cornwall

British Library Cataloguing in Publication Data
A catalogue record for this book is available from the British
Library

Library of Congress Cataloging in Publication Data
McKernan, James.
Curriculum and imagination: process theory, pedagogy and action
research/James McKernan.
p. cm.
Includes bibliographical references and indexes.
1. Curriculum planning. 2. Action research. 3. Critical pedagogy.
I. Title.
LB2806.15.M393 2007
375.001—dc22   2006100286

ISBN10: 0–415–41337–0 (hbk)
ISBN10: 0–415–41338–9 (pbk)
ISBN10: 0–203–94693–6 (ebk)

ISBN13: 978–0–415–41337–4 (hbk)
ISBN13: 978–0–415–41338–1 (pbk)
ISBN13: 978–0–203–94693–0 (ebk)

March 10, 2008

This book is dedicated to the
memory of Lawrence Stenhouse
(1926–82),
a curriculum Grand Master,
who gave curriculum research and development back to teachers.
Formerly Professor of Education, Director and Founder Member,
Centre for Applied Research in Education,
University of East Anglia, Norwich, England.

Contents

Tables

Preface

All educators have a passion to understand their work in curriculum. The field of curriculum studies has been a growth area of inquiry in recent decades in both the USA and United Kingdom. This is a book about how to design a curriculum, without objectives, on sound educational and rational values. It thus invites educators to the exercise of their art, not simply their managerial talent or technology. Amidst mutterings of thunder, teachers as artists still labor in pursuit of curriculum design and execution.

This is not a book which offers a critical, comprehensive review of the large corpus of curriculum literature. A review of a large number of curriculum books has been completed (Schubert, 1980; Schubert *et al.*, 2002). Sadly, Schubert did not take full account of the many curriculum books external to the USA, notably those in Europe, where a renaissance was taking place in curriculum work. There is a "transatlantic divide," I argue, in which American work is known in the USA, and on the other side of the ocean a different literature arrests those who think on the topic. The political economy of publishing as an enterprise contributes to this situation, despite noble efforts by publications such as the *Journal of Curriculum Studies* to bridge this divide since 1968. Lawrence Stenhouse, upon whom the model developed in this book rests, interestingly, contributed to the first volume of the *Journal of Curriculum Studies*.

A defining characteristic of this work is the attempt to plan without objectives educational experiences and utilize action research in this educational experience. No other book known to this writer has used a "process-inquiry" theory to promote curriculum improvement and linked this with action research as a form of procedural practical improvement. The value of action research is the provision of practical knowledge on which professional reasoning might be based.

One of the chief features of curriculum in the past one hundred years has been a lack of imagination in curriculum design. Since the early twentieth century, the dominant model has been a "technical" and managerial style of ends-means rational planning, by instructional-behavioral objectives. This age of efficiency and technical-ends-means planning began in the USA in earnest with Franklin Bobbitt in 1918 with the publication of *The Curriculum*, which advocated for the use of "activity analysis" and human performance outcomes that all good citizens would need to know, or be able to do. Bobbitt wanted schools to efficiently use plant and resources on a peculiarly engineering model of schooling.

During the mid-twentieth-century period, a more "practical" number of theorists pointed to the fact that curriculum development was a social and cultural practice and modes of deliberation and practical reason were required (Smith *et al.*, 1957; Schwab, 1969; Skilbeck, 1976; Reid, 1978). The curriculum paradigm was labeled as "moribund" by Joseph Schwab in 1969 and, today, the situation has become a monopoly of various forms of technical rationality and the objectives model at all levels, in most countries. The political context of curriculum planning, and the reasons why this model has been accepted, almost uncritically, require examination. The "objectives model" has been a monopolistic force, theoretically speaking, and has contributed to a stagnant status for curriculum theory.

The "critical" educationalist theorists emerged with a philosophic discourse linked with philosophy, social justice and equality enhancement through education and in the social sciences (Habermas, 1972; Gadamer, 1980). This was extended to education with equality-driven analyses of power and control and the over-emphasis on technical rationality, managerialism and social inequality (Freire, 1972; Apple, 1979; Carr and Kemmis, 1986). Some linked critical theory to an emancipatory teacher-researcher role (Stenhouse, 1975; Carr and Kemmis, 1986; Elliott, 1991; McKernan, 1996), while others formulated personal and expressive alternatives using conflict, existentialist, humanistic, postmodern and gender theories. Not all of which were interested in matters of curriculum design and theory. Not all of which were aimed at reforming schools in the USA, or in the United Kingdom.

A theory of curriculum is consistent with the meaning of the word education: "to lead out from ignorance." We must proceed in directions that are worthy. The main argument in this book is that a rational alternative process-inquiry model of curriculum can be employed to develop, implement and evaluate curriculum on a logic and pedagogy other than that of the dominant objectives model of curriculum planning by pre-specified outcomes. I argue that the objectives model contains serious flaws when designing programs of education, but does serve a limited utility when it comes to programs of training and instruction. I am not taking a content substantive position here – that some subjects or content is better than some other selection. That decision is always up to local authorities I believe. I am simply arguing that a process approach is more suitable than an objectives approach.

This book offers a practical and theoretical plan for curriculum-making without objectives. It concurs with the spirit and reality of the teaching profession today. A curriculum, like teaching, may be considered an "art."

There is a degree of intuition, creativity, situational understanding and practical and critical judgment in the work of educators who make professional decisions about their day-to-day work. Elliot Eisner has remarked that:

> Teachers are more like orchestra conductors than technicians. They need rules of thumb and educational imagination, not scientific prescription.
>
> (1983: 5)

This work represents several decades of personal experience in Northern Ireland, the Republic of Ireland and the USA in curriculum research and instruction. The book offers an alternative model for curriculum design: a process-inquiry model. The "Process Model," first advanced by Lawrence Stenhouse (1975), begins by suggesting that, as an alternative to planning by objectives, curriculum may be designed in a rational way by specifying an educational process which contains key principles of procedure, organized by a logic which is immanent in the conduct of education itself, and researched by an action inquiry educator. It is significant to note that before the twentieth century the objectives model of design did not exist. Educational psychology with its penchant for the measurement of behavior change is responsible, largely, for the current status of curriculum planning. It is time to go back to the rough ground and clear out the mediocrity. Such is the way of culture.

Principles for selecting content, for teaching and for evaluation of students are discussed. Thus, the process-inquiry model argues that a curriculum can be planned by a strategy other than by the ends-means model of stating pre-specified objectives or intended learning outcomes. It is valuable because it has educational values and processes, rather than outcomes, as its mission.

The principal reason for writing this book is to provide a rational and logical alternative to all educators, whether university professors, or classroom teachers, and others with an educational responsibility, who plan curriculum and do not wish to be held captive by a mechanistic, ends-means notion of educational planning in the form of the dominant objectives model. I understand the purpose of curriculum development to be that of extending alternatives to educators. Making decisions about pupil learning, pedagogy and evaluation invites the very best of the human imagination, for the curriculum is the most formal plan for educational experiences to happen. The provision of rationally planned "curriculum alternatives" and the freedom to decide on matters of content, pedagogy and evaluation need to remain with each educator, in each school.

In this work, I shall argue that a new and revitalized National Schools Curriculum Council, managed by educators and with the power to innovate, research, experiment and even forge policy, is urgently required in both the United Kingdom and at State level in the USA.

Another important development has been the political retreat away from teacher professional control towards central government decision-making in both the USA and United Kingdom. To wit, the demise of the Schools Council for Curriculum and Examinations in 1984 in the United Kingdom and Federal accountability legislation to control how much of what subjects gets learned. Sadly many educators, supervisors and even superintendents of local school districts agree the policies couched in the language of the *No Child Left Behind* law really endorses a mode of mediocrity that many believe results in *No Child Gets Ahead.*

Modes of planning curriculum have changed little in the past century. Tanner and Tanner (2007: 142) argue that the Tyler rationale, or objectives design model, is the standard for the field and "conversion to another model or paradigm awaits another revolution in the curriculum field." A paradigm is the standard acceptable set of procedures for doing work in a given field. This book is opposed to this technical/ends-means paradigm for planning and designing educational experiences. The position adopted here is that one may plan rationally without specific "objectives" by identifying worthwhile aims, procedures and research activities.

While conscious that any labeling of perspectives is very crude (as it often excludes, or overlaps) there would appear to be at least three domains of curriculum theory. First, the "technical" orientation, which would include authors such as Thorndike, Bobbitt, Charters, Tyler, Bloom, Popham, Taba and Beauchamp. Second, the "practical theorists" such as Schwab, Reid, Skilbeck, McCutcheon, Elliott and Walker, who argue that over-reliance on theory is misplaced and that what is required is attention to local and practical problems through sustained, school-based curriculum making.

Schwab, for example, advocated modes he called "practical" and "eclectic" that focus on who does what, when, and with what practical reasons in the practical situation of teaching and learning – a form of situational analysis. Skilbeck (1976) suggested that curriculum-making does not begin with the specification of objectives but rather a broad "situational analysis" of the setting, resources and personnel that must be undertaken as a first step before thinking about curriculum purposes. The aim here is not advancement of theory but improvement of a difficult and concrete problem that will improve practice and decision-making.

Third, arguments from critical theorists and existentialist reconceptualists (Pinar and Grumet, 1981; Pinar et al., 1995) as well as an interdisciplinary cadre of postmodern critics of schooling and some "teacher-researcher" idealists (Stenhouse, 1983; Elliott, 1993) and curriculum are considered. These are not only educationalists and curriculum thinkers but include an international array of philosophers, social scientists and others, some adopting alternative, and sometimes radical, views, such as Paulo Freire, Michael Apple, Henry Giroux, Peter McLaren, Joe Kincheloe, Jonathan Kozol, Pierre Bourdieu and David Gabbard, to name only a few. These critics view schooling as replicating inequalities and advocating against the "reproduction of culture": the reproduction of roles and statuses for those who wield power from one generation to the next. One aim of the critical school is to lay bare the tacit values underpinning educational policies and to engage in consciousness and awareness-raising. Yet, another curriculum book is desperately required to counter the monopoly held by technical rationalists who have dominated curriculum by imposing the behavioral-driven objectives model.

The book has several aims. First, it attempts to provide a perspective quite different from that of the ends-means logic advocated by outcome-based ideas of education. Second, it attempts to more fully inform the role of the teacher as a person committed to educating pupils, or students, by adhering to sound pedagogical "principles of procedure," and by examining the effects of one's curriculum implementation through evaluation conceived as curriculum action research. This work seeks to extend the breakout ideas articulated by Lawrence Stenhouse (1975) and his colleagues in the United Kingdom, and make his theory and practice more widely available. Teaching, curriculum implementation and evaluation are not separate entities but rather distinctly inter-connected. The process-inquiry model for curriculum outlined herein rests on a division of labor that unites teaching with researching one's practice; thus tying curriculum and evaluation together. One of the most confounded situations has been the separation, or division of labor, that exists between the concept of curriculum and that of instruction and evaluation. None should exist, as education suggests a unity of curriculum and instruction: a process that incorporates instruction and evaluation in its totality.

In this book both teaching and a research role for the teacher are focused on educational principles of procedure for realizing curriculum aims as its central foundation. Conceiving curriculum as a research proposal, or educational plan, that needs to be field-tested, the task of those who implement it is to determine its worth and utility. However, its chief contribution is to carefully outline how an educator can develop, and implement, a curriculum through a process-research approach to curriculum development.

Paramount among the tasks facing curriculum planners are: first, the need to select principles of procedure for selecting content; second, the need to research the effects of implementing a defined line of teaching, being faithful to these principles of procedure; third, deciding upon a pattern of organization for a curriculum: is it to be subject, activity or inquiry-discovery based? The idea is to follow the process of education as the basis for a theory of curriculum planning. Should curriculum content be derived from considerations such as society, the subject matter or the students? Alternatively, should curriculum count as the integration of knowledge, skills and values? Fourth, it is imperative that a pedagogy that is consistent with the educational values imbedded in the content be observed in teaching and learning. Finally, principles for improving curriculum through research and evaluation are described. Casting the teacher in the role of the researcher is at once professional and empowering. It is an appropriate role for the educator in an age of expanding teacher professional development.

This work rests on the ideas and philosophy of education presented principally by Richard S. Peters, formerly Professor of Philosophy of Education at the Institute of Education, University of London, an advocate for the analytic philosophy of education (principles of procedure). The book also presents the perspectives and legacy of Lawrence Stenhouse (process model and teacher neutrality), John Elliott (action research), Malcolm Skilbeck (school-based curriculum development), David Jenkins (alternative and qualitative evaluation) and Hugh Sockett (moral-democratic education), all of whom were honed on curriculum work in the United Kingdom. A curious collection of liberal, moral, practical and critical perspectives. I was fortunate to have known these men and to have worked with some of them.

Lawrence Stenhouse claimed that the objectives design model was seriously flawed as being overly instrumental, thereby defeating an essential principle of true education: education counts as being worthwhile for its intrinsic value. That is, education is worthy in its own right, not because it leads extrinsically towards the realization of some end-in-view, or serves some "instrumental" purpose.

Stenhouse worked out his theoretical and practical curriculum positions principally through the development and direction taken in his Humanities Curriculum Project (HCP), designed under the authority of the Schools Council for Curriculum and Examinations in England and Wales during the trial period of 1967–72. The HCP team, directed by Stenhouse, began to develop an innovative pedagogy and conception of curriculum based on what he called a Process Model of design. A colleague of Stenhouse, Hugh Sockett, once remarked that the pedagogy of the project would be its lasting legacy. Pedagogy held a special importance for the project team and its work. Teachers employing a common teaching strategy (neutral chairperson-ship) subjected their evaluation to the adherence of the principles of procedure outlined in the pedagogical strategy using discussion-based humanities work centered around controversial value issues, including a discussion-based strategy focusing on areas of interest such as war, poverty, gender relations and other themes. Thus, the pedagogy became the central focus of an educational process, rather than pre-determined outcomes. Leaning heavily on the intellectual scaffolding of Richard S. Peters, the English philosopher of education, Stenhouse argued that our everyday discourse about education does not assume that we are speaking of aims, or extrinsic outcomes, as so much of the outcomes-based education rhetoric and policy insinuates. Rather, according to Peters, we are referring to a value and set of principles; what he elucidated as principles of procedure that make for a true educational process. Aims refer in this sense to criteria embedded in the disciplines; principles of procedure which are realized "in" having the educational encounter, having an educational experience as it were, rather than as a "result" of an educational encounter. John Elliott (1993) suggests lucidly that many of the early curriculum reform practices embodied this "insight." What Stenhouse, Peters and Elliott have all attempted to do is to illuminate and articulate logic, in the form of an alternative form of practical rationality; a practical science for curriculum improvement, which rested upon a teacher committed to researching his or her professional work and gaining situational understanding of that practice. In brief, one might think of the principles of procedure governing a paradigmatic practice as one's objectives – but these ends are the process and not the product of education. Furthermore, with Dewey, if education is to be preparation for life, reflective citizenship and democracy, then value issues need to be a crucial ingredient in curriculum and thus a central component of content.

I have brought along with the notion of principles of procedure the idea that education is about intelligent action applied in a "critical reality experience." Furthermore, all education contains an ideological stance or preference. The theory here is embedded in the notion of social reconstructionism, which suggests schools as agencies for cultural change, and personal and professional empowerment. At root are principles of Pragmatism. It is of interest to note that Kant first coined the term "pragmaticism"; later on William James took over the concept from C.S. Pierce. Pierce used the term to differentiate his position from that of James. Pierce was interested in the methods and procedures of laboratory science. His argument was that the testing of ideas as hypotheses would attain a specific type of experience and that the purpose of "pragmaticism" (Bentley, 1963: 144–50) was to clarify conceptions of experience. He viewed pragmatism as a temperament.

Action research is a form of inquiry that seeks to solve practical problems, while forwarding human understanding experienced by practitioners. It is a style of research that can be effectively used to test our human actions in educational settings (Elliott, 1991; McKernan, 1996).

We need to begin our curriculum design situations not by asking what objectives we need to attain but rather, what kind of curriculum we need in the new Millennium that is relevant to the lives and intelligent action of our students. Whose interests do the knowledge, skills and dispositions selected for curriculum serve? How do we handle knowledge and value issues in a liberal democratic state? One of the great challenges of our time is to teach for understanding as distinct from memorization and to view education as the construction of personal meaning rather than the reproduction of meaning.

I was very fortunate to have had the experiences of working as a curriculum researcher and developer in Northern Ireland at a time when curriculum development and evaluation were enjoying a reconstructive resurgence in the history of education, particularly the school-based curriculum development reforms and initiatives that were sweeping through the Western European nations at that time. This brought me into contact with thinkers and teachers who substantially contributed to curriculum and theory, including Malcolm Skilbeck, an advocate of social reconstructionist theory long before even this idea was transformed as "critical pedagogy and theory" and school-based democratic curriculum making; David Jenkins, a rare Welsh wit and extraordinary evaluation theorist; and Hugh Sockett, curriculum and educational philosopher. These individuals were all colleagues at the Ulster University in the 1970s. I was very influenced by the curriculum theory of Lawrence Stenhouse, working out of the University of East Anglia at that time, who suggested that one could rationally plan without objectives and who demonstrated this admirably with his Humanities Curriculum Project that was internationally recognized. He also was one of the first to champion the notion of the teacher as researcher, re-constructing the earlier American initiatives at action research to improve school practice and university seminar work (Corey, 1953; Shumsky, 1959) initiated at Teachers College, Columbia University.

I have also been influenced by Professor John Elliott, of the University of East Anglia, who has been a champion of the teacher as action researcher movement internationally. Elliott has steadfastly advocated the teacher as action researcher process as the road to improvement and I am grateful for his rich descriptive accounts and professional collegiality as well as his affable friendship over the years. Elliott worked with Stenhouse on the Humanities Curriculum Project, where many of the teacher-researcher ideas were worked out. This work, with all its limitations, tries to forward this legacy.

Working as a teacher and educator since 1975, and being appreciative of the difficulty of curriculum planning, I have sought alternatives to the tech-nical objectives model on two continents. I believe the absence of clear alternative models of curriculum theory that are followed by schools has led the State Departments of Education to fashion curriculum around an objec-tives design. This is probably due to the dogged belief in a science-rooted idea of behavioral testing, but also to the politics of the paradigm. It is time to publish this reconstructed theory of planning a curriculum without objec-tives and for giving research and development of curriculum back to educators.

This book is offered as an alternative to the dominant objectives design for curriculum. There is a crisis in education in not only America but in the West, generally, that needs addressing. There is thus a sense of urgency about this process model of curriculum planning. What is flawed is the way we plan courses – the internal logic or structure hangs upon a naive belief in reaching targets.

Another set of important issues raised by this book concerns teacher education. The one thing I am certain of is that this book and its ideas are no better than a hypothesis that only demands the test of practical experience. It does not stipulate a blueprint for success. It humbly invites and requests educators to test its value.

Jim McKernan,
Greenville, North Carolina
May, 2007

Acknowledgments

I owe a profound intellectual debt to Lawrence Stenhouse, who first advocated for an educational process model in his curriculum theory work. I was introduced to the work of Lawrence Stenhouse by Professor Hugh T. Sockett, now at George Mason University, my doctoral supervisor at the Ulster University (Professor Stenhouse was External Examiner for my D.Phil thesis on teaching controversial issues). I also wish to acknowledge the influence of Professors Malcolm Skilbeck, David Jenkins and John Elliott, whose democratic notions of schooling, philosophy of education, evaluation and action research have had a lasting impact on my personal curriculum journey. Some of the value survey data contained in Chapter 11 was previously published (2002) as "Value orientations of teacher education students in Ireland, Palestine, Costa Rica and the USA," in *Irish Educational Studies*, 21 (3), Winter: 1–20. Quotations of Lawrence Stenhouse throughout the text used with permission of Harcourt (UK) Publishers. I am grateful for the ideas and support given by Rebekah King, an art teacher at Heide Trask High School, Wallace, North Carolina. Finally, I wish to acknowledge the assistance of my editors at Routledge, Philip Mudd and Lucy Wainwright.

J.A. McKernan
Greenville, North Carolina, USA
2007

Part I

Curriculum

The theoretic domain

Chapter 1

The curriculum and its ideological conceptions

> Definitions of the word *curriculum* do not solve curricular problems; but they do suggest perspectives from which to view them.
>
> Lawrence Stenhouse (1975: 1)

The problem of curriculum, and curriculum design in the main, is not the specification of objectives as targets to be attained by students; and then designing a course of study for achieving those objectives. A curriculum, to be truly educational, will lead the student to unanticipated, rather than predicted, outcomes. The problem of curriculum is rather a matter of experiencing a course of human action created through images and understanding related to the things that truly matter in life. Too many of the things that students experience in the school curriculum do not matter in the living of one's life. It is essentially the development of the powers of understanding in relation to the things that ultimately do count in life that is the real concern for educators and curriculum. A curriculum embodies the planning and implementation of educational experiences through carefully orchestrated procedures made from a judicious selection from the culture. To put it simply, education is not so much about arriving, as in hitting targets, as it is about traveling with passion, and being interested in worthwhile experiences at hand.

The problems of living are not technical concerns of taking a means to an end. They are largely moral, cultural and value-laden. One must choose wisely courses of action that are in harmony and consistent with a unified view of living that has purpose. Learning to choose, and value the "action turn," is central to learners, and teachers, who must develop situational understanding to be men and women of practical reason (McKernan, 2006). The curriculum must, if successful, ignite the human imagination. This idea of a curriculum as a unique and manifest mandate was ably put by Macdonald:

> Curriculum theory is what speaks to us "through it" and what we do is informed by theory; but neither the specific words of theory nor the

specific pedagogical acts of educators are the reality of education. What defines each is the spirit and vision that shines through the surface manifestations.

(Macdonald, 1982: 56)

This is a book about designing curriculum in the absence of objectives. The underpinning idea is to develop a curriculum based on a theory of educational experience, rather than behavior change. The central ingredient is experience, rather than behavior. The primary aim of a curriculum is to enable students to think and to make critically informed choices. William Schubert claims the role of curriculum work is a moral imperative. He put it this way:

> An educator is entrusted with the most serious work that confronts humankind: the development of curricula that enable new generations to contribute to the growth of human beings and society. This means that those who have chosen to devote themselves to curriculum must address the most basic questions that exist. What does it mean to live a good life and how can a just society be created?
>
> (Schubert, 1986: 423)

The curriculum is concerned with what is planned, implemented, taught, learned, evaluated and researched in schools at all levels of education. The word *curriculum* is from the Latin *currere*, meaning "a course to be run, or the running of the course," and usually is defined as the course of study at an educational institution. William Pinar (1975) argues that *currere*, as the Latin infinitive suggests, involves the investigation of the nature of the individual experience of the public: of artifacts, actors, operations, of the educational journey or pilgrimage.

The philosopher Richard S. Peters has argued that education involves the initiation of others into worthwhile activities in a morally acceptable manner (Peters, 1966). A curriculum is the educational policy proposal on offer by a school or college and is composed of the valued knowledge, values, skills and other dispositions that have been intentionally planned. The curriculum supports both training and education. This is a crucial distinction and the curriculum has a place for both. Basketball skills, classroom management techniques or computer processing do not involve development of intellect or mind in any depth and can be organized within an "objectives model" of curriculum as they speak to skills development and fall into a "training" sphere. However, areas that invoke knowledge and understanding, that is induction into forms of knowledge and the development of mind, are the sphere of education as distinct from training. The objectives model of planning is satisfactory for instruction and training but it breaks down in "education," where a "process-inquiry" model is more appropriate. My point is that we are not concerned solely with a cognitive mind development model in speaking of curriculum. In speaking of education we do better to support a process theory rather than a product theory, that is an objectives model of curriculum design. Curriculum can encompass mathematics, history and art as well as building construction and basketball; but not things such as pornography, methods of burglary or tiddlywinks.

In recent years a rather monopolistic view of curriculum design has emerged following the work of behaviorist planners and rational curriculum developers who have based their approach largely on the notion of behaviorist theory and, more specifically, planning by measurable outcomes. Franklin Bobbitt first introduced this concept of objectives into curriculum planning (Bobbitt, 1918, 1924), and Ralph Tyler (1949) popularized this idea for behavioral objectives with his simple syllabus for a course at the University of Chicago titled *Basic Principles for Curriculum and Instruction*. It is instructive to note in all fairness that Tyler does not merely describe how a curriculum actually occurs but how he thinks it ought to be developed.

This technical perspective is not only a curriculum problem but also a problem for teacher education. Giroux and McLaren boldly submit:

> One of the great failures of North American education has been its inability seriously to threaten, or eventually replace, the prevailing paradigm of teacher as formal classroom manager with the more emancipatory model of the teacher as critical theorist.
>
> (Giroux and McLaren, 1986: 286)

There are also political and cultural reasons for the way curriculum is mandated and implemented at present. The neoconservatives have sold policy-makers the notion that what is to count as "official curriculum" is a political strategy exercised to aid such causes as market ideology, personal choice of schooling, standards for literacy, school crime and violence: all decidedly away from the momentous concern for equality of educational opportunity which has been a hallmark of the political landscape, at least in the USA, in education, since the 1954 Supreme Court Case in Brown v. Board of Education, Topeka, Kansas. In fact there is evidence that re-segregation is now occurring at a growing rate.

Since the 1980s the call has come from the New Political Right in both the USA and the United Kingdom for accountability and a "back to basics," or essentialist theory; a notion of teaching and testing of pupils, alongside appraisal of teachers' performances and competencies in subject matter. An allied theme has been that of cultural patriotism and heritage restoration. This has all been achieved by taking power away from teachers and professors and giving it to special interest groups and government.

In the USA curriculum policy and educational provision are duties of the local state. There is no mention of education in the US Constitution. All matters not mentioned are given back to the individual states. Yet states are still subject to Federal Laws, to wit Title X of the Elementary and Secondary Education Act *No Child Left Behind* (2001). In the United Kingdom, although there are decentralized local education authorities there is a National Curriculum administered by the Department of Education and Science. More control over teachers, increased accountability and performance-based data has been a policy in both the USA and in the United Kingdom for the past quarter century.

The conception of curriculum design advanced in this book runs contrary to that of the technical rationalists' view. The process-inquiry model abandons the idea of education as the pursuit of specific instructional objectives and the concomitant ends-means production baggage in favor of *education as a process* and the assertion that the curriculum is really about being faithful to certain *key principles of procedure* in the conduct of education. The problem for curriculum today is that it is planned in an anti-educational and undemocratic way more often than not by government; and it leaves no discourse at the development and improvement level for those working at the grass roots level. We need, in brief, a political decision to allow for school-based curriculum reform and improvement to re-occur.

To my mind, the curriculum needs to be seen as a continuous educational experience: a process, rather than a product. That is, as an educative experience, rather than a behavior, or outcome of that experience. To this day the work of Lawrence Stenhouse, sketched in his *An Introduction to Curriculum Research and Development*, remains the clearest account of a Process Model put forward as a valuable alternative to the objectives model for curriculum design.

One consequence of the growth in the study of curriculum has been an increasing rhetoric of teacher professional development. Many key decision-makers call for the acknowledgment that the teacher, as a professional, at whatever level of the education system, has a role to play in curriculum decisions, inquiry and improvement. This fact is often overlooked in the USA and the United Kingdom, where the teacher does not figure in the actual planning and development of new curriculum, but rather only in the implementation stage. In fact, curriculum itself has largely been separated from instruction and assessment. This separation counts as an unhealthy and unprofessional division of labor. Teacher professional development, or empowerment, has been a recent goal for teacher education: "No curriculum development without teacher professional development" was the old adage. However, Michael Apple (1995) argues that teachers have been largely disempowered and raises the interesting question: "Is there a curriculum voice to reclaim?" Indeed, Apple argues that scholars have almost no impact on the field of public curriculum today, nor have they had any influence in the past number of decades in the USA (Apple 1995: 38).

Stenhouse viewed curriculum work as a creative entity:

A curriculum is more like a musician's folio than an engineer's blueprint.

It requires an element of aesthetic quality, as well as imagination. Stenhouse continues:

A curriculum, like a recipe for a dish, is first imagined as a possibility, then the subject of an experiment.

(1975: 4)

It is, essentially, an educational proposal, that invites classroom testing. This is also the link that makes the relationship between teaching and research clear. In order to test his or her curriculum practice, the teacher must adopt a research stance.

Like the concept of education, the curriculum is creative, unpredictable in its itinerary and path of growth: moral, intellectual, spiritual and constructive. It is crafted through the exquisite aesthetic virtues of teachers acting upon their own artistic and intuitive situational understanding about what is right and good. It operates best when practical reason is highly honed. Dunne (1997), an Aristotelian educational scholar, argues for practical reasoning and wisdom, noting we need to get back to this "rough ground." Indeed, this practical self-reflective mode of professional conduct, although well identified by Aristotle and Thomas Aquinas, has hardly been explored in the curriculum writing of the past century.

In spite of the many reforms, task force reports and the general debate related to education in recent years the theoretical model governing the design and nature of curriculum and assessment has remained virtually unchallenged and unchanged, dominated as it is by an unrelenting mode of theoretical behaviorism and technical rationality that intrudes deep into the national psyche and culture. Yet the possibilities of alternative rational models have been raised. This book charts an existentialist critical context for curriculum thinking.

Culture and curriculum

Every society sets up schools in order to induct students into the culture, that is, the ways of the society. The English philosopher John Locke held that the child's mind is blank, or *tabula rasa*, at birth and must begin to acquire the knowledge, habits and values of the group. Thus experience, particularly involving the senses, provides the basis for Locke's empiricism. The vocal tradition, especially folklore, stories, songs and the like, is more evident than the written word in this process. The curriculum then becomes a reflection of what the people think is valuable, what they do, and what they believe. Curriculum is necessarily a selection from the culture, and it is largely composed of knowledge. Now there is a great deal to select from the culture and this is the tricky task of curriculum developers and policy-makers. As one of my graduate students remarked, "The curriculum is like a library to which subjects are constantly being added but few are ever withdrawn."

There are also difficulties in applying the culture concept to education and curriculum because we live in a multicultural society with pluralist values. That is, American society, just as British society or French society, contains many customs, traditions and values, often incompatible, that are transmitted, learned and shared. In actual practice, most schools emphasize formal bodies of knowledge, arts, skills, languages and moral values in education. This is customary and conventional, and for good reason, as these formal subjects or disciplines of knowledge have come down to us from the ages: in the main from the great medieval universities. This curriculum is known as the *Trivium* and the *Quadrivium*, or "The Seven Liberal Arts," which were present in incipient forms in the schools of Greece, Rome and the Arab world. The *Trivium* comprised grammar, rhetoric and dialectic (logic); and the *Quadrivium* was composed of arithmetic, geometry, astronomy and music. Philosophy was relegated to advanced study – hence the tradition of the doctorate in philosophy degree.

What we need to appreciate about these seven "subjects" is that they did not approximate closely with what goes by these labels in the modern world. Grammar, for example, was more than the simple content found in grammar courses but also included a fair amount of literature, forms of expression and so forth. In modern times, the *Trivium* further added history and literature (Smith *et al.*, 1957).

The curriculum of our schools is also a product of politics and interest groups (Giroux, 1994). The theoretical basis of this book is grounded in a belief that educators are more than mere functionaries in a bureaucracy – they are the constructive agents of cultural renewal. Umberto Eco, the Italian art critic and social theorist, and other critical theorists, such as Jurgen Habermas, urge man to adopt a resistance theory towards the encroachment of technological communication (Habermas, 1976). Maxine Greene argues that the technical approach has frozen our imaginations (Greene, 1995: 379). It is an era of conservatism and theoretical frugality.

We observe the "back to basics" movement and the calls for economic accountability with a jaundiced eye. William James, in his celebrated work *The Will to Believe*, warned:

> Philosophers long ago observed the remarkable fact that mere familiarity with things is able to produce a feeling of their rationality. The empiricist school has been so much struck by this circumstance as to have laid it down that the feeling of rationality and the feeling of famil-

iarity are one and the same thing, and that no other kind of rationality than this exists.

(James, 1992: 514)

Thus, half a century after Tyler wrote his classic, *Basic Principles of Curriculum and Instruction*, the objectives model and the use of instructional objectives in both norm-referenced and criterion-referenced testing has assumed an air of infallibility, at least in the USA. It is a major contention of this book that this assumption is problematic and in need of critical re-examination. This author would align with Professor Kliebard:

> One wonders whether the long standing insistence by curriculum theorists that the first step in making a curriculum be the specification of objectives has any merit whatsoever. It is even questionable whether stating objectives at all, is a fruitful way to conceive of the process of curriculum planning.
>
> (1975: 80)

Kliebard goes on to assert the James notion of "the sentiment of rationality" in concluding his reappraisal:

> One reason for the success of the Tyler rationale is its very rationality. It is an eminently reasonable framework for developing a curriculum. . . . Tyler's version of the model avoids the patent absurdity of, let us say, Mager's, by drawing that blueprint in broad outline rather than in minute detail.

In North America, Europe, Australasia and many other parts of the world, the education system is most definitely at risk from the lock-step linear ends-means model of curriculum and assessment. It is at risk from an enemy within its own ranks; that enemy is a dogmatic aspiration to enshrine program-building and evaluation around a limited objectives model and its concomitant assessment technology. The value and quality of an educational system can be judged by an examination of three critical features: first its system of teaching and teacher education; second its system of assessment and evaluation; and finally, with regard to its curriculum.

This work is offered in the free spirit of inquiry intended to open the long overdue discussion on the topic of how to replace the moribund paradigm of the objectives model in curriculum. We cannot offer the entire cultural heritage for the curriculum and therefore a judicious selection is required. When one thinks about it, the curriculum is in the first instance a selection from the culture of a people and is primarily implemented through discourse and conversation.

Interpretations of curriculum and educational imagination are always the idea of an individual thinker; the idea emerges in the mind and then is disseminated by believers who see the process of curriculum-making in a new light. These ideas are most always processed by practitioners – educators who are concerned about curriculum teaching and learning. They are practical theories.

This is a book about curriculum design and theory. It is offered as an alternative to the dominant objectives model of curriculum design. As such, the process-inquiry model outlined here contributes to curriculum theory. Curriculum theory has been evolving during this century. After several decades of unprecedented curriculum change and innovation we have moved into a more static situation characterized not by dramatic change but by bureaucratic functionalism in which the technical objectives model has been imposed upon schools, colleges and indeed universities. The curriculum is the foundation stone of any education system. One of the hallmarks of curriculum change in recent years has been the increasing incidence of planning and preparation in curriculum development activities involving both pre-service and in-service education of teachers and administrators. Yet most of this planning has subscribed to a single monolithic view of ends-means rationality and has limited rather than expanded the imagination and potential for curriculum experimentation. Curriculum work is artistic at its best. Bertrand Russell remarked:

> The teacher, like the artist, the philosopher, and the man of letters, can only perform his work adequately if he feels himself to be an individual directed by an inner creative impulse, not dominated and fettered by an outside authority.
>
> (Russell, 1950: 159)

The technical rationality-driven outcomes-based education (OBE) movement has subjugated self-autonomous thinking in preference for predetermined outcomes, standards and specifications. This is in total opposition to the concept of the educated mind principally because it is in opposition to the rights of students and teachers to exercise intellectual and moral judgment. I believe further that the virtue of the individual, and in fact humanity, is greatly diminished when judgment is over-ruled by the warrant of authority. In a democratic civilization, education allows the student and teacher to be entrusted with the responsibility of reflective judgment and a firm commitment to emancipation and freedom, not the promotion of a conception characterized by targets and predetermined outcomes mandating the limits of knowledge and human speculation.

A curriculum is something of taste and judgment, testing the power of creativity, research and evaluation, calling upon our best powers of *imagination*. In the past, at least before the twentieth century, curricula were seen as of two kinds. First, was the curriculum that was offered to the common schools, and second, a different curriculum that was offered to fee-paying, elitist, academy/private schools. One prevailing conception was that the curriculum was whatever was taught and actually experienced in lessons. This reality-based "actual" type curriculum was set out as the "timetabled curriculum." A second sense that emerged was that the curriculum involved all the learning that was planned and guided by the school. Thus we have on one hand a limited, and on the other a more expansive, notion of what is to count as a curriculum.

The curriculum is, above all else, the proposal for an educational process. I am loathe to set up strict definitions but to satisfy critics I shall offer a tentative one here and several standard definitions found in the literature:

Some definitions of curriculum

All the learning which is planned and guided by the school, whether it is carried on in groups, or individually, inside or outside the school.

(Kerr, 1968: 16)

The curriculum is a structured series of intended learning outcomes. Curriculum prescribes (or at least anticipates) the results of instruction.

(Johnson, 1967: 130)

We see the curriculum as a desired goal or set of values that can be activated through a development process culminating in experiences for students.

(Wiles and Bondi, 2007: 5)

The total experiences planned for a school or students.

(Wiles and Bondi, 2007: 347)

The term curriculum would seem to apply most appropriately to the program of activities, to the course run by pupils in being educated.

(Hirst, 1976: 183)

The curriculum of a school, or course, or a classroom can be conceived of as a series of planned events that are intended to have educational consequences for one or more students.

(Eisner, 2002: 31)

Curriculum is often taken to mean a course of study. When we set our imaginations free from the narrow notion that a course of study is a series of textbooks or specific outline of topics to be covered and objectives to be attained, broader more meaningful notions emerge. A curriculum can become one's life course of action. It can mean the paths we have followed and the paths we intend to follow. In this broad sense, curriculum can be viewed as a person's life experience.

(Connelly and Clandinin, 1988)

Curriculum is such permanent subjects as grammar, reading, logic, rhetoric, mathematics and the greatest books of the Western world that best embody essential knowledge. An example is that of the National Curriculum found in the UK with three core and seven foundational subjects, including specific content and objectives for student achievement in each subject.

(Marsh and Willis, 2007: 9)

A curriculum is an attempt to communicate the essential principles and features of an educational proposal in such a form that it is open to critical scrutiny and capable of translation into practice.

(Stenhouse, 1975: 4)

Stenhouse's idea of curriculum as a hypothesis invites scrutiny and testing. This casts the teacher and students in the role of investigators or researchers with a view to improving social practice or curriculum. It is also very faithful to the notion of action inquiry, which seeks to solve problems in social interaction. My definition is similar in adopting a process rather than specifying the results of teaching and learning. A curriculum is a proposal setting out an educational plan, offering students socially valued knowledge, attitudes, values, skills and abilities, which are made available to students through a variety of educational experiences, at all levels of the education system. As a proposal, the curriculum is a hypothesis inviting a research response.

The above definition does not separate curriculum from assessment or evaluation, nor from instruction as is so often the case in contemporary thinking. There is no division of labor here. Just as the curriculum includes evaluation and inquiry by the teacher into her or his work there is no theory and practice divide. The theoretical aspect is incorporated in the proposal which has grown out of practice and is validated by concrete evidence of practice. It is also substantiated by thirty years of my own teaching practice. I am claiming that a procedural values position does better than a teaching-to-the-objectives style. It is really a question of liberating students. What I mean is getting students to not be dependent on my authority, to accept the need to justify their own reasoning and evidence for their judgments. It was Peter Abelard, the eleventh-century Parisian speculative philosopher, who said that we must reside in the belief of using speculative reason operating upon human doubt as the means to advance the truth.

With critical educationalists like Paulo Freire (1970, 1972) the process theory permits an educational policy that is concerned with liberating human reason and granting freedom; to use Freire's language it is a "pedagogy of the oppressed"; and with Antonio Gramsci, correlative of the notion that:

> The last phase of the common school must be conceived and structured as the decisive phase, whose aim is to create the fundamental values of "humanism," the intellectual self-discipline, and the moral independence.
>
> (Gramsci, 1971: 32)

A curriculum is, above all else, imagined as an ideal. Should we fit curriculum out with a design that includes key concepts and electronic student portfolios? Alternatively, should it be based on an inquiry-discovery pedagogy? Thus, it is a grand experiment. Like a cooking recipe, it might have a good or bad taste. However, we can modify a curriculum like a recipe by adding virtues like the concepts of courage or cultural nationalism. Yet it is at once a compelling task of the human imagination. It is, at base, simply a hypothesis that invites being put to the test of action. It is never a finished entity but open to modification.

The curriculum must not be regarded as a final prescription or blueprint; it is nothing more than an idea, and ideal in the form of a proposal that it represents some worthwhile plan for leading us out of ignorance and thereby resulting in further growth through education. As an ideal, it springs from the imagination. It is conceived as an image, the purpose of which is to facilitate learning and education.

John Dewey (1916) argued that the purpose of education is simply the continuing growth of the person. This perspective is helped by teachers who understand that the aim of education is to have students become participants in that process – as opposed to being mere spectators – and to rely on the use of a process of inquiry for resolving difficulties, thereby allowing them to lead themselves out from ignorance through self-expression, critical thinking and the motivation of curiosity (Dewey, 1910, 1938). Aristotle held that the aim of education is to allow students to like and dislike what they want. Such a perspective grants autonomy to the student. It is not one in which the student is passive and the only authority is the teacher.

Curriculum as a social practice

Education is a social practice. Teachers and students meet in social interaction within the institution of the school. Curriculum is not exclusively a theoretical matter but mainly a practical matter involving the actions of humans that will make a difference. As such, it constitutes a challenge for praxis – a commitment to using principles in action. A practical action theory seems to be a fitting rationale for curriculum. This "practical" element, and the "action turn" (Reason, 2006) has a strong connection with both Pragmatism and Critical Realism. It was Charles Sanders Pierce who first used the word "pragmatism," which is from the Greek word *pragma* meaning "action," in an article in *Popular Mechanics* appearing in 1897. Pierce's idea is that unless some action makes a real difference then it is insignificant and one should be able to re-trace the consequences of actions, as they impact, to determine this difference on an empirical footing.

Who, when, why and how become key questions that need to be answered in negotiating and implementing a curriculum. The whole subject of education is practical, social and very much a highly moral matter more than the current weight given it as a "technical" matter. It is a great mistake to reject educational theory and indeed a curriculum on grounds that they cannot be proved. After Aristotle, one must not demand more rigor than the subject matter is fitted for. The curriculum is created, tried and judged. As such it is above all else an idea worth testing – a hypothesis the rational educator might proffer. Like the culture concept, a curriculum is created, shared and transmitted to others embodying values and knowledge and skills and a host of dispositions. It is found in the normative realm of beliefs and rituals and in the physical artifacts of texts and materials.

Curriculum, as a term, is a rather recent concept if we accept the *Oxford English Dictionary* (*OED*) as an authoritative source. The term was used originally to describe courses of study at universities and in schools. One might refer to the law or engineering curriculum in the university, or the history or reading course in a high school.

In terms of the American experience, Lawrence Cremin argued that a founder father of curriculum reform in the USA was William Torrey Harris, who as Superintendent of St. Louis public schools began a rigorous curriculum change movement around 1870 onwards. Whilst holding distinctively rationalist values he argued that the purpose of education was a process "by which the individual is elevated into the species," or by which a self-active human being is enabled to become privy to the accumulated wisdom of the race (Cremin, 1974: 28). Harris (1898a, 1898b), subscribed to a view which accorded import to a process of widening concentric circles involving family education, formal schooling, vocational induction and civic and political education as well as the religious education of the student. He advocated the use of the textbook as the vehicle *par excellence* for public education. In this, Harris paid a tribute to the emergence of psychology and to science in education in the preparation of teachers and the school curriculum. The age of curriculum thinking and making had arrived by the turn of the twentieth century.

The curriculum is concerned with what is planned, implemented, taught, learned, evaluated and researched in schools at all levels of education. To experience a curriculum is not to arrive at a particular destination, but to have traveled with a different view. It is in the journey and its experiences that a curriculum is realized, not in the act of alighting from the train.

Anyone who studies curriculum theory and history is bound to be very soon faced with the question of whether the logic of the literature coincides with the experiences of teachers and pupils in the schools. There is a vast difference between the two. There is the "official" curriculum and the "actual" curriculum in this debate: what is supposed to happen and what actually is happening, to be blunt. In addition, there is the "hidden curriculum" which describes the latent values which are unplanned but which exert a powerful effect on pupils and teachers.

Elliot Eisner has stated that "the quality of school curricula and the quality of teaching are the two most important features of any educational enterprise" (Eisner, 1983: 1). However, there is not a general consensus as to what constitutes quality in teaching and curriculum. Here I wish to suggest that two separate but complementary social practices were regenerated out of the curriculum reform movement in Europe, mainly under the aegis of first-generation innovatory programs: first, the design of curriculum without behavioral objectives and second, revitalization of the teacher action research movement. Both movements emerged due to a large-scale assault on the technical model of curriculum design, which had become distanced from democratic classrooms and teacher practices seeking excellence in evaluation.

The lost democratic ideal of school-based curriculum development

One of the most important questions is "Who should improve curriculum?" During the early years of the twentieth century, there was a widespread interest in educational circles for school-based curriculum development linked with the concept of democracy, particularly in the USA and Britain (Dewey, 1916; Whitehead, 1929; Skilbeck, 1984). In fact, John Dewey set up a "Laboratory School" at the University of Chicago for his experiments with democracy and education.

This is a rather profound democratic ideal, which granted autonomy to local schools and teachers for creating and recreating their curricula. In the United Kingdom, Labour Government policy had empowered teacher unions and local schools to exercise a right to reform their own school programs and to develop experimental modes of curriculum and evaluation under work commissioned by the Schools' Council in the 1960s and 1970s. Sadly, neo-essentialism and conservatism has clawed back power from schools and teachers and placed it with government.

It is quite clear that schools in the USA do not have the freedom of deciding the curriculum at the local level of the school. I was able during the 1970s to enjoy working with schools committed to school-based curriculum development in Northern Ireland. The concept was widely taken up by a number of secondary/comprehensive schools, at that time, throughout the United Kingdom of Great Britain and Northern Ireland outside of the selective grammar schools who were strongly tied into the GCE O- and A-Level examinations which permitted little experimentation.

Wolfgang Klafki (1975) wrote a Council of Europe paper on the topic of localized school-based curriculum development as action research, which Klafki saw as an alternative to empirical research. An early example of action inquiry related to curriculum development in Europe.

Other recent influences have come from the critical philosophy of Jurgen Habermas challenging the primacy of technical and analytical positivism in favor of a more critical social theory of hermeneutics and interpretive models. In education, this critical theory was introduced by Wilfred Carr and Stephen Kemmis in 1986 with their book *Becoming Critical: Education, Knowledge and Action Research*. The role here would be to advance human emancipation and justice to rid institutions of inequality through action research.

Advances in educational program evaluation contributed significantly to curriculum thought as qualitative approaches were added to the standard quantitative styles. Evaluation as "illumination" (Parlett and Hamilton, 1972), or as "literary criticism" and "connoisseurship" (Eisner, 2002), or as "democratic evaluation" (MacDonald, 1971). Michael Scriven (1973) offered "goal free evaluation," acknowledging that programs often attain unanticipated effects, and Robert Stake produced "responsive evaluation" (1967). All of these creative evaluators have allowed practitioners to better understand their actions and involvement through "thick description" rather than bean counting and number crunching of the behavioral style of evaluation.

While at a professional meeting in Scotland I was informed by an American professor of curriculum that most American educationalists did not know anything about how curriculum, or indeed education, was studied and practiced in Britain or Ireland; or indeed, elsewhere in Western Europe. This may have been an exaggeration but it certainly is true that, as regards higher education in particular, and the manner and means by which curriculum and the foundations of education are pursued, one might readily conclude that either side of the Atlantic two completely different fields or subjects are being studied.

Stenhouse crafted his Process Model as opposed to the objectives model of curriculum design and with his reconstructed version of teachers as researchers, manifest through the Humanities Curriculum Project (HCP). Stenhouse acted as External Examiner for my own D.Phil thesis, which dealt with controversial issues in curriculum. John Elliott, a member of Stenhouse's HCP team, which first advanced the "teacher-researcher role" in the United Kingdom, has been a champion of educational action research on an international scale, and Jean Rudduck, an HCP member and, later, life partner of Lawrence Stenhouse, has written on teacher research and reflective practice in teacher education (Rudduck, 1989).

When I arrived in Northern Ireland in 1973, Professor Malcolm Skilbeck was Director of the Education Centre at the New University of Ulster and, as my doctoral supervisor, he counseled me to surround myself with what he called "about fifty great books." Skilbeck was a scholar of Dewey and of the social reconstructionist theory of education. Reconstructionists believe that schools can rebuild a culture in crisis and are the genuine forerunners to critical theory. Skilbeck first mentioned Kurt Lewin's work in solving conflict and his notion of action research, and we discussed the possible role of action research in our Schools Cultural Studies Project aimed at peace education in Northern Ireland secondary schools. This was during 1974 and the second cycle of the educational action research movement had not yet begun in earnest at this time. The first cycle began during the 1950s in the USA (Corey, 1953). Action research fizzled out as educational research became dominated by the scientific method and Research, Development and Dissemination (R, D & D) styles of work became the norm (Hodgkinson, 1957). We did have the already-documented experience of the Schools Council curriculum projects, and the Humanities Curriculum Project made forays into promoting the "teacher as researcher" notion.

As a postgraduate research student attached to the Schools Cultural Studies Curriculum Project in Northern Ireland in the mid-1970s I was concerned with curriculum development in social/cultural studies within secondary schools aimed at promoting peace, tolerance and mutual understanding. The now UK-wide goal for promoting "education for mutual understanding" (EMU) as a policy aim was first forged by our project at Ulster University. Thus, "conflict resolution" was a central interest. Skilbeck organized an Education Centre Seminar for faculty and postgraduate research students at Ulster University around the theme "Education and Conflict in Northern Ireland." It is within this seminar that I began to forge some ideas about how the teacher and curriculum could be used as a significant aid for cross-community understanding. One of Skilbeck's first suggestions was for me to read Kurt Lewin's (1948) book *Resolving Social Conflicts*, in which he first argued for action research as an applied form of inquiry that would solve social problems.

At my D.Phil research sessions with Professor Skilbeck, and later with Professor Hugh Sockett, I would be handed several books at a time and told to go away and read, and come back months later and discuss these in preparation for lodging a doctoral proposal. There were no classes to attend for it was assumed my basic grounding in the knowledge and skills of education and research methodology had been adequately completed with a good undergraduate degree and a Master of Arts degree as preparation. I would conduct field work, write a chapter, and make an appointment to see my (by then) supervisor, Professor Sockett, who had studied under Richard Stanley Peters at London and was an analytical philosopher of education with an abiding interest in curriculum design. He would leave no stone unturned, drafting long critical pages of typescript critique for me of my draft chapters to take away after having discussed my writing. This process continued for several years. Now this graduate education differs markedly from that in the United States. In the USA, students attend classes, and perhaps seminars at graduate level. There is rarely individual tutorial type work, which to my mind is a great pity and demerit in the American system. Ben Bloom (1995) has concluded in research on student learning that the tutorial is the most effective method of learning. If we accept this to be true then it will dramatically affect the way in which the curriculum will be organized and implemented. Tutorials are noticeably absent as a mode of teaching in the USA.

Giving teachers the role of curriculum development and research is an ultimate act of democratic education for it admits to authority and power to change at the local level and requests educators to operate within a reflective research and professional development brief. Teachers logically must be researchers in such a change scenario. The most amazing hypocrisy is that on the one hand Colleges of Education argue for the development of "professionals committed to reflective practice" and on the other the teachers and administrators are stripped of their professional autonomy.

The school-based model advanced by Skilbeck (1984) admits five stages to the process of curriculum development: situational analysis; specification of goals; organizing content and program building; creation of learning experiences; and feedback and evaluation. Skilbeck held that logically, teachers, when faced with curriculum change, do not set about the task by addressing goals and objectives first – but rather they take account of the situation that they find themselves in ("Situational Analysis"). I found that teachers do, in fact, ruminate over the constraints they face, say a public examination system, and discuss resources available and other immediate concerns before outlining any targets they hope to achieve. This stage is concordant with the artistic awareness of constraints and resources, or a situational understanding. This is not a theoretical matter, nor indeed a technical concern, but rather a practical and at once, professional choice.

The failure of large expert-led national curriculum projects to create teacher-proof resources and materials packages led ultimately to a strategy of bringing teachers into the mix of school-based curriculum developments. This conception of curriculum planning derives from the needs of learners in the first instance and the need for the freedom to learn by students and teachers is a necessary condition of this work. It further suggests that schools are responsible, as human communities, to being responsive to their own environment. In addressing this environment, it is vital that teachers be researchers and curriculum developers in adapting learning to its own idiosyncratic ecology.

Given this experience and the wide-scale acclaim attributed to school-based support groups it remains a marginal strategy in the face of large production type packages of school curriculum innovations today. I would argue with others that there could be no effective curriculum development without teacher development.

The objectives model and technical rationality

Our present paradigm of curriculum-making is the direct result of the beliefs and assumptions of those engineers and psychologists such as Bobbitt, Thorndike and Charters, and technologists who have dominated curriculum thought over the past one hundred years. These beliefs are deeply rooted in a scientifically based educational technology and practice. The contributions of Thorndike and Dewey reflected this scientific orientation. In 1910 the first issue of *The Journal of Educational Psychology* contained an article by Thorndike titled "The Contribution of Psychology to Education." This used measurement of intellect and character and ultimately the prediction of behavior, an ends-means notion relying on a strict regimen of behavioral testing which has come to have a politically connected high profile in Western nations.

One can locate the origin of educational objectives notably in the work of Franklin Bobbitt, who was an engineer by training, and in his two principal works *The Curriculum* (1918), and *How to Make a Curriculum* (1924). The advent of management orthodoxy and scientific planning in the years after the First World War cemented this perspective. Bobbitt held the Chair of Education at the University of Chicago, as did Ralph Tyler and later Benjamin Bloom, who applied principles of behaviorism to instructional design.

In recent years a rather monopolistic view of curriculum has emerged following the work of behaviorist planners and rational curriculum designers who have based their approach largely on the notion of behaviorist thinking and more specifically according to planning by "objectives." Ralph Tyler (1949) popularized this idea with his simple syllabus for a course at the University of Chicago titled *Basic Principles for Curriculum and Instruction.* Regrettably, the objectives model has been championed dogmatically and aggressively, not only in North America, but also internationally.

Interestingly, Tyler appears far more direct and liberal than the host of psychologists who have put their stamp on curriculum since mid-century, including Popham, Gagne, Bereiter, Carroll, Bloom, Anderson, Block, Guskey and others who come offering educational blueprints of a technical nature. Such a view of curriculum restrains the human imagination simply because it sets limits or boundaries to what is learned, and tested. The curriculum equates with tested knowledge. Content, or the material covered in a course, becomes the means to the stated objectives. Thus, most courses reduce content to an instrumental role. This is a serious problem. Let us accept that education can, in certain senses, be seen as an introduction to disciplined forms of knowledge like mathematics or philosophy. If we accept this then we can see how education can be viewed as being justified by being faithful to the forms, or principles of procedure, equated with these disciplines. To work as a mathematician, or philosopher, is to work in accordance with and fidelity to these *principles of procedure* rather than in accord with some pre-specified objective, which is external and extrinsic to the activity itself. Thus, the model outlined here is that if one defines the content, that is, the knowledge base, the key concepts, the methods of doing philosophy, its tests of proof, and then set out an acceptable teaching procedure and standards to judge students' work, then one would be planning without utilizing objectives. I believe this to be the prized model for work in the disciplines of knowledge because the principles of procedure then become our objectives, if you like, and this is the best way to communicate the essence of these endeavors. Disciplines allow us to determine the input into the educational process rather than the outputs. Eisner (1981) argues that there have been at least six consequences of behaviorist curriculum powered by positivism and scientific control:

1   The utter dominance of a scientific epistemology in education that has excluded all other notions of inquiry. (Indeed the recent Federal Law passed with the self-recommending Title X, *No Child Left Behind* (2001) has eliminated all but the most scientific and quantitative methods of educational research.)
2   Educational research has been preoccupied with control.
3   There has been a preoccupation with standardized outcomes – such practices undermine students' creative idiosyncrasies.
4   Little role is accorded students for participation in the creation of their own learning programs.
5   The consequences of being interested in issues of control and measurement has led curriculum makers to break up curriculum into small micro-units of behavior and in so doing to render much of the curriculum meaningless and irrelevant to pupils.
6   So much of curriculum is characterized by humorless and devastatingly sober quality writing in both research and educational practice. Eisner concludes:

The tendency towards what is believed to be scientific language has resulted in an emotionally eviscerated form of expression; any sense of the poetic or passionate must be excised.

(Eisner, 1981)

This conception of writing is in opposition to the view of R.S. Peters (1966), who urges students to work with passion with educational tasks at hand. Passion is a precious possession for the student and for the teacher.

Deliberation and curriculum

Deliberation is a significant concept associated with the whole field of the "practical" in curriculum studies. The curriculum is a deliberately planned practical activity. Several writers (Reid, 1978; Sanders and McCutcheon, 1986; McCutcheon, 1995b) have exhumed this concept in some depth. The authors question how practical wisdom can be facilitated and developed. The position is that professionals do develop practical theories out of their own hard-won experience. McCutcheon (1995a: 5) states that there are at least nine characteristics of deliberation. A deliberative activity is one that embodies decision-making at its core. Deliberation:

1 considers alternative possible solutions;
2 envisions the consequences and outcomes of each alternative;
3 considers facts and values, and means and ends simultaneously;
4 takes action within time constraints;
5 is a moral activity;
6 is a social enterprise consisting of responsibility, social interactions, anticipation of events and trends;
7 is simultaneity – that is, as we think and speak many things vie for attention. Deliberation is mistakenly thought of as a linear clear rational activity when it is often a muddle;
8 involves presence of interests;
9 involves presence of conflicts.

Further, McCutcheon discusses teachers' use of "practical theories," that is, their explanations of their thinking, and she has summarized an important literature dealing with "professional knowledge of teachers" (Elbaz, 1983), or "personal knowledge" of their work (Connelly and Clandinin, 1988). This vein of research is crucially important if we are to understand the "situational understanding" held by the practitioner. A complete new literature on teacher knowledge about teaching has come forth from this area of "practical theory."

Some of this theoretical knowledge is arrived at through autonomous independent thought, which McCutcheon (1995a: 147) labels "solo deliberation." Other theories are arrived at through a socially constructed knowledge in interaction with others in our culture. Thus, curriculum development is a deliberately planned activity through which courses of study or other educational patterns of activity and experience are designed and proffered as proposals worthy of implementation and evaluation in practice. These ways of developing and deliberating vary from one national system to another. In Ireland, we used to have a fair amount of school-based curriculum development. In the USA, the state is increasingly deleting the amount of control teachers and schools have to make changes.

Imagination and curriculum

Mary Warnock, the English philosopher of education, has remarked that:

> Quality in education is measured by the degree to which the imagination is exercised. To exercise the imagination is to keep it in practice, by giving it, to attend to, in detail, objects which are worthy of attention; and all objects are more worthy of attention in detail than superficially.
>
> (1973: 121)

The imagination, on Warnock's view, is akin to "free-thought," and therefore, if we neglect imagination, then we are in a strong sense neglecting a student's freedom. Thus, a curriculum must provide opportunities for students to think critically and freely for themselves. Given that curricula emerge from images of desired and ideal practices we need to introduce another powerful concept, often neglected in education, and that is the concept of *imagination*. Imagination is central to the educated mind. It permits the possibility of the creative.

The work of Elliot Eisner (2002) and Kieran Egan (1990, 1992, 2005) stands out as singular in dealing with the concept of imagination, particularly with reference to good curriculum and evaluation in education. Eisner advocates a new form of curriculum evaluation positioning educators as connoisseurs of practice who reveal their qualities through literary criticism. Egan has launched an Imagination Educational Research Group out of his base at Simon Fraser University to promote the development of students' imagination through curriculum reform. Eisner works at encouraging new forms of expression in evaluation as literary criticism and private savoring of quality through educational connoisseurship.

The cultivation of imagination is one of the most important aims of education yet it is rarely discussed in a meaningful way. By imagination, I mean two things: first that the student becomes intrigued and seduced by a subject, so much so that the student makes it his or her territory. The student, moreover, feels compelled with the need "to go on" with his or her individual inquiries. Second, they acquire tools that allow them the ability to develop their knowledge, skills and abilities after they leave the guidance of the teacher. This is particularly true of college-level education. Students at university, or college, need to learn research skills so that they can follow a line of inquiry that has been pursued by others but with their own questions. Above and beyond this, they need to know that this is really what they are doing. If they can make a genuine and concrete contribution to knowledge they need to understand this to be the case. This is one reason that instead of a formal examination I require my graduate students to complete a piece of educational action research as applied to their day-to-day professional life and work. My students come to understand, albeit gradually, that they are doing research that will improve their practice and therefore make a difference. I think that some research in education does do this but I feel this is the exception to the rule generally. The purpose of education and of imagination is to seek the freedom to "go on" in the study of the subject. A good education, or what some might refer to as "quality" then might be evaluated by the extent to which the student's imagination is worked. It is akin to freethinking, which is critical. Therefore, if we neglect the imagination then we shall be putting constraints on our freedom. By allowing students the opportunity to think freely for themselves we shed our being in authority and give this as a right to the student. This is what is emancipatory about education; it frees the student from the *patria potestas*, or the parental jurisdiction. This is at the core of the concept of education, which my *OED* informs me comes from the Latin *educere*, "to lead out from ignorance," thus setting one free from the warrant of authority. Education is implemented through the curriculum in schools and it is the great emancipator in liberating us from more than the parental jurisdiction.

In this chapter, I have been touching on aims of education, which raises questions of philosophy. The philosophers that I have been influenced by are the sort who ask questions like "What do you mean?" and "How do you know?"

> The poet Shelley thought it was imagination, in the end, which made love and sympathy possible. Poetry for Shelley was influential because he thought it directly appealed to imagination.
>
> (Warnock, 1973: 112)

Part of the problem of curriculum is that our concept or image of education has been one of consumers and products, no doubt located in the obsession with capitalist motives and market production; or an image of the school as a corporation or factory utilizing quality control mechanisms and treating education as a consumer beltline. This reasoning has led us directly to the present "market ideology" which drives curriculum and assessment in American schools. Making products is technical, but I would submit that education has more to do with pastoral care and a caring pedagogy. Indeed surveys of teachers show clearly that the main motivation for entering teaching is to care and help children grow and learn (Ornstein and Levine, 2006).

Pedagogy, or the art of teaching, is a word that is not in vogue much in the USA. Yet the concept of pedagogy still has widespread currency in Europe. The etymology of the Greek word pedagogy comes from the root "ped" or foot, and means literally "leading children." The pedagogue was originally an escort to the pupil between home and the Ludus, or Roman school. Some of these pedagogues were actually slaves of some education who acted as tutors, thus diminishing the place of the father and supplementing the teacher over education (Gutek, 1995: 63).

Teachers "educate" if the leading is grounded in care and love. This is the basis for an educational relationship between teacher and student. Aristotle commented that the relationship between a teacher and pupil was characterized by this special care and was a loving relationship.

The idea of curriculum posited in this book runs contrary to that of the instrumentalist notion in that it abandons the idea of education as the pursuit of specific instructional objectives and this ends-means production baggage in favor of education as an educational experience crafted by adherence to certain processes and that the curriculum is really about being faithful to certain key principles of *procedure* in the conduct of education. The curriculum is the mechanism enabling the education of students. Education is a process embodying key principles and values – it is in the realization of these embedded values that one is educated: not through the attainment of trivial outcomes seen as products.

Because curricula are at base mere proposals, or hypotheses, and not finished products, there will always be unresolved questions and no one can write the last word on the subject. We are all, as educators, faced with curriculum questions, some more tormenting than others. In facing these questions, we have to engage serious thinking, which can be done well or badly. It is the task of curriculum theory to help us think better on these questions and issues. A central issue is that of *rationality*. We have practical and technical versions of rationality. We can ask, "Which rationality shall prevail?" In all cases, a first step towards answering questions of curriculum rationally is to understand the question. Understanding is often the goal or purpose of teaching and learning and is always seen to be a crucial aim of curriculum. Yet understanding itself is fraught with difficulty, even for philosophers. I can hold any of the following positions tenably:

> "I understand fully what you say."
> "I do not understand what you say."
> "I do not fully understand what you have said."
> "I think I understand what you have said."
> "I understand what you say but your understanding is wrong."
> "I misunderstood what you have said."

Stenhouse (1975) contended that we could decide on designing the curriculum by three means:

1 *Planning* considering *epistemological issues* of knowledge. The "Content Model";
2 *Planning* by consideration of the *pupil's characteristics*. The "Process or Learner Development Model"; and
3 *Planning by objectives*. The "Objectives Model."

That is, we can plan with reference to the knowledge, student or outcome desired.

Designing a curriculum is like designing a building. First, what will be the purpose of the building? Thus, its function is considered. Second, how much finance is available? Thus, the practical concerns are paramount in design.

Policy-makers are notoriously obsessed with the concepts of cost, effectiveness and efficiency, and not only in education. Curriculum and schooling must be managed scientifically, echoing conduct in corporations, factories and finance institutions. Such engineering is said to be "rational," namely taking a means to a specified end. But Dewey (1910) and Oakeshott (1966, 1981) have both argued that such thinking, first posited by John Stuart Mill in *On the Logic of the Moral Sciences* (1843), is fuzzy indeed. Mill's account of rational action is the basis for the scientific rationale for planning, and it is true that many educators see themselves as behavioral scientists. Mill argued that rational action is *planned action*. One should first consider the *end* to be achieved and select this carefully. You should then determine, with the aid of science, what will enable you to achieve your end. You then have to act on that knowledge. Mill argued further that actions that deviate from this procedure are that much less rational.

Michael Oakeshott (1966, 1981) is perhaps the harshest critic of Mill's account of action. For Oakeshott it is inconceivable that we could detach ourselves from our ends quite independently of the context in which they were aimed at. Our actions are part of our ways of proceeding, of going on in a situation, just as there are ways of continuing in a debate or game. Oakeshott's central thesis is that actions cannot be taken away from or detached from their social context. What makes an action rational for Oakeshott is how far it conforms to the "idiom of the activity," that is, the context in which we act. Supporters of Tylerian notions of rational curriculum planning must defend against these criticisms. Arguably, there have not been that many critics of technical rationality and educators are often hounded by the ends-means rationality embodied in our system of schooling and education. Teachers are often seen and view themselves as functionaries in a bureaucracy. This becomes more visible when they are shrouded in state accountability standards, and of course test results and the like.

Much Western education could be evaluated theoretically as being behaviorist and neo-essentialist in nature. There is a newfound belief in basic subjects, core curriculum, testing, control and accountability through the achievement of outcomes specified in behavioral terms. Beginning around 1980 with conservative education policies, arguably imported from Britain, where Margaret Thatcher, herself a neo-conservative, and former school-teacher, implemented the social market perspective, at all levels of British education. It was a shift in policy away from local control and choice towards government education policy control – often under-resourced and incoherent.

In the United States this might be called "The New Federalism" characterized by five trends: (1) more choice for parents; (2) deregulation of rules; (3) cutbacks and downsizing at all levels and programs; (4) consolidation of agencies and elimination of programs; and (5) establishing national standards. This latter is somewhat at odds with the more decentralized concerns of the other trends striving for national standards and testing where teachers and students are accountable for performances. Thus one can analyze a shift in American Federal education policy that might have been categorized as reconstructionist or, at least, progressive rather than traditional-essentialist.

The current debate about curriculum needs to acknowledge that the use of instructional objectives as the ultimate basis for planning is seriously flawed, not only as a planning model, but as an assessment model of student learning. This picture of student learning is also criticized by Dewey (1916) in arguing that our results – what students actually achieve – are different from our intended ends-in-view – what we were aiming at. In the course of trying to achieve our ends-in-view all sorts of interactions occur, changing our course, and we must not, as he said, be under a "tyranny of ends." For Dewey the aim of education was not in reaching some standard, or end, but in "achieving growth and more growth." Sockett (1976) has outlined these objections in his attack on the Mill account as it relates to curriculum design.

In most nations, citizens are demanding more and more of their education system. Schools are requested to establish drug education programs, to teach critical thinking, character education, technology education, to combat inequalities, racism, crime, and even prepare students to accept death, besides fulfilling the traditional role of imparting the culture and cultural heritage.

Conceptions of curriculum

By the notion of a "conception" of curriculum, I refer explicitly to a defined orientation, or values, embedded in a curriculum perspective, which characterizes the most prized virtues connected with a curriculum style or practice. Several curriculum researchers have worked this idea (Eisner and Vallance, 1974; Schubert, 1986; Eisner, 2002; Marsh and Willis, 2007). I believe it is very difficult to pigeonhole persons and policies into a labeling system; however, in thinking about this one must necessarily see that all curricula are based on a conception or vision of desirable qualities, or values. Eisner (2002) provides an in-depth discussion of the notion of curriculum *ideologies*. He suggests competing conceptions, or ideologies: Religious Orthodoxy, Rational Humanism, Progressivism, Critical Theory, Reconceptualism and Cognitive Pluralism.

Ideologies are thus more than models – they have a political essence at their core. The base of values from which decisions are made about what and how to teach. These ideologies are often construed as philosophical orientations such as perennialist theories.

Six curriculum ideologies

I have identified six major curriculum conceptions, or ideologies, which correlate remarkably and mesh closely with the six value orientations of teachers I independently derived from survey work with teachers' value systems around the world (see Chapter 11). I believe there is great significance between the theoretical constructions posed in the literature and the actual data found from teachers in four nations which requires greater exploration and explanation. The six curriculum ideologies are:

1   intellectual-rationalist (Greek/Roman/medieval);
2   theo-religious (Christian-Scholastic, Islamic, Jewish);
3   social-romantic (child-centered);
4   technical-behavioral (science-efficiency);
5   personal-caring (Existentialist-self-growth and self-realizing);
6   critical-political (equality-meliorist).

The history of education shows pretty well clear patterns of preference in moving from an intellectual rationalist tradition that merges with the rise of Christian education to the humanistic child-centered tradition of the Enlightenment. In the modern period the concern for a science of education led to technical and behavioral conceptions. Running parallel was a concern by some curricularists to focus on the personal values and growth of the student as a person. I call this tradition the "personal-humanistic" and it can be seen in the work of Jean-Jacques Rousseau, Friedrich Froebel, A.S. Neill, William Pinar, Carl Rogers, Sidney Simon and others. Since 1945, there has been a conscious attempt to employ curriculum to achieve equality of opportunity and with the rise of curriculum research into inequality has emerged a new vibrant "critical-political" ideology for curriculum.

From where does the content, usually called the "subjects," offered in school come from? What should be in the curriculum? What knowledge is of most worth? Whose knowledge is most worthwhile? These questions invite our imagination to work. An overview of various conceptions or curriculum ideologies follows:

1. Intellectual-rationalist ideology

This conception of curriculum was the earliest and is seen in the development of education in the Greek and Roman states and with the curriculum of the early universities in Europe based on the seven liberal arts, or the *Trivium* and *Quadrivium*. Intellectual rationalism holds to the view that the function of education is to cultivate the intellect and to further intellectual growth by subjecting students to the most rational forms of subject organization that have been consistently passed on. This is a knowledge-driven enterprise with development of mind as a virtue. One strand of this is perennialism, or the idea that character is permeated with a search for the truth and it contains the best of the cultural heritage and is therefore "perennial" in nature. This is the idea that truth will always be the same and these studies (mathematics, music, etc.) have stood the test of time and should be permanent studies in the curriculum. This is undoubtedly the oldest form of curriculum organization dating at least to Platonic Idealism. The idea is that the curriculum requires an elite selection of true knowledge; schools do not exist to meet all forms of social need or special extracurricular activities for these would ultimately take away time required for intellectual and worthy academic pursuits.

2. Theo-religious ideology

The oldest known schools were in the Tigris Valley in what is modern Iraq around 6000 BC. These were known as *Edubba*, or "Tablet Schools," whose purpose was religious training of young boys using a cuneiform stone tablet for the text (Webb *et al.*, 2003). Similar religious schools were also characteristic of education in Egypt from 3000 BC, for educating religious or temple scribes. In the Western tradition, the Monastic Schools arguably kept the lights of civilization from going out altogether during the Dark Ages of AD 500–1000. The "Cathedral Schools" also demonstrated the primacy of religion in education after Charlemagne. Following the rise of the universities around AD 1100, Thomas Aquinas, a Dominican priest and professor of theology at Paris, advanced deductive logic as a primary reasoning model by meshing Aristotelian thought with Roman Catholic Church doctrines. However, the supremacy of Scholasticism was devastated by the ideals underpinning the Renaissance, and the shift from religious values to the educated courtly gentleman.

In North America, religion was the central galvanizing factor in the rise of both private and public education. The historian E.P. Cubberley (1934) argued that three types of religious influence were transplanted from Europe to America. First, the Church–State type founded in New England by Puritan Congregationalists, for example the establishment of Harvard as a Divinity College in 1636 and the passing of the "Old Deluder Satan Act" of 1647 which made towns responsible for building Town and Latin Grammar Schools. Second, the Parochial tradition of both Protestants and Catholics in Pennsylvania and Maryland, and third, the tradition of Charity and Sunday Schools found in Virginia and the Carolinas. One need only look at the fact that all of the Ivy League colleges were religiously endowed. In fact, there was not a public university until after the Republic was established. The University of North Carolina, of which East Carolina University, where I labor, is a constituent institution, was founded in 1789. Even today some 12 percent of children attend mostly religious endowed private schools in the USA and, Eisner (2002: 57) states, "In America about 90 percent of all private or independent elementary and secondary schools are Roman Catholic."

3. Social-Romantic ideology

This ideology focuses upon the needs and interests of the child rather than the subject or content to be taught. Part of the message is that students need to be made ready for being with others in society – to be democratic and sociable. Exponents range from Comenius with his passion for peace and justice to the Romantic naturalism of Rosseau and the work of Johann Pestalozzi and Froebel's Kindergarten. Progressives of the twentieth century would include, but are not limited to, A.S. Neill in Britain, John Dewey and William Kilpatrick in the USA, and Maria Montesorri in Italy.

Notably, Dewey longed to teach students a "logic of inquiry" with which to solve problems. This is the essence of Pragmatism, the philosophy that drives much of the experimentalism of Dewey and his followers. Deweyan Progressivism adopts a scientific method of thought and action (Dewey, 1910). For Dewey, curriculum does not begin with knowledge as the source, but with the child and his or her nature. Professor A.V. Kelly (1989: 87) boldly asserts: "the fundamental values of education are to be found in the nature of human development and its potentialities." These theorists have also pointed to the profound changes in the role of the teacher using a child-centered human development approach. From subject expert to facilitator; from judge to advisor; from text master to inquiry-centered teaching role.

4. Technical-behavioral ideology

This is a set of values that encourage students as consumers in the capitalist system: producing, consuming, measuring and vocationalism. Students are seen as contributors to the market economy and being readied for participation in globalization. The high emphasis on curriculum for career work and the premium bunting applied to those aspects of curriculum governed by technology courses are evidence of these values. Indeed the way in which the curriculum is measured for both students and teachers bespeaks of this emerging accountability concern. Students and teachers get the message that they will be held accountable for the results of their performance and there is a widespread view that education is at base preparation for the world of work – that is, it is instrumental in leading students to this transition.

5. Personal-caring ideology

Perhaps the most widely ascribed ideology by teachers is the caring orientation (see Chapter 11). It is found in curricula and personnel who advocate for the care and welfare of the child.

The Metropolitan Life National Survey of teachers' motivations for entering teaching showed that the number one reason folks enter teaching is to help children grow and learn (Ornstein and Levine, 2006). This ideology has found intellectual advocacy from writers such as Jane Roland Martin with her three Cs – care, concern and connection – and in the writings of Nell Noddings and William Pinar within the USA. In Britain, the traditional emphasis on programs of pastoral care (Hamblin, 1984) in schools has become part of the structure for curriculum. Pastoral care emphasizes the role of the teacher as shepherd, caring for the total needs of the students from guidance advice to education for life (McKernan *et al.*, 1985).

The personal ideology is concerned with the growth of the student as a person. It signals an emphasis on self-actualization, inner harmony, self-respect and the dignity and worth of persons. In this latter sense, it can be seen to exercise its humanistic curriculum features. It answers the questions "Who am I?" "What are my values?" "How can I learn to clarify my values and beliefs?" Existentialist and Reconceptualist educators would see this as a priority for curriculum – a spiritual form of values education and personal identity construction. Eisner (2002: 31) has stated that in the self-actualizing ideology content is important only to the extent that it helps the individual student personally – not as it is defined by outside experts.

One salient feature of the personal-caring curriculum ideology is the belief that students need to learn how to make moral decisions and choices – choices that ultimately affect their personal well-being, for example "Who am I?" "Should I do, or not do, drugs?" In the Schools Cultural Studies Project high school students in Northern Ireland were given opportunities to exercise making decisions about their values and to choose from competing alternatives. Dewey's method of valuing – a process of choosing, prizing and acting on choices – was used as a values clarification process by others (Raths *et al.*, 1966). Values and moral education are central in the humanistic ideology.

This caring and humanistic ideology also has a concern for the development of the student as a spiritual being. Philip Phenix (1974) calls this the dimension of transcendence – the idea of the student going beyond any limitless state or realization. It is akin to infinitude – limitless exploration. The student, on this ideology, is committed to inquiry and getting beyond the boundaries so as to grow even more, in accord with Dewey's goal of growth (Dewey, 1916).

6. Critical-political ideology

The critical-political ideology attempts to lay bare and expose the underpinning values of the curriculum – it has taken on the brief formerly attempted by social reconstructionist thinkers that views schools as agencies of political and cultural renewal.

Critical ideology would carefully consider issues that underpin equality in the school, for example gender relations, or analyses of social class backgrounds that affect school performance.

Eisner suggests:

> Critical theory provides one of the most visible and articulate analyses of education found in the pages of educational journals and in books devoted to the state of schools. It is for this reason – its salience in the intellectual community and its potential for reforming the current priorities of schools – that it is included here as an ideology affecting education in general and curriculum in particular.
>
> (2002: 73)

This perspective gained currency with attacking some of the social inequalities that serve as a sort of "upside down core social curriculum" after the Second World War in both Britain and the USA. Problems of intergroup conflict, racism, anti-Semitism, environment, poverty, gender issues, led some to call for active roles for schools to help transform culture by teaching about equality and conflict resolution. At school level, the Schools Cultural Studies Project mentioned above promoted student understanding of controversial issues and attempted to advance processes of conflict resolution and values clarification. One direct result was the extension of "education for mutual understanding" to all other teachers in the United Kingdom. Critical ideology would seek to empower all who work in the school – teachers, administrators and students. Yet as Eisner notes they tend to emphasize the negative and not the positive – and their strident critiques probably do not have much impact on policy.

In conclusion it may well be that the best way to unearth and exhume the values of a school curriculum is through the direct exploration of the priority the curriculum gives to any or all of the above six curriculum ideologies.

Curriculum development

Political, economic, social, legal and technological change in cultures during this century have caused the curriculum to be modified, adapted and radically altered in educational institutions. These changes have affected the meaning of education. Curriculum development has been the means by which responsible groups have tried to deal with changing the educational experiences students at school enjoy. Curriculum development is a systematic and critical process of realizing educational values as ideals and worthy images and transforming these into proposals for action in the form of programs of teaching and learning that will hypothetically be realized in reality. Such a view sets up the curriculum development work as a research enterprise inviting our inquiry. Our imagination is fueled by our environment, experiences and language. If we prefer to talk of "outcomes" rather than aims, of feedback rather than evidence, of products rather than learning, we shall become slaves to technical rationality. Johnson has adopted a technical view of curriculum development as the processes by which a set of objectives, or intended learning outcomes, are to be realized in the classroom. I would assert that the term curriculum development is a concept denoting deliberately planned activities involving the design of courses: their aims, content, methods and modes of evaluation and styles of organizing students in courses of study and patterns of educational experience as worthwhile proposals intending to educate students. To venture a definition I would proffer that curriculum development is the process of planning, implementing and evaluating courses of study, or patterns of educational activity, which have been offered as proposals for improvement.

Philosophical considerations and the role of values in the educational ideology proposed is of crucial importance to our understanding of curriculum and education. The conception of education entertained by planners, teachers and others is instrumental in how these courses are developed. Whatever the philosophy or ideological base, a curriculum involves a good deal of rigorous and systematic planning. Curriculum development rests on several assumptions. First, that the improvement of education and experience is possible and indeed justifiable. Accepting this means that current practices are not complete or perfect.

A second assumption is that individuals with an educational responsibility will have access to resources and other forms of support that will allow them to contribute to worthwhile endeavors in a positive direction. Third, that ongoing change in technology, culture and indeed even knowledge make curriculum development an imperative.

Teachers, parents, students and administrators are the partners in curriculum development for improved education. These partners need to establish quite clearly what purposes they have. This statement should not be confused with the technical specificity fostered by the objectives model approach, but rather involves a statement of aims: directions worthy of proceeding in.

These curriculum actors require significant support. Styles of supporting curriculum change vary widely from one culture to another. In Britain the Schools Council for Curriculum and Examinations was established in 1964 after an attempt by the then Ministry of Education (now the Department of Education and Science), a remarkable agency for making resources available for experimental programs. The purpose of the Schools Council was:

To undertake in England and Wales research and development work in curricula, teaching methods and examinations in schools, and in other ways to help teachers decide what to teach and how to teach it. In all its work it has regard to the general principle, expressed in its constitution, that each school should have the fullest possible measure of responsibility for its own curriculum and teaching methods based on the needs of its own pupils and evolved by its own staff.

(Schools Council for Curriculum and Examinations, 1975: 7)

Such a statement is curiously similar to one made by Alfred North Whitehead in the introduction to his book *The Aims of Education*, published in 1929. Of course, today the Council is gone, and this sort of democratic thinking has been replaced by a National Curriculum. The role of central government has been stepped up and is certainly more powerful today in modern Britain than in the 1960s and 70s.

In American schools the degree of autonomy held by teachers in designing curriculum varies considerably from state to state, yet does not permit a totally free hand in the way that British teachers historically had before the advent of the Great Educational Reform Bill (GERBIL) and new National Curriculum of 1988 which eliminated much of that independent judgment and decision-making in curriculum concerns at the school level. Alas, the Schools Council has gone to the wall and the curriculum is now "telegraphed to the provinces."

Curriculum development is a process; usually involving several steps or stages. Ideologically speaking I believe it is best undertaken by each school through working teams of participants in the spirit of practical deliberation. Schwab (1969) not only provided a model or practical approach to curriculum development but he gave a new language. One of the principal problems with curriculum is the antiseptic technical nature of curriculum theory at present. Perhaps the best statement of this idea is rendered by Whitehead in *The Aims of Education*, where he argued that each school needed to define and plan its own curriculum. Would this not be a reality in a true democracy? There are numerous starting points for curriculum development. For example:

1   The knowledge domain. Here we examine the epistemological issues connected with the discipline or subject we are developing. The working party draws upon all informed judgment and sources of knowledge and through a careful examination arrives at course aims or goals.

2   Identification of methods or strategies for teaching. Here we are concerned with the art of teaching the proposed curriculum. This is its pedagogy.

3   Creation of materials in the form of units. This is the action of structuring the knowledge and affective and skills components so that they have an internal logic.

4   Judging or evaluating the curriculum in practice. For example, student assessment through structured essay writing, subjective examinations and so on.

5   Informing the project team through feedback and further deliberation and reflection on the curriculum in action.

The above criteria imply no one particular starting point, as is the case with identifying specific objectives. It has been my experience that teachers do not think of objectives first and when asked to they have great difficulty in doing this. Rather they think of content in the form of unit themes, topics and material they would include. The curriculum, like education in general, is a rational and purposeful activity. However, the purposes, or virtues, of curriculum vary with philosophers and ideologies. For Aristotle, the aim of education is to allow the student to both like and dislike what he or she ought.

Imagination

The concept of *imagination* is crucial to the purposes of education. It "is the faculty by means of which one is able to envisage things as they are not" (Warnock, 1973: 113). What this suggests is that experience encapsulates more than we can see or predict. Lawrence Stenhouse once remarked that "education as induction into knowledge is successful to the extent that it makes the behavioral outcomes of the student unpredictable" (1975: 82). Stenhouse has grasped an important nettle of curriculum theory here. What he argued for is that the educated mind does not simply arrive at pre-determined outcomes but rather at unpredicted outcomes because it uses knowledge to construct unique meaning. This is the challenge of education and the human imagination. It is a constructivist operation.

The acquisition of new vistas requires a reflective imagination and mind. Maxine Greene has taken the position that the arts are the most likely content areas for releasing the imagination and capacity and give it play. There must be authentic and wonderful engagement of aesthetic experience for the imagination to have play. Maria Montessori recognized this with her theory of education based on storytelling, which ignites the curiosity and imagination of the pupil. Art strikes us as being more than simply objects, as Jean Paul Sartre suggested:

> The work is never limited to the painted, sculpted or narrated object. Just as one perceives things only against the background of the world, so the objects represented by art appear against The background of the universe (T)he creative act aims at a total renewal of the world. Each painting, each book, is a recovery of the totality of being. Each of them presents this totality to the freedom of the spectator. For this is quite

the final goal of art: to recover this world by giving it to be seen as it is, but as if it had its source in human freedom.

(1949: 57)

Sartre thus sees many ways in which students having encounters through curriculum in the arts can use imagination to renew and extend their experience and knowledge. All too often, however, the arts and the curriculum are conceived as a repository or urn of the banking notion of curriculum in a postindustrial society serving the needs of technology. The alternative view is to allow young students to find their own values and voices. A few theorists have developed this existential idea of curriculum. William Pinar (1975; Pinar *et al.*, 1995) writes of the personal nature of curriculum. While the curriculum may be experienced as a private personal encounter, Pinar does not believe that curriculum can be planned for others. This is not a helpful principle when curricula are indeed planned for all pupils.

What is stated here is that curriculum study and planning is as much for the teacher as it is for those with a responsibility for planning at a local educational authority, district, state or national level. The creation of teaching and learning units broken down into daily lessons is at the base of sound curriculum planning. A curriculum is not the equivalent of a syllabus which is a mere list of topics, which has perhaps led to the view of curriculum as "content" to be covered. There are at least three aspects to curriculum:

1   The *intentions* – these are the aims, purposes, values and direction in which it is believed education should be progressed.
2   The *transactions* or encounters that happen while curriculum is being implemented. The "lived" or actual curriculum.
3   The *effects* of curriculum – the results of what transpires because of the teaching and learning.

Types of curriculum

1   *Formal curriculum*. The planned academic courses of study offered by the institution. The content, goals and arrangements formalized for learning.
2   *Informal curriculum*. The "extracurricular activities" which are organized around the formal curriculum such as societies, sports clubs, games.
3   *Null curriculum*. This is the curriculum that schools do not teach but that is perhaps equally as important as the formal curriculum. Eisner (2002: 97) argues that one important dimension is the intellectual processes that schools emphasize and then neglect their implementation and another is the subject matter that is absent in formal curriculum.
4   *Actual curriculum*. This is the curriculum that is actually implemented

and transacted and which may not have fidelity with the formal plan for curriculum.

5   *Hidden curriculum*. The curriculum that is latent or covert but present in school culture. Kids learn lots of things the school doesn't plan for, for example how to cheat; it also embodies key values, for example in a religious private school where the unwritten rule is that "silence is golden." The hidden curriculum is mediated through implication rather than direct teaching and is embedded in the culture of the school. It strikes me as interesting that some of the things I recall best from my early school days had nought to do with formal or informal curriculum but with the hidden curriculum. For example "Where do pupils congregate and why?" "Who holds the keys?" "What access exists to Principal and Teachers?" "Who has control of finances?"

Conclusion

There exist competing and conflicting ideas of planning the curriculum alongside competing ideologies. It is not the purpose of this work to say what the substantive content curriculum should be for all pupils – that is a task for each school and community to decide. The point of this work is to propose a model for curriculum that focuses on the educational process and in-built principles of procedure that can bring education about, helped by a teacher being careful of implementing a teaching strategy that has fidelity with these principles of procedure monitored through an action research brief. The process-inquiry model for curriculum design can be used both with disciplines such as mathematics, music and philosophy (forms of knowledge) and with subjects and interdisciplinary modules (fields of knowledge, e.g. geography, engineering, social studies).

Chapter 2

Curriculum, quality and freedom

> The first requisite for educational reform is the school as a unit, with its approved curriculum based on its own needs and evolved by its own staff. If we fail to secure that, we simply fall from ... one dunghill of inert ideas into another.
>
> Alfred North Whitehead, *The Aims of Education and Other Essays* (1929: 21)

One might readily recognize that Whitehead was an advocate for freedom and choice via school-based curriculum development and the freedom of the local educators to effect reforms democratically. Alas, the England of Whitehead's day is not that of modern times, which resembles closely the American model of disempowering the school and teacher of curriculum development powers and responsibilities. Rather teachers perform more as functionaries in a top-down bureaucracy. It is my task to show something of the messy situation, particularly in schools and colleges that are embedded in the quality wars, the advent of technical rationality and the clash that has arisen when faced with a practical reflective driven model of education. There is a lot of waste and confusion. Philosophers and curriculum scholars must begin to debate the way out. In this chapter, my plan is to discuss critically:

1 a conception of *curriculum* and *quality* briefly;
2 the idea of school-based curriculum freedom that allows for curricular and teacher development;
3 the enormous wastage of resources, particularly in teacher preparation and retention;
4 differences in academic freedom and curriculum development for teachers and professors.

Yet there are significant critics that argue (Apple, 1995) that the present curriculum situation is dominated by conservatives, technicians and bureaucrats and that it is somewhat mythical to presume that curriculum scholars ever have had a "voice" of any significance in impacting curriculum change. Apple has asserted:

> The Right has done a good job of showing that decisions about curriculum, about whose knowledge is to be made "official" are inherently matters of political and cultural power.
>
> (1995: 39)

Moreover, Apple contends that within the past forty years it is difficult to find more than a few instances where scholars specifically within the curriculum field have had any significant impact on the debates (1995: 38–39). The political "Right" is doing well. Neoconservatives have succeeded in marginalizing the voices of women, the poor and minorities and it continues to take power away from educators who have been disrespected as "intellectual liberals" who are seen as part of the problem. It has become "the survival of the richest" given that educational resources and scholarships are more unequally distributed to those who already have high socio-economic status and resources (McKernan, 2004).

The central task and the intellectual challenge of the moral and intellectual life is to discuss ways in which the true wealth or equity that we hold in education may be reclaimed and how these ideas are related to curriculum, quality and choice in the present critical situation.

I must also preface my remarks with the comment that this is a task that philosophers have not impressed very well upon educational policy-makers. This chapter extends my arguments about the "rhetoric of quality" in American education and the "value dilemmas" thesis, which I constructed as a quality war between two competing rationalities: the dominant technical-management-minded brokers and those engaged in practical and critical hermeneutics.

The ideological quality war may be illustrated by reference to the following value dilemmas: standards versus expression; productivity versus excellence; measurement versus understanding; training versus education; control versus freedom; unity versus diversity; objectivity versus subjectivity; and uniformity versus imagination. Suffice it to say that the curriculum wars are wars over values: technical rationality is in full control of our national and state system of education. Yet this should not deter the mind of the educator from seeking improvement in intention and reality.

The public curriculum

In Chapter 1, the question was raised "How should curriculum be understood?"

The curriculum should be seen as a symbolic and meaningful object like Shakespeare's first folio in that it has meaning and communicates that which is valued in the culture. It has been won through research and the curiosity of scholars. In the same sense that these scholars did not know what they would find in advance of their inquiries – so too students should not be told what it is they will know, find and be able to do as a result of their inquiries. Which leads me to the central argument for this book: a curriculum can be planned without recourse to behavioral objectives. Indeed this was the situation that existed prior to the twentieth century. It was the introduction of measurement via educational psychology that changed this within the past one hundred years.

In our current situation of accountability, and control by top-down policy-making hierarchies, there is little prospect for a way out of curriculum confusion other than the extension of freedom to practitioners to experiment with alternative curriculum ideas that will enable the imagination and art of teachers to teach a view of knowledge that is the conception and essence of the process of education. An art can only be improved by the exercise of art. So my conception of curriculum argues for a reconstruction of curriculum development as school-based development and research by educators, utilizing our collective understanding of equity, freedom and choice and addressing barriers to that development as they are contextualized in the narrow bondage of curriculum as currently based in which teachers are given the freedom to develop as artists. A curriculum is embodied as artifact and as symbolic art where teachers are artists and the way one proceeds is by the careful testing of curricula as hypotheses. The terrible sadness is that most teachers and educational authorities do not view curriculum as art in the way musicians or artists do and they do not share my enthusiasm for teaching as research or the importance of experimentation in education as Dewey did, or indeed their role in it.

Philosophers of education now have an opportunity to enlighten policy by furthering understanding of alternative plans conceived by local and state authorities along with teacher educators. A curriculum is a proposal that invites critical scrutiny through testing in practice. That makes us all researchers. This also allows educators to exercise their situational understanding and judgment.

Thus the issues and questions are: What do we mean by curriculum and how can it be improved? What freedom do we require to deal with enhancing choice and quality curriculum in our schools? What machinery would best be utilized to undertake this task? A Schools Council for curriculum? How do we deal with the enormous wastage of public resources and incredibly inefficient mechanisms underpinning teacher education at present?

Quality as a concept in education

The first thing that needs to be said about quality in the curriculum is that it must ignite imagination. That is, we should not be bored or paint on a canvas that is so broad that students fail to gain any depth of specialization. The poet Shelley spoke of the imagination as making love and sympathy possible; it was for this reason that Shelley found poetry so valuable, because it influences human imagination. It seems to me that students are often bored by curriculum offerings and are not stretched. Quality amounts to learning something in great depth in my view, and students not offered a specialization are treated not as responsible thinkers in their own right, whereas many are indeed most competent to think and create for themselves. Recall that *educere*, from the Silver Latin, means to lead out from ignorance. In this sense, imagination comes into play.

In the USA secondary pupils study more than half a dozen subjects each term; a scenario in which it is impossible to build any real depth of knowledge or acquire specialization. With the "Block System" of timetabling, where students are grouped for ninety-minute classes over half the year, rather than the full academic year, students are being exposed to even more courses. Mini courses cannot lead to depth of understanding nor to specialized knowledge. The French system usually admits five subjects for state examination and the British system three. The latter are far better suited to student specialization and choice – as students select these at Advanced Level themselves. I am not convinced by the arguments for a general education with the decreasing number of core subjects. The argument that a general education tries to teach students a little of everything cannot be justified as its leads to complaints of boredom and no depth of understanding or knowledge. Boredom is the awareness of limits while the imagination is, by definition, limitless. A student hooked on learning history is not bounded by frontiers or walls and that is the beauty of specialization.

To have quality, then, we need to allow room for the inquiries that are indeed fired by imagination, so that students can get far beyond the knowledge that we trust we have so that they can get to the places they will claim. This is essentially a "constructivist theory" of individual educational autonomy. Knowledge is always provisional. This freedom to "go on" is the essence of education. This brings us to a very practical question: Will some students be bored by some subjects? The answer is inevitably yes. That is where choice comes in. Here I refer not to taking the odd elective but to allowing the choice to study two or three subjects in high school on an equivalency with, say, the British A-level system of curriculum and examinations. My own son took ten different subjects in his first year at university – this to me was a quite absurd intellectual task.

Quality, then, can be determined to the degree that imagination is evident and exercised. Free and unrestricted thought is required. The capacity to think can be advanced by allowing subject specialization, rather than delaying it, in areas chosen by students, with a fair amount of freedom to roam and claim the subject as their own. I find that students entering my classes are not fully prepared by the schools for free thought. We have postponed specialization and that seems to me to work against high standards and what counts as excellence.

The curriculum is a powerful selection of values from contemporary culture. On the view of Mary Warnock, the imagination is the extent to which students and teachers have the capacity for free thought, and to neglect imagination is to neglect pure freedom (Warnock, 1973: 121). We must acknowledge that all educational and curriculum decisions involve matters of choice and value. These are matters of enduring moral concern requiring moral deliberation, and not merely a technical response. In a profound sense, we suffer what can graphically be described as a "paralysis of imagination." A curriculum is like a recipe, whether we wish to add quality features like a half dozen key concepts, or intellectual specialization, is a question of design and value.

The "wealth" or "equity" that we hold in a real cultural capital sense may be recovered and suggests a strategy for dealing with the inefficient use of resources in teacher education. The pyramidal systems of governance we embrace stifle imagination and initiative at the grass roots level. The central feature of a school that wishes to become better is this: there is an unashamed inspirational character that is "hungry" and wants to succeed. Setting the conditions for inspiration and hunger are what a Schools Council can rightly support.

Constraints on quality: time and work overload

The most significant constraint acting on the teacher as a reflective professional and action researcher is *time* (McKernan, 1996). Teachers experience a serious work overload and do not have time for research or curriculum improvement. A significant feature of modern higher education is that fewer resources are allocated yet faculty are asked to do more and more. "Downsizing" is a word that was coined only recently to reflect this concept and activity. At a time when research funding is drying up class size rosters are increased; and more publications are demanded for promotion. The emphasis in public universities has been to concentrate on teaching – to teach more classes and larger classes. This perspective places a premium bunting on increasing productivity by all workers. At East Carolina University faculty are expected to teach four courses per semester (term), or twelve clock hours per week, per semester, and one must explain and defend teaching loads that do not meet this standard, which is about double that of the traditional research university loadings. The irony of working in a department of Curriculum and Instruction is that undergraduates and postgraduates do not have a required course in curriculum theory, development or action research at times when all are calling for "extended reflective professionals."

Academic positions are created on the basis of ever-expanding full-time education equivalency (FTE) indexes. Some believe that information technology will help to achieve more work more efficiently. Privately, I have heard deans discuss how smaller classes could be consolidated into large audience-type classes with technology and distance education mechanisms. What suffers most in making small educational encounters into large auditorium-type encounters is the quality of the educational relationship between tutor and student. In Britain, the National Curriculum demands that teachers cover more content than previously and they will thus have to teach far more effectively and efficiently. Teachers are expected to work "smarter." In conducting an international survey (England, Ireland and USA) of constraints on action research and curriculum it was discovered that the chief constraint on practitioners was lack of time, followed by lack of resources, school organizational features and research skills (McKernan, 1996).

There is also the hope that Information Technology (IT) will enable a restructuring to manage with fewer teachers. This all flies in the face of what research tells us about learning in larger and larger classes with fewer teachers. One solution might be to delete some of this expanding content, but it seems that the curriculum resembles the library; books are always added and none are ever withdrawn. There is universal agreement among social market enthusiasts that the system can continuously be improved.

There is also the widespread belief that all education must be measurable. Some programs, courses and values are not always amenable to measurement. For example, when we think about measuring the effects of programs designed to increase sensitivity, tolerance and mutual understanding among and between schoolchildren the measurement problems are considerable if not insurmountable. Education has many purposes and values which make measurement susceptible.

Lack of freedom in planning: state versus the reflective practitioner

We say that we value freedom and democracy and that we have a system of decentralized education yet our system is run by a top-down model of bureaucracy. Our planning at state level more closely resembles the Stalinist notion of ten-year "mega state plans" for a central communist regime of the archaic past than the democratic reflective practitioner. Behind such a notion is an implied distrust of the teacher as a professional. We need to be about enhancing professional autonomy and trusting educators. By disempowering teachers, we reinforce this semi-competent image of the educator; State Departments of Education that really allow very little in the way of school-based curriculum development, leadership and empowerment. I am not advocating that we not have a state curriculum, or a state department with a mandate to set standards, inspect and fund public education. Having said this I feel that policies affecting how a school may wish to develop its curriculum is really a local matter, for example social studies, mathematics and gender sensitive education should be left to individual teachers and schools. We talk about reflective practice and teacher empowerment and then we implement the social market policies of the New Right with universities being seen as service providers to clients (i.e. students) and as production units through the work of their Colleges of Education. This is a long way from the reflective autonomous empowered professional we say we are seeking to develop and these efforts, if anything, subtract from any autonomous professionalism.

The need for a Schools Council for Curriculum and Examinations

During the halcyon days of curriculum development beginning in the 1960s in the United Kingdom, total control over curriculum and examinations was in the hands of the Schools Council for Curriculum and Examinations in England and Wales (Scotland always retained their own state provisions), a teacher-controlled body. I cannot adequately describe what a rich and fruitful period of innovation this was, not only for curriculum, but also for advances in curriculum studies, evaluation and theory. Projects sponsored by the Council reached into every community throughout the United Kingdom. This was largely linked to the tenure of the Labour Party and was abruptly overturned by the New Right with the ascendancy of Margaret Thatcher. The Conservatives deleted the Council and returned power to the state, thus taking control of curriculum away from the schools and teachers and returning it to the Department of Education and Science (DES).

What is required today is the re-establishment of a Schools Council for Curriculum and Examination Reform in the United Kingdom and the setting up in each of the American states with a State Schools Council, with control over curriculum assessment and evaluation placed in the hands of educators. It is unlikely that such a body will reappear in any state where conservative politics rule, I should think, but it would be unfaithful to my idea of democratic education not to suggest the possibility of establishing a Schools Council for Curriculum and Examinations. The purpose of such a Council would be to involve practitioners, meaningfully, in curriculum development and research work that affects their practice, and to suggest "alternatives" to present curriculum and evaluation policies.

In recovering the "wealth" in education I wish to state that five conditions should be present: First, in terms of true freedom, and school choice, teachers, parents and community need to be more centrally involved in shaping the curriculum and school choice options based on the needs of their community. We need a school system that is driven by curiosity, imagination and hunger when it comes to learning, curriculum and teaching. We love to talk about excellence in the USA but look for untrained teachers to replace our attrition rate figures each August. In North Carolina, we are losing 14 percent of teachers annually to attrition. This means that half of the teachers who started teaching will not be around three to four years later when they have earned "tenure." A terrible waste.

Second, in terms of equity, extraordinary resources should be recovered and not wasted in the preparation of pre-service and in-service teachers. It is a fact that a significant number of all those who study education to degree level never enter teaching. Of those remaining some 50 percent leave within the first five years of their professional life. These losses are expensive not only in terms of the financial implications but also morally, in terms of teacher morale in general. We need a "contract" with teacher education students to stay the course. We need to find induction teachers and in-service teachers more resources to be supported and retained in school.

Third, in terms of quality we need less government intervention and control of curriculum and more responsibility for educators in curriculum development and assessment. We cannot morally mandate that Professor A.N. Other will use an objectives model of curriculum design when academic freedom permits diversity, yet that is what it has come down to in North Carolina, even for university professors. Faculty are told to write syllabi listing instructional objectives and competencies. When such a policy is mandated, academic freedom is threatened.

Fourth, an agency that supports curriculum development is required. I would suggest the establishment of a Schools Council for Curriculum and Examinations, governed by teachers, which would sponsor experimentation in new curriculum development and assessment, including the evaluation of individuals, programs and even systems. The Council I envisage would operate under the control of a Professional Board of Educators and all others with responsibility in the community for education. If we were truly serious about partnerships and collaboration this would be the best policy horse to back to improve learning, teaching and curriculum. In my view, the reconstruction of curriculum, teacher development and assessment has become a social market strategy because the traditional view of teacher educational policy has been managerial and technical-rational and not hermeneutic, practical and reflectively professional. In recent times, we have witnessed a concerted and persistent emphasis on the effectiveness, efficiency and cost economics of education and the keeping of records as social indicators of the health, and dare I say wealth, of education systems. This social market mentality ensures the "survival of the richest." That is, that those endowed with major social and economic advantage, continue to lay claim to the scholarships, prizes and higher echelons of achievement. Cultural capital is not distributed equally (McKernan, 2004).

Education is measured in terms of indicators like output, scores and costs.

Quality is never free. It is a bottom-line business nowadays. Outcomes, and not the process, seem to matter most. We are asked to be "bottom-line workers." The growth of interest in vouchers, tax credits, outcomes-based curriculum, high stakes testing, quality management and so on is without question a political concern reflecting the trend towards accountability, social indicators and increased efficiency. This is the new "social market ideology" of education where conservative values rule. Under this guise of increased choice and equity innovations there has been a persistent search for performance indicators in education. The efforts to improve education and its accountability mechanics are often presented as non-partisan, neutral technical purposes when in fact they are deeply held concerns about educational theories and political initiatives. Furthermore such activities are indisputably, yet are not acknowledged as, moral endeavors. All aims in education are moral. We are told we have freedom and choice when we are shackled to systems that deny true democratic curriculum-making by prescribing curriculum by mandate.

To treat education as a balance sheet is a poor version of cultural wealth. Pressure of a political nature did not originate from within the education community but from outside agencies as a means for establishing a surveillance technology over the performance and control of schools and students, and teachers. One must ask if these indicators are really quality indicators at all. We need a philosophy of educational discourse that strengthens the notion that a culture essentially holds its values, beliefs and dispositions as the central aspect of its life – not just the objects and art it creates. To limit our work to the ABCs of a handful of utilitarian school subjects is to strip us of our cultural inheritance and wealth. Along with the three Rs I would add Jane Roland Martin's 3Cs (care, concern and connection) of the "School-home" project, particularly in this time of uncaring, impersonal attacks, violence and abuse. So what should be in the definition of cultural wealth? This form of ideologically-driven control and accountability has little to do with improvement of education but is more about proving market choices and consumer values. It does not seek to remedy and enrich, but rather to cut and slash programs and personnel.

The other thing that deeply troubles me in the present climate of choice and unbelievable investment in education is the fact that educational authorities ignore a basic market mechanism, and that is this: if you wish for quality teachers with good credentials then you must pay the market price. US teachers are paid well below the other top GDP nations. Because of this, and for other reasons, teacher attrition rates are soaring in the USA. The market pressures take a telling revenge. Take for example the honors graduate with a good mathematics degree and teacher certificate (license). This graduate needs to be compensated so that she or he does not resign for a higher paying post in the industrial sector. Teachers need to be paid market force wages and other forms of teacher reward and remuneration. Teacher attrition is perhaps the greatest problem faced today by public schools in the USA. As mentioned above it is estimated that in the USA, almost half of the teachers who take up jobs leave within five years, the vacant positions being entrusted to poorly trained, alternatively certified slap-dash pedagogues. This nurtures a cult of inefficiency, the true cost of which to taxpayers needs to be made more widely known by the economists of education.

Yet the call is for *excellence* in education. Oddly, all the models of "professional development" conceive of teachers as implementing "teacher-proof" programs that have been developed by the state, with specified blueprints for strategy and outcomes. This is truly a "de-professionalization" of the curriculum. I suppose this call for excellence is premised on the idea that if we keep repeating the concept long enough the citizen will think he or she has it. Excellence assumes quality and quality is not cheaply bought. Here I wish to challenge the idea that our teachers and administrators are free at all to decide about important curriculum issues. We need to move to a more decentralized system of curriculum control and accountability to the state.

Education is a form of capital in that it secures future status and wealth. Western societies, based as they are on market economies, have an uncanny ability to reproduce the social class system over and over. Can important values be measured readily? There is the assumption that important goals can be treated as measurable products and that production targets in the form of student outcomes form a complete technology. And that schools and teacher education colleges should be regarded as production units whose performance is regulated by consumer choice. Such managerialism has been readily sold to the public and the legislatures and it is a terrain to which philosophers of education have paid little attention; to their peril, I might add. Cultural wealth as education has stock value. Freedom and equity remain elusive for educators and professors who serve as mere functionaries in a cost-benefit bureaucracy.

Two things bother me greatly about education in society. The first is the over-arching and dogmatic preoccupation with technical rationality as an accountability tool – the achievement of targets, for example learning outcomes, as evidence of learning these *technical* concerns which in fact are *moral* problems. The second is the reliance on essentialist and behavioral theories – the poverty of educational theory in dealing with complex and diverse problems. This has led to poverty in contemporary curriculum, learning and education. We need to recover from this present state by acknowledging those aims that recognize that education is in fact moral education and that if we wish to recover then we will need to redouble our efforts at things like value and character.

As I mentioned in the last chapter, during my doctoral research, my supervisor, Professor Hugh Sockett, would lend me books, and ask me to report back on these readings. He was an analytically trained philosopher of education, and one of the last research students taken on by Richard Stanley

Peters, the English analytic philosopher and psychologist, of course, an exponent of scholarship, lucid writing, discipline, critical inquiry, rigorous evidence and other values embedded in scholarly modes of procedure. At the time I could not comprehend this drill – I was so close to it I could not see that these values were *procedural educational values* that would contribute to my own education in research and to not heed them would be to advance at my peril. Value was further added by the educative nature of the student–supervisor relationship under the British Ph.D. model. This academic/acolyte apprentice system eschewed doctoral coursework in favor of an intense tutorial relationship favoring research; it is a remarkable system and comes closest to what I think Aquinas and Aristotle must have had in mind when they spoke of the educative nature of the relationship between a student and a tutor. Aristotle thought of the relationship between teacher and student as a loving and caring relationship. We have lots to gain from such a system, which in my mind is infinitely more moral than, and generally superior to, our large group-based system of teaching in overcrowded classrooms and the impersonality of online teaching and distance education, advocated for, largely, by administrators with an eye on the "bottom line."

We do not implement such a postgraduate system as I have described above because it is costly. Thus, the economics of higher education and education in schools goes for productivity, cost-cutting, large units of work; all political directions that have led to what must be considered a *loss* of wealth. Education is in poverty as a result.

The diversified nature of our culture's assets is seldom acknowledged because Western culture embraces a very narrow definition of its own wealth. There is an interesting parallel to be drawn between the eighteenth century's far too narrow definition of economic wealth and our own overly narrow definition of cultural wealth. When in 1776 Adam Smith inquired into the wealth of nations, he expanded upon the earlier concept of economic wealth as money or gold and silver by broadening the definition to include not just the wealth of kings, or even the wealth of the merchant class, but the goods that all people in a society consume. In rejecting the present definition of cultural wealth as "high" culture, or the "higher" learning, I take similar action. Of course, high culture is a part of our cultural wealth. However, there is far more to a culture's wealth than the acknowledged classics of art, music and literature; more even than philosophy and economics, history, science and psychology.

I wish to propose that the wealth of our culture is to a very considerable degree dependent upon the wealth of our educational system and the school curriculum. What does this focus on education entail? John Dewey characterizes the task when he writes:

> What we want and need is education pure and simple, and we shall
> make surer and faster progress when we devote ourselves to finding out

just what education is and what conditions have to be satisfied in order that education may be a reality and not a name or a slogan.

(1966: 360)

To become philosophers of their own education students cannot leave these tasks to others but must devote themselves to "finding out just what education is" for them and what conditions have to be satisfied in order that education may be a "reality" for each of them. In so doing, learners cease to be merely students *in* education; they become students *of* education.

I am not saying most people need to become professional academics, or should undertake study in the technical traditions and texts, ancient, modern and postmodern, associated with advanced work in the field of educational philosophy – although I would certainly not discourage anyone from doing so if they were interested in or inclined to take up these studies. However valuable I consider an in-depth study of our field to be this is not my primary agenda here. Nor am I suggesting that we turn the education of young children or of youth in general over to their own charge. I quite agree with John Dewey's view that we neglect our responsibilities to the young if we carelessly free students from adult structures and guidance only to leave them abandoned to the whims of their own uncontrolled desires, to be manipulated by sophisticated media, pressured by peer groups and tossed about by inward impulses.

Some feminists have recognized the poverty of the curriculum and I note with interest the calls by Jane Roland Martin for the three Cs curriculum of *care, concern and connection* in education and the creation of moral communities which she calls the "Schoolhome" (see Mulcahy, 2002). I believe that the work of Martin and many other female educational philosophers has been ignored by the status quo on several grounds not limited to race and gender. Martin's design merits a fuller explanation than she herself has elucidated, especially regarding its place in the curriculum at national and local state levels. Moral education used to be a large part of the official curriculum in Britain and, no doubt, these values continue in a far less controversial manner than in the USA.

Let me sketch my idea of a common core curriculum that takes account of the moral shortcomings of contemporary curriculum. Curriculum must be rational and therefore purposive. It used to be that aims were the thing; today we have much talk of micro outcomes-based learning objectives, which I have been critical of in other papers. John Dewey had the audacity to state:

A narrow and moralistic view of morals is responsible for the failure to recognize that all the aims and values which are desirable in education are themselves moral.

(1966: 359)

Educators who wish to preserve a liberal humanistic educational ideology will need to face up to the challenges of the social market ideology and this will not be conducted successfully through direct opposition to the new social market privateers. We need "creative resistance" and a more profound rhetoric of educational philosophy as a way of responding to these political mandates. My colleague Professor David Gabbard has just begun a new online journal devoted to such an aim titled *Public Resistance*. A reflective discourse will allow parents and the public to become partners in the educational discourse in clarifying the aims and means of education.

Dewey went on to remark that it wasn't "good enough for a man to be good; he must be good for something," letting us in on the emergent utilitarian value that education was perceived to confer. Of course Dewey did not advocate this perspective; on the contrary he thought of education as the capacity for enabling man to live as a social member so that what he obtained was balanced by what he contributed. Education for Dewey was not a means to an end. He wisely remarked:

> Education is such a life. To maintain capacity for such education is the essence of morals. For conscious life is a continual beginning afresh.
>
> (1966: 360)

In this sense, Dewey's idea is that curriculum and education is essentially moral education. Perhaps the last word should be left to Dewey:

> Interest in learning from all contacts of life is the essential moral interest.
>
> (1966: 360)

The cult of inefficiency and teacher education

Only a small fraction of students who enter initial teacher education are serving as teachers ten years later. We are facing a national crisis in the USA regarding teacher supply. Erskine Bowles, President of the University of North Carolina system, has made this his top priority. However, the rush to get more teachers into classrooms may endanger standards and quality.

It should be of enormous concern that approximately half of the students who enter initial teacher education in the USA shall leave within three to four years after starting as teachers in state schools. In North Carolina 45 percent of teachers leave within the first three years. The situation is not uniform across school districts. In North Carolina the annual attrition rate is 14 percent. In 2005, one eastern school district (LEA) had almost a 50 percent teacher attrition rate in one school year. Added to this is the alarming finding that nearly half of all students who intend to become teachers never in fact teach a single day after their graduation from college. The state invests an enormous sum of money in the education of students. If they choose not to use their education then this has been a great waste of resources. We need the researchers to conduct a searching empirical inquiry into the loss of those who for all good reason wished to become teachers, or did become a teacher, and then left the profession. This is a truly staggering attrition cost to the states and the nation.

Education is thought of in most European nations as an investment that will improve the quality of life and culture. The US attrition rate speaks directly to a massive inefficiency in the use of public funds. It is estimated that in the USA 2.4 million new teachers are needed before 2010. This projection jumps to 2.7 million when we factor in declining student/teacher ratios. In high poverty, urban and rural districts three quarters of a million teachers are required in the next ten years. Here is a chilling fact: in the USA, we spend billions on education and accountability mechanisms and then hire in most cases unlicensed teachers and teachers who have not been inducted through traditional teacher education programs. Teacher compensation is a real constraint on retention. The starting salary for a graduate with a Bachelors degree and a teaching license is a mere $26,000 per annum paid over ten months in North Carolina on the 2006 pay year scale (www.ncpublicschools.org).

We need quality, and that entails excellence and learning that places a premium on specialization. In the USA, students who graduate after a four-year program with a Bachelors degree and a teaching license at best have a year of in-depth study of a major/minor teaching subject. A Bachelors degree ordinarily entails the completion of about 128 semester credit hours and requires four years of full-time study. About sixty to seventy-five credits are devoted to a General Education/Liberal Studies program over the first two years. About thirty-six credits are taken up with a major area of special knowledge and about twenty-four devoted to professional "education" classes. Thus, one year is spent out of four studying the subjects one is to teach. This compares very unfavorably with teacher education programs in the United Kingdom, and Europe at large. In Germany, for example, normally a six-year period of study is required to become a teacher after secondary education. Our counterparts in some West European nations produce graduates with advanced levels of three subjects upon university entrance where they study for a Bachelors degree focusing on a major subject at honors level. In North Carolina, only a third of our teachers hold a Masters degree.

We have a messy, inefficient system of teacher education based on spurious notions of schools as production units and education cast as a production technology. There are no courses in curriculum development and no required courses in action research for prospective teachers at East Carolina University. Quality is not cheap. We are not receiving a fair return on current investment.

Academic freedom and curriculum development

There is a huge difference in the freedom to plan curriculum enjoyed by college faculty and those who labor in schools. Academic freedom is an ancient and revered principle. The *Studium* of the University of Paris intended to be the vassal of neither the *Regnum* nor the *Sacerdotium* in the time of Aquinas (Donohue, 1968). This theme of freedom to teach was important for secular professors in a religious administration.

Schoolteachers on both sides of the Atlantic today perform more as functionaries in a top-down bureaucracy. Not only are teachers constrained in their curricular development briefs but also learners are restricted in terms of using their academic freedom to pursue genuine inquiries. Otto Von Bismarck once remarked that there are two things that no one should ever see being made . . . politics and sausages.

Philosophers sometimes make a distinction between it being the case that I "ought" to do something, and my having an "obligation" to do it. That education is not merely a technical operation, but rather a moral enterprise, brings us into the realm of moral philosophy. To become clearer about this I have to address legal and moral rights. In brief, legal rights are the easier to comprehend for there are decision procedures for determining the law and justness of decisions. The thing about moral rights is that there is no such decision procedure. Many of our intractable education disputes – for example, should we support vouchers or busing pupils for racial equity in education – come about because they arise where a moral right is being claimed, not a legal right, which can be addressed by a court. It involves moral thinking because the question of what rights to academic freedom a teacher or professor has is a moral question.

I wish to state that I find it illogical to differentiate the academic rights of Kindergarten through 12th grade (K-12) educators from professors on academic freedom rights. In what follows I will endeavor to show what legal cases currently exist for academic freedom, and since *prima facie* moral principles are needed for the conduct of those who administer law, then the legal and the moral are not mutually interdependent but are linked.

The East Carolina University Faculty Manual indicates that professors are empowered with curriculum improvement rights; yet our State Government Department of Education, despite recent rhetoric about educating "professional" teachers, does not extend these rights to K-12 educators. It is a major contention of this book that K-12 educators do not enjoy academic freedom to the extent that tertiary educators do and that, it seems to me, is both illogical and immoral. Educators have a great stake in both questions of academic freedom – teaching evolution, for example – and those of "tenure." Interestingly, both of these sacred contractual concerns originated with teachers in our schools, not with university professors. Moreover, even in the universities both here and abroad the academic freedom of students and faculty is under attack.

Academic freedom is perhaps the key legitimizing concept of the entire enterprise of higher education. It consists of the rights of faculty and teachers to speak, write and select materials relevant to their teaching and research programs. Yet the phrase "academic freedom" is more often invoked ceremonially than deeply understood. The 1940 American Association of University Professors (AAUP) statement on academic freedom is a classic piece in the literature. Curiously, it does not mention freedom to develop curriculum but focuses upon freedom in teaching and learning. While the Supreme Court has not ruled on teachers' academic freedom, it has commented that teachers do enjoy constitutional rights to freedom of expression. Indeed the First Amendment protects such rights.

The legal concept of academic freedom may have first been recognized in Germany around 1850, so it is not an ancient concept. The Prussian Constitution of 1850 declared that "science and its teaching shall be free." In Germany, academic freedom is known as *Lehrfreiheit* – the right of faculty to teach on any subject. There are two related concepts in Germany: (1) *Freiheit der Wissenschaft*, freedom of scientific research, and (2) *Lernfreiheit*, the right of students to attend any lectures, and the absence of class roll calls. In many European nations roll calls are not usual for student attendance, although they are mandated in most US colleges.

Academic freedom applies to both teaching and research. Freedom in research is fundamental to the advancement of truth. Academic freedom in its teaching aspect is fundamental for the protection of the rights of the teacher in teaching and of the student in learning. It carries with it duties correlative with rights.

In the USA college and university teachers are entitled to full freedom in research and in the publication of the results, subject to the adequate performance of their other academic duties, but research for pecuniary return should be based upon an understanding with the authorities of the institution. However, primary and secondary teachers do not have such protections. Teachers are entitled to freedom in the classroom in discussing their subject, but they should be careful not to introduce into their teaching controversial matter, which has no relation to their subject. Limitations of academic freedom because of religious or other aims of the institution should be clearly stated in writing at the time of the appointment. College and university teachers are citizens, members of a learned profession, and officers of an educational institution. When they speak or write as citizens, their speech is protected by the US Constitution.

There are many differences between the rights of K-12 teachers and university/third level instructors in curriculum decision-making, including the facts that:

1   Teachers in public schools in the USA use textbooks that are chosen by
    state educational committees. University professors make their own
    selection of textbooks for classes that they teach.
2   Teachers in public schools in the USA are required to follow a standard
    syllabus that comes from the state education authority. University
    professors mainly create their own syllabus and determine for themselves
    the course content, methods, and so on.

Patriotic correctness and the university

The USA and United Kingdom are presently at war against terror. The
AAUP created a Special Committee on Academic Freedom and National
Security in Times of Crisis in order to examine how the war on terror has
affected academic freedom. The Patriot Act weakens student protections
under the Family Educational Rights and Privacy Act (FERPA). During
2002, the FBI sent a letter to colleges asking for information about foreign
students, including "names, addresses, telephone numbers, citizenship information, places of birth, dates of birth, and any foreign contact information"
for the past two years. The letter declared that the USA Patriot Act "has
further granted educational institutions authority to release information to
the federal government for use in combating terrorism." In October 2006,
President Bush renewed the Patriot Act, allowing for telephone and internet
spying on citizens as routine surveillance.

The essence of freedom

The essence of freedom, then, signals to me the intellectual, spiritual and
moral autonomy which we recognize when one rejects paternalism and
authority and we hold ourselves obliged to appeal to judgment. Our collective humanity is reduced when judgment is over-ruled by authority. Yet the
situation today is that K-12 schoolteachers do not share in the academic
freedom to develop curriculum that university professors have. Government
departments of education have always been in charge of developing the
curriculum for children in primary and secondary schools. In the United
Kingdom the last vestiges of teacher control were excised with the passage of
the Great Education Reform Bill (GERBIL) in 1988, which was a direct
result of conservative educational policy which called for the demise of the
Schools Council for Curriculum and Examinations (an agency that extended
curriculum reform to teachers throughout the country). It is my task to
show something of the messy situation, particularly in schools and colleges
that are embedded in the "differentiated professionalism" of teachers and
professors. Suffice it to say that technical rationality is in full control of our
Federal and State Departments of Education. Yet this should not deter the
mind of the educator from seeking improvement in intention and reality.

Recommendations

What is required, straightaway, for state schools is the re-establishment of a Schools Council with control over curriculum, assessment and examinations, to be put in the hands of educators in both the USA and United Kingdom. It is unlikely for such a body to reappear in any state where conservative politics rule, I should think, but I cannot be faithful to my idea of education and not suggest the re-introduction of an American Schools Council for Curriculum and Examinations. In recovering the "wealth" in education I wish to state that six conditions should be present:

1   In terms of true academic freedom, and school choice, teachers, parents and community need to be more involved in shaping the curriculum and school choice options based on the needs of their community. We need a school system that is driven by curiosity, imagination and hunger in terms of learning, curriculum and teaching.

2   In terms of equity, extraordinary resources should be recovered and not wasted in the preparation of pre-service and in-service teachers. It is a fact that many of those who study education to degree level never enter teaching. Of those remaining some 50 percent leave within the first five years of their professional life, at least in the USA. These losses are expensive not only in terms of the financial implications but also morally, in terms of teacher morale in general. One radical solution has been proposed by Whittle of Edison Schools infamy – fire half the teachers and pay the remaining half about $90,000 per year.

3   In the USA at least, we need a "contract" with teacher education students to stay the course. We need to find induction teachers and in-service teachers more resources to be supported and retained in school.

4   We need to endow pre-service teachers with curriculum improvement and research skills (in other words, enable them to become reflective practitioners).

5   In terms of quality, we need less government intervention and control of curriculum and more responsibility for educators in curriculum development and assessment. Curriculum improvement is essentially about realizing alternatives to current practice and policy. We are told to write syllabi in terms of departmentally agreed instructional objectives and "competencies" that are endorsed with the Good Housekeeping Stamp of Approval by the National Council for the Accreditation of Teacher Education (NCATE) – who act as external examiners of teacher education institutions by visiting every program once every five years – and the North Carolina State Department of Public Instruction (SDPI) – who certify teachers in the State. Such nonsense all in aid of the "technical rationality" that drives the autocratic hierarchy.

6   A Schools Council for Curriculum and Examinations should be estab-

lished, which would sponsor experimentation in new curriculum development and assessment, including the evaluation of individuals, programs and even systems. The Council I envisage would operate under the control of schoolteachers largely but include Professional Boards of Educators, external researchers and professors, and include parents and community delegates. If we were truly serious about partnerships and collaboration this would be the best horse to back.

Conclusions

In my view, the reconstruction of curriculum, teacher development and assessment has become a technical social market strategy because the traditional view of teacher educational policy has been managerial and technical-rational, and not practical and reflectively professional. There is an unreal rhetoric of excellence that does not have any fidelity with education practice in schools. Our current policies thus fly in the face of true autonomy and teacher professionalism. This clash of values – one supporting instrumentalism and technical style curriculum, the other supporting hermeneutic/practical science and individual growth – co-exist.

The efforts to improve education and its accountability mechanics are often presented as non-partisan neutral technical purposes when in fact they are deeply held concerns about educational values, theories and political initiatives. Furthermore, such activities are indisputably, yet not acknowledged as, moral endeavors. All aims in education are moral. We are told we have freedom and choice when we are shackled to systems that are state-mandated bureaucracies.

There are two things that bother me greatly about education nowadays. The first is the over-arching and dogmatic preoccupation with technical rationality – the achievement of targets, for example learning outcomes, as evidence of learning these *technical* concerns, which in fact are *moral* problems. The second is the reliance on essentialist and behavioral theories – the poverty of educational theory in dealing with complex and diverse problems. This has led to poverty in contemporary curriculum, learning and assessment and education. We need to recover from this present state by acknowledging those aims that recognize that education is, in fact, moral education. I wish to propose that the health of our schools and curriculum is to a very considerable degree dependent upon the quality of academic freedom permitted all teachers and professors. There should be no difference in the academic freedom of educators. All should enjoy equal rights.

Chapter 3

Curriculum design and theorizing

> We believe that our curricula should be revised, but we do not know where or how to begin. Our susceptibility to educational fads has become notorious.
>
> Boyd Bode, *Modern Educational Theories* (1927: 232)

Designing a curriculum is at once an artistic venture, a political event and a value-driven exercise. The purpose of this chapter is to explore theory and design perspectives in curriculum. However, given the dominance of the behavioral theoretical tradition we may do better to deal in perspectives or models rather than full-blown theories of curriculum (Marsh and Willis, 2007).

Curriculum is a field of study that has both theoretical and practical knowledge. Theory yields up rational explanations for worthy models. Models function as representations of theory. They may be illustrated linguistically, through physical forms, through graphic representations or mathematically. Curriculum consists of ideas imagined by educators and others with the responsibility for making education "better," that is, for curriculum development. It is above all else about form or design. Curriculum is thus like a musician's or artist's portfolio. Should the curriculum have behavioral outcomes expressed as objectives, or should it be designed on another form of logic? All curricula have "content" in the form of publicly valued knowledge, often included with skills, values and dispositions. Curriculum developers have usually approached design from one of three perspectives: The nature of subject knowledge; the nature of society; or the nature of the learner (Kelly, 1989; Marsh and Willis, 2007).

Teachers are licensed in areas of public knowledge – whether history, or mathematics – and, at least in the USA, all teachers under the *No Child Left Behind* law of 2001 must hold a Bachelors degree, a teaching license and show competency in their licensed areas of curriculum specialization.

Teachers are licensed, by virtue of their education, in subject (content) specializations. How to organize "content" has been a perennial problem for curriculum developers. Is the content to be arranged traditionally in the shape of subjects, or disciplinary knowledge? Should there be an essential "core" to the curriculum stressing mathematics, reading, science and technology? Or, is the curriculum to be seen as inter-disciplinary, allowing for an inquiry-discovery approach to learning where knowledge is integrated across subjects and disciplines? These are all questions that curriculum designers have to deal with. The intent of this chapter is to outline some of the possible designs available – without an assumption of completeness – simply as hypotheses worthy of consideration.

A further observation needs to be made now. Curriculum design rests to a considerable degree upon the exercise of practical reason and deliberation; it is not simply a procedural or a technical response to problem solving. It is an act that is made *in situ*, that is, on the spot, by a practitioner employing deliberate thought. As a practical matter, curriculum decisions need to be made skillfully based on an accumulated situational understanding on the part of the teacher. As such, it is at once personal, social, political and theoretical. Macdonald suggested:

> I suspect that in many ways all curriculum design is political in nature; that is, it is an attempt to facilitate someone else's idea of the good life. By creating social processes and structuring the environment for learning, curriculum design is thus a form of "utopianism," a form of political and social philosophizing and theorizing. If we recognize this, it may help us sort out our own thinking and perhaps increase our ability to communicate with each other.
>
> (1975: 293)

Sources for the curriculum

1. Epistemological (traditional)

Curriculum may be designed with reference to its epistemology: its knowledge or subject base. This has generally come from two basic forms: the traditional "disciplines" or forms of knowledge approach and "fields of knowledge," defined by their subject knowledge, rather than their distinctive "form," for example geography, sociology, psychology. The advocates of this traditional approach to curriculum argue that these disciplines and subjects will develop appropriate character and qualities of mind (Kelly, 1989).

2. Learner-based

Some have argued that it is the child, or student, upon whom design should be based. The source of curriculum would be the needs, interests and human development of the individual. From the time of Comenius there has been a concern for the student, rather than the subject, as a source for planning. The child-centered movement began with thinkers such as Erasmus, Comenius, Rousseau, Froebel and Pestalozzi and has culminated in a modern progressive theory promoted by Dewey, Montessori, A.S. Neill and others. The personal-progressive perspective is based upon what is important for the child and student as a person.

3. Objectives-based (technical-scientific)

The objectives model derives from a view that efficient technology, teaching and resources aid the attainment of specified outcomes. This output or "product" idea of education is based upon behavioral change in students. Tyler, for example, has stated "the most useful form for stating objectives is to express them in terms which identify both the kind of behavior to be developed in the students and the context or area of life in which this behavior is to operate" (Tyler, 1949: 46–47).

4. Society and problem-centered

Based on the difficulties of living, the problem-centered design attempts a form of life-adjustment education using personal, group and institutional issues and problems. Curriculum addressing social problems such as racism, inequality, terrorism and so on would fall within this design.

Curriculum theorizing

The twentieth century has been productive in putting forward a number of alternative theories relating to curriculum. Comprehensive reviews of these theories can be found in several texts (Reid, 1978, 1994; Schubert, 1986; Kelly, 1989; Marsh and Willis, 2007; Tanner and Tanner, 2007).

One of the more detailed and elaborate classifications and discussions of curriculum theory is found in the work of William Reid (1978) and adapted and modified in Colin Marsh and George Willis' comprehensive book which deals with alternative curriculum approaches (2007). In the USA, William Schubert (1986) and, in the United Kingdom, Vic Kelly (1989) have written large synoptic curriculum texts addressing curriculum theories based on content, objectives and personal development. What I propose is to attempt to merge these analyses into categories and authors that capture not the totality of contributors, but the essence of each orientation: personal-progressive; academic-rational/liberal; technical-behavioral; practical-deliberative; critical-political; critical-artistic; and finally critical-Existentialist-gender. Thus, these are not pure curriculum theorists, but writers who have influenced philosophy of education, curriculum studies and research with an impact on policy and design of curriculum as a result. These classifications also reflect the values underpinning competing ideologies; a further continuation of ideologies is contained in Chapter 11 with the empirical survey of teachers' values.

Curriculum perspectives

Table 3.1 Personal-progressive

Bode (1927)
Dewey (1900, 1902, 1916)
Froebel (1896, 1899)
Kilpatrick (1918)
Montessori (1949, 1967)
Neill (1960)
Rogers (1983)
Rugg (1927)

Table 3.2 Academic-rational/liberal

Hirst (1965)
Hutchins (1968)
Mulcahy (1981)
Peters (1966)

The academic rationalists favor the development of mind and the traditional, general humanities studies aiming at intellectual experience of association with knowledge and a liberal education. This is perhaps the oldest of the Western education traditions going back to the idealism of Plato and realism of Aristotle – the foundation of Western philosophy and curriculum.

Table 3.3 Technical-behavioral

Beauchamp (1975)
Block (1971)
Bloom (1956, 1981)
Bobbitt (1918, 1924)
Charters (1923)
Davies (1976)
Herrick and Tyler (1950)
Mager (1962)
Popham and Baker (1970)
Pratt (1980)
Tyler (1949)
Wheeler (1967)

Born out of the rise of behavioral psychology, efficiency-oriented administration, performance assessment and the Science in Education movement of the late-nineteenth and twentieth centuries, the technical perspective has moved "outcomes-based education" to the forefront of policy and curriculum development in the modern world.

Table 3.4 Practical-deliberative

Elliott (1991)
McCutcheon (1995)
Reid (1978, 1988)
Schwab (1969, 1971, 1973, 1983)
Skilbeck (1976)
Walker (1971)
Westbury (1972)

The practical deliberative tradition marked a radical new departure towards the practical work of teachers and others with a responsibility for curriculum change with the four classic critical papers by Joseph Schwab in the 1960s, 70s and 80s. In the United Kingdom, work by William Reid and Malcolm Skilbeck gave new meaning to the practical in terms of school-based curriculum development. This perspective argued for extended professional development and teacher research in their professional settings. The practical perspective argued that education, and curriculum, is an act of significant social practice and teachers and others are best placed to undertake such tasks in the school.

Table 3.5 Critical-political

Anyon (1980)
Apple (1979)
Bourdieu and Passeron (1977)
Freire (1970, 1973)
Giroux (1982)
Kemmis (1986)
Lawn and Barton (1980)
Whitty (1980)
Willis (1981)

Table 3.6 Critical-artistic

Eisner (1974, 1979, 1991)
Eisner and Vallance (1974)
Stenhouse (1975)

Table 3.7 Critical-existentialist-gender

Greene (1975)
Grumet (1981)
Huebner (1975)
Macdonald (1971)
Martin (1984)
Noddings (1984)
Pagano (1992)
Pinar (1975, 1980)

Some curricular design models

1. Subject-disciplines designs

This is the oldest design model for curriculum. Since at least the time of the Sophists, master teachers of the *Trivium* (grammar, rhetoric and logic) in ancient Greece, knowledge has historically been packaged as fragmented subjects, organized into discrete disciplines of pure "forms of knowledge" (Hirst, 1965). The development of mind was key to the oldest philosophy – Idealism as conceived by Socrates and Plato. The search for truth, wisdom and the development of mind was a primary concern of disciplinary design – sometimes referred to as academic rationalism.

Many educationalists would say that education is mainly concerned with the transference of knowledge to students. This relates to the notion of the development of the mind, reasoning and thinking. This raises the distinction that has been made by a host of curriculum theorists such as Phenix, Schwab, Hirst and Peters that curricula are concerned with public forms of knowledge – the disciplines. A discipline consists not only in body of knowledge but also in the respected methods of inquiry which produced the knowledge as well as the accepted "principles of procedure" adopted by those in this venerable community of scholars. Disciplines do not need justification on instrumental (objectives) grounds as they have their own in-built criteria recognized as sufficient.

There is no need for a detailed set of outcomes or targeted objectives to be achieved to demonstrate competence – the good teacher of literature will be able to recognize success or mediocrity, or indeed failure, according to whether the student applied the standards of those who work within the discipline – these principles of procedure then are the real aim of education and they will be different from discipline to discipline. This is an important point and one which if accepted makes the entire curriculum model of planning by objectives fall like a house of cards.

Curriculum-making, astonishingly enough, was accomplished without the use of instructional objectives prior to the twentieth century and was the chief model of the early Greek, Roman and Muslim institutions of learning.

Content has traditionally been seen to be knowledge packaged as disciplines or subjects to be learned by students. More recently the seven liberal arts have been forms of knowledge owing to their logical and conceptual structure and Bruner's notion of "Structure of Disciplines" argued that these unique scholarly modes of knowing represent the best scaffold, or structure, in the form. Thus, the "disciplines" are aptly named because the knowledge contained therein has been won through rigorous testing and research. Disciplines, according to Paul Hirst (1965), have four characteristics:

1   a distinct logical structure;
2   a thread of key concepts;
3   ways of gaining new knowledge;
4   methods of testing knowledge claims.

Hirst calls these disciplines *forms of knowledge* – mathematics, physical sciences, history, religion, literature, the fine arts, and philosophy. Hirst also distinguishes *fields of knowledge* such as engineering or geography. Geography is in a class of theoretical study while engineering and curriculum are examples of "practical study." The subject design also has wide currency and credibility because teachers are professionally licensed to teach specialist areas, say mathematics or Latin.

2. Interdisciplinary/broad fields designs

The broad fields design brings together cognate areas or subject fields into one broad arm of knowledge. Social studies is such a field, using history, economics, geography and sociology. The "humanities" is another example of a broad fields design and might include art, Latin, music and areas that illuminate man in culture and his achievements. There is some effort to "integrate" separate fields that have logical connection. In elementary grades the "language arts" contain reading, composition, speaking, grammar and so on. The broad fields design appeared in the twentieth century (Ornstein and Hunkins, 1993: 245). In a sense, its use is a way of integrating subjects that have a close connection, such as the physical or social sciences.

Broad fields designs have also been advocated by blue ribbon agencies such as the National Society for the Study of Education, which advanced a broad fields model including the natural sciences, language and literary studies, art, social studies and mathematics for all students.

3. Student- or child-centered designs

Student-centered approaches suggested that it was the child's own needs, interests and curiosity, and not the discipline, that should be the subject of curriculum design and improvement. This was largely influenced by child-centered theorists such as Rousseau, Herbart, Pestalozzi, Froebel and Montessori and later by the Progressive theorists in the USA including the work of John Dewey, William H. Kilpatrick and others. Dewey's *The Child and the Curriculum* (1902) is a classic piece on the model. Learning must satisfy the child's curiosity about the world. Such a model was bolstered by the concept of the "activity curriculum" that children learn what they experience. The teacher on this idea is not cast as an instructor but as a partner in inquiry and as a guide, rather than a judge or expert.

The activity-centered design has been very popular since the beginning of the twentieth century and most specifically with pre-school and elementary/middle grades curriculum planning. In the 1960s the British and Irish primary school curriculum underwent re-organization and settled exclusively on a child-centered and highly integrated model for curriculum, attributing this to the influence of Dewey's thought. The most significant aspect of child-centered curriculum is its treatment of knowledge as not unified by disciplines but being more like a "seamless robe." Thus, inquiry and discovery and the breaking down of subject barriers are chief characteristics of this design.

The model also gained favor from such advocates as Paulo Freire who was critical of the type of school and curriculum often referred to as "banking theory," where students' heads are conceived as urns into which knowledge is poured. These radicals insist that more importantly a self-realization and "conscientization" need to be a major aim of curriculum and pedagogy. Freire's *Pedagogy of the Oppressed* (Freire, 1970) is indicative of this school of educators who see emancipation and cultural criticism as major aims of education.

4. Core curriculum designs

The *core curriculum* first came about as a result of concern with social problems (Taba, 1962). It was deemed imperative that curriculum explore national problems like race, economics, equality and so on. Thus, it was seen to be largely an affair of social reconstructionism and favored subjects from the social sciences in examining issues that were problematic in society.

In recent years, however, the term "core" has been associated with those areas of experience or subject areas that it was deemed imperative that every child have exposure to while at school. This is largely tied up with the notion of a core set of knowledge and areas of experience that are equivalent to a basic "national curriculum." This is a popular trend and national curricula have been adopted by most European nations to date as well as Australia, and there is a mandated "core" for each of the American states. It will be interesting to watch if the USA moves towards harmonization by adopting a core curriculum for all the states, though the difficulties would be profound for such an educational policy.

Core curricula have been adopted by a number of nations as a mandatory framework for a National Curriculum in all schools. Some nations with a core curriculum design include the United Kingdom of England and Wales (Northern Ireland and Scotland have their own system arrangements).

5. Integrated designs

The argument has been made that knowledge is more like a seamless robe – that is, there are no pure boundaries or compartments in terms of disciplines and subjects. That if we take seriously the notion of inquiry learning then the pupil will cross over boundaries in the search for answers. The curriculum might be organized around themes such as "the weather," thus allowing the teacher to touch upon the theme as found in literature, mathematics or geography. Such designs are more often found in early childhood education.

6. Process designs

In process designs, emphasis is placed upon those procedures by which students or teachers can conduct educational inquiries. For example, in a social studies class a pupil might be encouraged to pose the sort of question that might be asked by an historian; or in history learn the research methods used by historians. These designs usually are more related to how students learn rather than subject content. For example, what procedures can be employed to help pupils to think critically?

7. Humanistic designs

Arguing that curriculum was too subject-centered, the humanists wish to focus on values, morals and the existentialist question of how to live. This design was very prominent in the 1960s and 70s, with emphasis on teaching about personal qualities, character and values clarification. Deriving from existentialist third force psychology (Ornstein and Hunkins, 1993: 253) it was a clear reaction to the dominance of behaviorism in influencing curriculum. The aims were helped by the work of psychologists like Carl Rogers and William Maslow who worked with the notion of education for self-actualization – where a student is in touch with his or her inner harmony and spirituality.

The National Curriculum

The idea of a common core National Curriculum gives central authorities great control of curriculum reform and examinations. The key questions relate to what shall be taught and how it shall be taught – not why it is taught.

England and Wales National Curriculum

Curriculum in the United Kingdom after the Great Reform Bill of 1988 divided content into a number of "areas of interest." The Curriculum is offered in age blocks for pupils:

- art and design
- citizenship
- design and technology
- English
- geography
- history
- information and communication technology (ICT)
- mathematics
- modern foreign languages (MFL)
- music
- personal, social and health education (PSHE)
- physical education
- religious education
- science.

At ages fourteen to sixteen the core is: English, mathematics, science, MFL, design and technology, ICT, physical education, religious education and whatever other subjects are available from the staff of a school. It is interesting that religious education must be on the curriculum by law but it is also true that students may be excused from this area if they wish.

From sixteen to eighteen students take three subjects at A- or advanced level in preparation for entrance to higher education.

The North Carolina Standard Course of Study (2006)

In the USA, the Federal Constitution does not discuss education or its provision – this is left up to the individual states, which have the authority and legal power to administer public education as they see fit. In North Carolina, therefore, the state has responsibility for curriculum. A standard course of study detailing some 1,649 pages has been provided since 1898 and encompasses the following areas:

- arts education – four disciplines (visual arts, theatre arts, music and dance)
- career technical education
- computer/technology skills
- early childhood
- English as a second language

- English language arts
- guidance
- healthful living
- information skills
- mathematics
- science
- second languages
- social studies.

The emergence of the national curriculum concept has equity, standards and centralization issues at its base. The "Common School" idea was developed in the early years of the American Republic so that children of all backgrounds and social classes would receive a common curriculum experience, and because a national core curriculum would be more easily evaluated. Centralized curriculum systems would afford comparison say between pupils aged thirteen years old in different regions. The argument is that apples would not be compared with oranges in a common core system.

Roots of the objectives model in the USA

Scientific life analysis studies

While Ralph Tyler (1949) is regarded as the person most closely associated with the objectives model for curriculum, there were a number of individuals, reports and surveys undertaken as early as 1910 recommending a behavioral-scientific approach to curriculum planning, some recommending the use of behavioral objectives (Bobbitt, 1918, 1924), in the USA. Serious efforts to reorganize curriculum along "scientific" lines began in 1911 with the work of the National Education Association's Committee on the Economy of Time, which proceeded to adopt an analysis of the "life needs" of pupils. Thorndike, the psychologist, had made a study of pupil handwriting in 1910; and later, in 1921, produced an appropriate word list for pupils. Between 1923 and 1927, W.W. Charters undertook job analyses. The idea that the curriculum should have hundreds of objectives was also endorsed by David Snedden, a sociologist, with regards to the essential condition of whether the purpose was that of production or consumption (Snedden, 1921).

In 1918, Professor Franklin Bobbitt, the champion of the movement for "efficiency in education," argued for "activity analysis" of life activities as the basis for determining objectives in curriculum (Bobbitt, 1918). It is with Bobbitt that the demand for objectives was ushered into curriculum design. In 1924 Bobbitt, based on his activity analysis data, divided the broad range of all human experience into ten areas of focus from which to plan curriculum:

1 social intercommunication
2 maintenance of physical efficiency
3 efficient citizenship
4 general social contacts and relationships
5 general mental efficiency
6 leisure occupations
7 religious attitudes and activities
8 parental responsibilities
9 unspecialized practical activities
10 occupational activities.

Bobbitt realized that techniques for curriculum experience were required for learning in these fields and suggested the following:

1 undirected observations
2 the importance of practical performance
3 reading
4 oral reports
5 pictures
6 repeating one's experiences
7 problem-solving
8 generalization.

The idea was that in working on these techniques pupils would gain experience in life's most satisfying and valuable activities, and that further, pupils should receive no specialized education until these general educational experiences were completed. This trend may have laid the groundwork for the character of general education that American pupils receive to this day. Bobbitt (1924) furthered this life activity analysis study with a major inquiry into analyzing how adults use activities to come close to living a full and satisfactory life, publishing his results in *Curriculum Investigations.*

Surveys and annual Yearbooks of the National Society for the Study of Education

With the influence of science in education, the survey method was seen to produce sound data that could be used in curriculum development. The 1926 Yearbook of the National Society for the Study of Education (NSSE) castigated various committees for not using sound scientific data in making recommendations:

> The members of these national committees (1892–1926) have used subjective and *a priori* methods in arriving at their recommendations

and, with two recent exceptions, have ignored the results of curricular research.

(NSSE, 1926)

Gwynn (1945) notes that major surveys were taken up in various curriculum subject fields including classical subjects (1924); social studies (1934–41); foreign languages (1930); English (1935); and business subjects (1929). He continues that between 1920 and 1930 various Reports of the NSSE recommended the use of objectives in instruction that linked aims to the actual experiences pupils would have in classrooms. Perhaps the most famous for curriculum was the Twenty-Sixth Yearbook (NSSE, 1927) in two volumes: Part 1: *Curriculum Making: Past and Present* and Part 2: *The Foundations of Curriculum Making.*

Emergence of the unit method for teaching and curriculum organization

Perhaps the greatest single innovation in curriculum, besides that of the objectives model design of the twentieth century, has been the introduction of the *unit technique.* Morrison (1926) first introduced a "Unit Plan" and offered a new teaching procedure encapsulated within his five-step lesson plan. Thus, by tightly defining the concept of a unit and specifying an adapted version of Herbart's five-step model of teaching, he gave new impetus to curriculum design in his book *The Practice of Teaching in the Secondary School.*

In the early part of the century, the most prominent method used was that of Johann Herbart, the German educationalist who proposed the five-step lesson plan emphasizing moral character development. Herbart, unhappy with Pestalozzian theory as incomplete, had a great impact on American teacher education efforts through his influence on Horace Mann, Superintendent of the Board of Education in Massachusetts, who led the movement for a "Common School" in the 1820s in the USA (Ornstein and Levine, 2006).

Due to the increasing interest in psychology of education and scientific planning, Johann Herbart fell out of favor. Morrison argued that the curriculum of the US secondary school had three major curricular orientations: *scientific,* in which objects would be derived from mathematics, physical, biological and social sciences, and commercial subjects; the *practical arts,* which had objectives that enabled manipulation of appliances, materials and mechanical devices – domestic subjects such as cooking, sewing, and vocational and mechanical subjects; and the *appreciative type,* primarily areas that are value laden such as appreciation of art, religion, literature and ethics.

It is instructive to note how Morrison viewed the unit technique. He defined a unit as a comprehensive and significant aspect of the environment, of an organized science, of an art or of a conduct, which being learned results in adaptation in personality. This definition suggests that Morrison was after behavior change and that the unit would be an economy device to organize subject matter so that the objectives desired could be achieved. Curriculum planning would never be the same after the unit method was introduced.

Morrison believed that subjects should be organized into discrete units and taught according to his five-step procedure for teaching. The Morrison Plan also offers five steps:

1   exploration of topic
2   presentation by teacher
3   assimilation (classroom activities, e.g. discussion)
4   organization of the material or content
5   recitation.

Thus, the unit method has been the basic building block for most curricula, with the class lesson the primary base for the unit plan.

Chapter 4

Some limitations of the objectives model in curriculum

Education as induction into knowledge is successful to the extent that it makes the behavioral outcomes of the students unpredictable.

Lawrence Stenhouse (1975: 82)

There is little doubt that education is a purposive and rational activity. In earlier periods of educational history "aims" were the thing rather than the more specialist idea of targets, such as intended learning outcomes or behavioral objectives. Some philosophers have even queried the need for such aims. R.S. Peters (1959, 1963) queried the use of "aims" as extrinsic ends. He believed that it was not absolutely necessary for an educator to have an aim. However, he did suggest that aims are values that give direction – that is they are ideals the teacher is committed to in educating a student. Aims function as procedural values. This is a crucial point for an understanding of the alternative theory proposed in this book.

More discussion and literature has been devoted to the topic of educational objectives than any other concept relating to curriculum design. In fact, the curriculum literature has established the "objectives model" as the paradigm for curriculum planning and few have departed from this mold. I believe that the monopoly of this outcomes-based education movement has been detrimental to education not only in the United States but internationally. The movement can be traced from the prized position given to technical rationality and classical education as a science, which took root around the beginning of the twentieth century. Two works in particular stand out marking this model, *The Curriculum* (1918) and *How to Make a Curriculum* (1924), both by Franklin Bobbitt, who brought engineering and managerial orthodoxy to the field of public school education. Bobbitt had endeavored to analyze precisely the day-to-day life activities of an adult in an attempt to more carefully glean the purposes of American education.

This chapter is concerned with pointing out some of the problems and limitations of the objectives model. My main thesis is this: in programs of education, as distinct from training, objectives are inappropriate (if we are

dealing with rudimentary training then the use of objectives is permissible).
Tyler offers the classic definition of a behavioral objective:

> One can define an objective with sufficient clarity if he can describe or
> illustrate the kind of behavior the student is expected to acquire so that
> one could recognize such behavior if he saw it.
>
> (1949: 59–60)

The objectives model has become synonymous with the work of Ralph Tyler
and particularly the rationale he laid out in his celebrated syllabus for
Education 360 at the University of Chicago; perhaps one of the most widely
published books, *Basic Principles of Curriculum and Instruction* (Tyler, 1949).
Yet one could hardly take issue with the assertion that Tyler's book is "the
most influential curriculum book of the twentieth century" (Marshall *et al.*,
2007: 3). Others, such as Mager (1962), solidly ensured that goals would
have to be specified in strict behavioral terms.

Kliebard (1975) informs us in his compelling reappraisal of the Tyler
rationale that although Tyler's claims for the book are modest, the fact is
that over time the Tyler Model has been elevated to the status of *revealed
doctrine*. Tyler argued:

> If we are to study an educational program systematically and intelli-
> gently we must first be sure as to the educational objectives aimed at.
>
> (1949: 3)

We need to be clear as to what precisely he meant when talking of objectives.
For Tyler education was about changing human behavior. Hence, he remarked:

> The most useful form for stating objectives is to express them in terms
> which identify both the kind of behavior to be developed in the student
> and the content or area of life in which this behavior is to operate.
>
> (1949: 46–47)

He devised a commonsensical mode of product control as a mode of evaluation. Evaluation for Tyler was fundamentally focused upon:

> The process of determining to what extent the educational objectives are
> actually being realized by the program of curriculum and instruction.
>
> (1949: 69)

Some criticisms of educational objectives

Generations of teachers, professors, parents and students have uncritically
accepted the use of specific instructional objectives because it is so rational

and self-recommending. What one must understand however is that we do not have objectives per se but rather we make a decision to conceptualize our outcomes and behaviors by using objectives. Thus, objectives are merely a conceptual framework; they are not an object themselves. It seems that curriculum text writers have chosen to reify objectives as the only conceptual scheme available, which, of course, they are not. We can also choose not to have objectives while still being fully committed to rational planning. This demand for target behaviors and outcomes is therefore largely unquestioned. One can see that it is a salutary request to require teachers to set priorities, to scan their work and get clearer about what they are about. Yet education is a highly complex and diffuse endeavor in which many people engage without being completely clear about what they are trying to do. Education, as I have argued in Chapter 1, involves two kinds of criteria: those involved in characterizing the educated person, its outcomes or results, and those concerned with the procedures and processes by which students are gradually educated. Education then picks out processes involved in students becoming "better" persons as a result of their education. Thus, education is initiation into desirable or worthwhile qualities of life. It is mainly connected with values and principles that lead to qualitative development in individuals.

The adoption of the objectives model by practically all school districts, state departments, colleges and so on in American education raises fundamental questions and issues concerning the very nature of education as a process.

The following criticisms of the objectives model have been derived through critiques offered previously by Stenhouse (1975), Macdonald-Ross (1973), Eisner (2002) and from personal experiences which I have set out in an article describing the limits of outcome-based education (McKernan, 1993).

1. Objectives do not exist in reality

A crucial understanding is that we do not really have objectives at all. They do not exist in reality as objects like textbooks or laptop computers. Objectives are a conceptual creation – not a real thing. As educators, we should not engage in the reification of such outcomes. As one alternative curriculum designer (Stenhouse, 1975: 71) has remarked, "We do not *have* objectives – we choose to conceptualize our behavior in terms of objectives; or we choose not to."

2. Uncritical acceptance of objectives and the problem of simplification

In planning a curriculum, one must understand the realities of life in classrooms. Stenhouse (1970) reminds us of, first, achieving a value consensus as a basis for action and, second, turning that consensus into practice. The objectives model seems therefore to rest upon the assumptions, first, that by presenting lists of objectives to teachers they will agree with the objectives and, second, that they will be able to realize these in classroom work. Yet objectives are inadequate as definitions of value positions because an objective claims to embody value positions and interpret these in terms of student behaviors; it is presumed that an objective is a ready means of interpreting values in action, when in fact many experienced teachers fail to do this despite Tyler's assertions that it is rational and simple.

3. Objectives reduce education to a scientific activity, incorporating management orthodoxy and a view of human nature and concept of education that many find unacceptable

This model of planning is objected to by many who view it as scientific and human engineering; treating students as products that need to be molded and modified without in fact considering the views of children themselves in this process. Objectives are the specifications contained in a master blueprint framed by leading voices in Behavioral Psychology. Those who object see children as free, responsible and rational human beings in charge of their own destiny. The objectives model denies the free will of students as an alternative to molding the student in the eye of the human engineer and is more in keeping with a conception of *indoctrination* than of *education*. Thus the use of objectives contains an inadequate conception of what counts as being "human" and what counts as good "education."

4. Confusion about the nature of ends, or outcomes

Kliebard (1975: 79) cleverly reveals some of the difficulties with Tyler's thinking:

> One of the difficulties lies in the nature of an aim or an objective and whether it serves as the terminus for activity in the sense that the Tyler rationale implies. In other words, is an objective an end point or a turning point?

Dewey argued for the latter:

> Ends arise and function within action. They are not, as current theories too often imply, things lying outside activity at which the latter is directed. They are not ends or termini of action at all. They are terminals of deliberation, and so turning points *in* activity.

> (1922: 223)

If Dewey is correct, and there is supporting evidence brought by R.S. Peters (1966), then it would mean that Tyler is wrong to start with objectives. Rather, one should begin the process of designing a curriculum with the *activity and the experiences* (what Peters referred to as "principles of procedure" as values embedded in the process of education itself) and whatever objectives appear will arise within this process, that is, within the activity itself. Seen this way the process of evaluation is not one of matching outcomes with preplanned or anticipated consequences but of applying and describing standards of excellence to the activity itself. Dewey wrote that:

> even the most important among all the consequences of an act is not necessarily its aim.
>
> (1922: 227)

On this logic, Dewey held that ends are not really ends at all, but merely provisional turning points.

5. Education is wrongly viewed as an instrumental activity: taking a means to an end

To treat the curriculum as instrumental is to dismiss a crucial possibility: that the justification for education lies within the process itself. That is to say, that education is intrinsically worthwhile and desirable in itself, not because it leads to some extrinsic goal or reward. I have argued elsewhere (McKernan, 1993: 339) that the student who is educated will arrive at unanticipated ends which cannot be predicted in advance. Indeed, Stenhouse held that:

> Education as induction into knowledge is successful to the extent that it makes the behavioral outcomes of the student unpredictable.
>
> (1975: 82)

What about the myriad ends that are achieved without anticipation in the educational experience? This is a line of argument made also by Peters, who argued that certain forms of knowledge have in-built criteria, which justify their use – they do not need to be validated through targets to be achieved. It is these in-built standards that Peters calls "principles of procedure" (Peters, 1966).

6. Curriculum cannot be systematically broken down into objectives because this is destructive to the epistemology of the subject knowledge

Perhaps one of the most trenchant objections to framing educational objectives relates to the distortion this causes for the underlying structure of knowledge: its proper epistemology. The objection here is that the translation of the deep structures of knowledge into lists of instructional objectives is one of the principal causes of the distortion of knowledge in schools noted by Young (1971), Bernstein (1971) and Stenhouse (1975). The filtering of knowledge through the use of objectives sets up artificial parameters and limits the speculation of student and teacher by defining boundaries of fields of knowledge. A teacher's role then is changed into that of a master of the school's agreed version of that field rather than the curious student role demanded by the process of education. The objectives model attempts brazenly to reduce the epistemological structure of a subject such as history into lists of acceptable behaviors and "exit outcomes." Knowledge and understanding cannot be reduced to mere lists; it is open-ended, inviting further inquiry. Knowledge is not about reaching targets but going on with inquiries with passion. This is a particularly significant shortcoming of the technical objectives model, which has substantive implications for philosophy of education and the structure of knowledge.

7. There is the assumption that the curriculum is determined by systematic hierarchies of objectives that branch into larger goals or exit outcomes

The view is widely held that subjects are broken down into learning episodes, lessons plans, through units to courses and larger domains, each with outcomes. This linear, step-by-step notion is absolutely too tidy for the ultimate reality of knowledge, which is speculative and provisional at best. Learning is perhaps more developmental than sequential and linear. The idea of a field or discipline having this threaded, neatly organized hierarchical structure is epistemologically absurd.

8. It is erroneous to assume that the quality of education is improved by using an objectives design

What I mean to convey here is that while the objectives model is an ambitious theory of instruction – by arranging and organizing knowledge, skills and dispositions as content, it serves a certain usefulness through such organization by improving the structure of a lesson or classroom learning experience – it does not necessarily follow that we have a better or improved curriculum because of its presence. There is no evidence that the objectives model functions more effectively than alternative models of curriculum development. In point of fact it is of more than passing interest to note that a great deal of higher education, particularly outside the USA, is not engaged with an objectives model of teaching, learning or curriculum organization. It is my conviction that the absence of objectives may be associated with a more intellectually demanding and consequently a higher quality curriculum. In my twelve years as a lecturer in the National University of Ireland, I never once witnessed a colleague employing an objectives design for the college courses.

9. Objectives are most often stated as low-level recall or "trivial" outcomes

It is well known that trivial learning behaviors are most easily mastered, particularly simple "recall items." The objectives that then are assembled are regarded as the really important goals. A corollary of this is that if an objective is difficult or impossible to detect then it probably is not important if it cannot be operationalized. A result is that teachers tend to spend more time teaching facts and the specifiable outcomes to which all are directed. This is an ever-present danger. Many end-of-course tests are confined to the lower three levels of Bloom's Taxonomy of Educational Objectives for the cognitive domain (1956) of knowledge recall, comprehension and application.

10. Predetermination of objectives limits or prevents the realization of instructional opportunities – it is a constraining system not allowing "teachable moments" to be pursued

If a teacher feels compelled by state law to cover a wide range of content and objectives he or she may have second thoughts about permitting students to undertake inquiries arising out of issues and problems that surface during teaching and learning. The reality of school teaching nowadays is that one must "cover the ground" at a furious pace. Such a mentality leads to a non-critical lockstep de-professionalization of teaching given its reliance on a non-critical mechanical "teacher-proofing" of curriculum. The objection also relates to the notion that good educational experiences will produce unanticipated opportunities for inquiry that will lead to unanticipated learning for both students and teachers. To avoid the exploration of "the teachable moment" – that point in the lesson where a student is driven by a new line of inquiry to explore new questions – is, I suggest, anti-educational.

11. Setting educational objectives in advance of instruction is not democratic

This criticism has emerged in discussions with some practitioners. It may be considered autocratic for an external agent apart from the teacher and students to set out the objectives of education. It can be argued that all partners in the enterprise should have the democratic right of deciding the purposes of education. This has been a feature of most state control of innovation in curriculum, which tends to make innovations as if they were large-scale building blocks when what is really required is to allow teacher changes at the micro level.

12. Objectives are often perceived as having equal value when in fact some values, that is, goals, are of greater significance for the student

We have not enjoyed the sort of philosophical analysis of the kind that Herbert Spencer made (1860) when he asked "What knowledge is of most worth?" Is it more important for a teacher to be fair or well dressed? That hierarchies of value exist is not in question. The task of curriculum selection is to order these priorities. Is it more important that a student can recall the names of state capitals or critically discuss poverty among and between the states?

13. Objectives serve to reinforce the values and interests of groups interested in exercising hegemonic-political control

Some critical theorists (Apple, 1981; Giroux, 1995) have argued that some groups or classes of people adopt hegemonic practices in order to dominate others. These critics argue that mainstream curriculum developers often view curriculum as an objective text that merely has to be imparted to pupils.

Theories of curriculum defined through the eyes of those who believe in operationalism, behaviorism and the new technical rationality of corporate management have been the victors in the past struggles to cast schools as areas where teachers produce workers. This conception is weighted heavily in favor of those ideologies that hold the power and authority to legitimate varieties of accountability, basics and control in education: the new *ABCs* of education. The real issue is not what subjects are most worthwhile but whose interests does the curriculum ultimately serve?

The dominating group, or oppressor, has sought influence and control, either consciously or not, in order to legitimate its position, status or interests at the expense of the oppressed. For those engaged in a "pedagogy of the oppressed" (Freire, 1970), objectives function as a hegemonic apparatus in direct and manipulative ways by controlling for example what boys and girls will study. Teaching which careers are appropriate for girls and which for boys is a prime example that serves the values and interests of sexist curriculum makers. Most discussions of objectives have focused upon technical matters rather than a far-reaching critical examination of the self-interests of those setting educational objectives.

14. It is difficult, if not impossible, to formulate all objectives

In calling for "goal-free" evaluation Michael Scriven (1967) suggested that programs are achieving myriad objectives beyond those actually set out in the development phase. To focus only upon stated objectives denies and deletes efforts to understand the precise effects of education upon students, thus de-legitimizing the unofficial or null curriculums. Many outcomes are indeed realized – many are unintended. In teaching about war, I cannot identify all the outcomes students will realize – one student came to meet me and asked how many species of flora and fauna were extinguished forever by the American bombing of Vietnam. This student was thinking "outside the box" about war's effects.

15. There is a problem regarding the origins of objectives

Teachers often ask "Where do the objectives come from?" Advocates of objectives have never satisfactorily answered this problem. Tyler (1949) argues that objectives come from three sources – students, subjects and society – and are then siphoned through two filters – the philosophy and psychology of learning – something that seems opaque at the least for the classroom teacher to engage in. Even when criteria like the six categories of Bloom's Cognitive Taxonomy are employed, it is difficult to see how these can be applied equally to all students and to all curriculum subjects. Objectives, like it or not, are the historical results of political, economic and religious forces at state, local and federal levels who exercise an onerous control and influence over teaching (Apple and Christian-Smith, 1992). The politics of education probably accounts for the majority of objectives as a point of focus.

16. Lists of objectives do not reflect the internal logic, or structure, of the disciplines of knowledge

A major problem is that the structure of knowledge, its epistemology, is not represented through an objectives model. Knowledge and understanding presuppose a coherence among ideas so that a meaningful whole emerges that embraces processes, values and key concepts that are not articulated in mere lists. Behavioral objectives in particular do a disservice to the inter-relationship of ideas and the complex higher order structures of knowledge. The practice of designing curricula around objectives serves to advance the destruction of the internal logic of the discipline.

17. An objectives design represents a poor model of teacher and student interaction

The objectives model requests students to arrive at destinations predetermined by teachers, or whoever sets the objectives for a course of study. At a superficial level the objectives model supports a relationship of "banking" education by which teachers alert students to important facts and use test situations so that students may recall these facts, demonstrating mastery. Now this *mastery* is not the kind that true education advocates in which students do research and mount inquiries that may lead to unpredictable outcomes and novel and unique experiences. For example, the arts are not concerned to reach targets or goals once and for all but to deepen appreciation through the rational development of judgment, criticism and standards of taste. Now teaching is essentially concerned with the relationship between the tutor and the taught. That relationship is one based upon trust, love and a great deal of respect. Journeys of curiosity and imagination do not have destinations predictable in advance.

William James in his *Talks to Teachers on Psychology* reveals something of the uncertainty of destination when he states:

> I say moreover that you make a great, a very great mistake, if you think that psychology, being the science of the mind's laws, is something from which you can deduce definite programs and schemes and methods of instruction for immediate school-room use. Psychology is a science and teaching is an art; and sciences never generate arts directly out of themselves. An intermediary inventive mind must make the application, by using its originality.
>
> (1992: 717)

18. Infidelity of stated objectives with test items

One commentator (Macdonald-Ross, 1975: 367) has remarked:

> Unless the objectives are actually identical (synonymous) with the test items, some degree of ambiguity must and does remain.

We can make the distinction between behaviors, for example movements, and actions (which must meet specific criteria). In fact, statements of behavioral objectives are not really statements of behaviors at all but, on the contrary, they set up criteria, which specify the results of behavior. It logically follows that the behavioral objectives, then, are not behavioral.

19. Objectives are not interpreted equally in terms of significance and meaning

Certain objectives do not constitute a foolproof system of communication. Objectives are interpreted differently by those who have attained the objective – for example, teachers – but they may hold a different meaning for students not familiar with the meaning of certain terms. This may be so because they are ambiguous, as noted above. Yet the main limitation here is the assumption that everyone will have the same understanding of the meaning of the objective.

20. Objectives are non-reflexive in nature – they are non-self-evaluating

By this is meant that any system of objectives as targets does not encapsulate reflexivity; and this objectives approach does not critically examine itself, but, rather, exists to determine if a means is taken to an end or not.

21. Teachers do not plan this way in reality – teachers rarely specify their goals, empirically, in terms of measurable objectives/behaviors in planning

Teachers, in my experience, are more concerned with content and methods when they plan curricula, not with precise targets. I have found this true in all countries in which I have worked and, further, teachers do not find the specification of objectives to be the best starting point to becoming engaged in curriculum development. A reflective *situational analysis* (Skilbeck, 1976) is more preferable and, indeed, the usual starting point when groups of curriculum planners first sit down to discuss curriculum change.

Teachers argue (McCutcheon, 1995) that, if the objectives are published in guidelines and other materials, why should they then think about or write them down again in their lesson planning?

22. Objectives are unscientific

There is a sense in which the objectives model is unscientific. Oakeshott (1962) argued:

> Why travel if there is no prefigured and final destination? But, it may be replied: why suppose that the analogy of a journey towards a prefigured destination is relevant? It is clearly irrelevant in science, in art, in poetry, and in human life in general, none of which have prefigured final destinations and none of which are (on that account) considered to be "pointless" activities . . . To describe the enterprise as "keeping afloat

and on an even keel" is to assign it an office neither to be overrated nor despised. (Cited by Macdonald-Ross, 1975: 373)

23. The limits of discourse as a constraint

Elliott Eisner (2002) identifies several limitations of behavioral outcomes. The first he describes as the limits of discourse itself, by which he means that much of what we aim at is not amenable to description in terms of clear language. Eisner gives as an example the difficulty in describing a person who has the trait of "sensitivity" and the fact that we attempt to articulate in words what we know non-linguistically (2002: 113).

24. Those who evaluate objectives often fail to distinguish between applying standards and making judgments

Eisner (2002: 113–14) suggests that there is a problem for those who evaluate in distinguishing standards from judgments. A standard is unambiguous – a student can either run ten laps of the track or not. I can spell Mississippi, or I cannot. But what about the judgment of the aesthetic qualities in a student's art work or the persuasive logic in a student's essay? While such work may not be amenable to "standards," it is open to critical judgment.

25. Objectives presume that pre-specification of goals is the most rational, or "scientific," way of proceeding with curriculum planning

Finally, Eisner suggests that we have become enslaved by a tradition of "scientific" technical rationality rooted in Western technology, so that to not have such goals is to court accusations of "professional irresponsibility" (2002: 115). He argues that some work needs to be deliberately explorative in that it does not have a pre-determined end. After Aristotle, Eisner quotes the remark "Art loves chance."

26. Unanticipated, or unplanned, objectives or outcomes are always being achieved

One of the best insights offered was the idea by Stenhouse (1975) that education is successful to the extent that unanticipated outcomes are being achieved. These "unanticipated" objectives are the stuff of learning with a critical-inquiry-driven mind. New knowledge is precisely that – it was not known beforehand and is created by the educational process and the passion of a learner committed to constructivist activity. This is akin to the null curriculum, which is not taught, or planned, but learned as a result of education.

Standards and curriculum

Apart from the foregoing discussion of instructional and behavioral objectives one can say that we must proceed in our work rationally. In the end, education is really an initiation of students into worthwhile activities. These worthwhile experiences are aim-driven and contain a variety of standards. Dewey wrote:

> The child is the starting point, the center, and the end. His development, his growth is the ideal. It alone furnishes the standard. To the growth of the child, all studies are subservient; they are instruments valued as they serve the needs of growth . . . Literally, we must take our stand with the child and our departure from him. It is he and not the subject matter which determines both quality and quantity of learning.
>
> (1956: 9)

Curriculum is often fragmented and lacking in coherence. Some powerful forces have implemented a variety of projects aimed at raising "standards" and we find new standards not only for students but for teacher education programs, professional bodies, assessment practices and so forth. Many argue that this rationalization is leading us down the road to a National Curriculum like that found in Britain, Ireland, France and other nations from which we have drawn many educational influences. Governments not only in Western Europe have been attracted to the *social-market* perspective due to its emphasis on cost-cutting economies, accountability and behavioral indicators of performance. Thus the concept of "standards" nowadays is linked with efficiency models rather than a more nostalgic and traditional concern for academic standards. In 1983 the National Commission on Excellence in Education published its report *A Nation at Risk* and concluded that educators had to "adopt rigorous and measurable standards and higher expectations for academic performance and student conduct."

Concluding comments on objectives

The objectives model is the dominant form of curriculum planning in use internationally. Those who advocate for the objectives model are those interested in evaluation, and not course design or pedagogy. As Stenhouse has remarked, the objectives model is a "marking model" rather than a "critical model" for assessment (1975: 94–95). In all fairness it does seem that the objectives model is indeed appropriate in areas of the curriculum that focus on training and skills, while the process model is more appropriate in those curriculum areas that focus on knowledge and understanding. Perhaps some sort of a compromise is possible.

One would like to believe that education is a democratic and local matter, yet we would be wrong on both counts. Instruction, by its very nature, is undemocratic and to pretend that classrooms are democratic would be untruthful. Outside of prisoners in jail, students are conscripts and in school not by choice. The curriculum is externally imposed. Clever publishing companies in the USA often track adoption policies for their texts and exert powerful influences over the objectives of the curriculum. It is a rare teacher who recognizes that equality is urgently required in classrooms. By their very definition, teachers are both "authorities" on a subject and exercise an "authority role" in the execution of their work.

State government departments of education control curriculum now enshrined in policies of accountability, basics and control (ABCs). While the state curriculum may be implemented as the "official curriculum" there is also an informal curriculum where teachers can make contributions to development of resources and units, but the pressures of planning by objectives have become wedded to schooling as the only option mainly because it is believed that is the epitome of good management (Sockett, 1976: 125).

The notion that education must be validated through a system of objective testing has given Educational Psychology a firm grip over the control of curriculum. Schubert (1986) notes that measurement and psychometrics have played a major role in the impact of educational research and practice through the growth of the testing industry. Practically all schools use standardized tests of achievement and cognitive development and the results of these tests drive educational policy and accountability. As noted above, too often an examination-driven measurement or "marking model" seems to be favored over a "critical" model that goes for understanding.

Chapter 5

A process-inquiry model for the design of curriculum

> It is idle to criticize the objectives model as a strategy for the design and development of curriculum if no orderly alternative can be found.
>
> (Stenhouse, 1975: 84)

For me this chapter is of crucial significance. Here I shall endeavor to outline the process-inquiry model and I shall offer my ideas on how schools and curriculum can be improved by students, teachers, administrators and parents. Stated briefly the proposition is that the curriculum can be substantially reformed and improved through the practice of "the arts of the reflective practitioner," involving members of the school community. The notion here is that curriculum development and the act of research and critical reflection belongs to the members of the school community – not to external agents and agencies. I am simply suggesting that in designing any curriculum, whatever ideology one subscribes to, one must consider a basic design question: "Do I use objectives or not?"

There is little doubt that teachers are the key operators in this movement for reform. Stenhouse argued:

> It is not enough that teachers' work should be studied: they need to study it themselves.
>
> (1975: 143)

Action research is perhaps the most suitable research methodology for investigating and solving curriculum and practical classroom problems. I take as a definition that of Elliott (1993: 69):

> Action research may be defined as the study of a social situation with a view to improving the quality of action within it.

At base action research seeks to inform the practical judgment of actors in real situations that are problematic. It is not so much concerned with the production of theory and conceptual frameworks as it is in obtaining useful results that improve practice for individuals in difficult situations.

I further argue that the field of curriculum, both in theory and practice, depends to a large extent upon evolving a critical process of research and development by teachers, using other professionals to support the work of these inquiring educators. Action, and reflection on that action, is the responsibility of teachers. They need a research tradition based on classrooms rather than laboratory experiments. Such a research tradition will feed teachers ideas and be eminently accessible to them. It is difficult to believe that classrooms and curriculum can ever be improved without the participation of teachers in that improvement.

The process-inquiry model

Perhaps the most trenchant question we can ask is "Can curriculum and pedagogy be organized satisfactorily by a logic other than that of the ends-means (objectives) model?" What one is asking is whether a curriculum can be designed without recourse to using objectives, and the answer is, most certainly it can. Stenhouse (1975: 84–97) offered a Process Model as an alternative to the product-driven objectives model (see Table 5.1). The latter

Table 5.1 Contrasting characteristics of outcomes-based and process-inquiry models for curriculum

Outcomes-based model	Process-inquiry model
Exit outcomes: unit/lessons	Statement of broad aims/understanding
Behaviors of students stated as what student will know, or do	Content selected upon the procedures and criteria embodied in discipline
Units sequenced in logical mode	Unit method not necessary
Curriculum sequenced into micro-units	Teaching viewed as reflexive practice
Instruction towards objectives	Inquiry/discovery strategy – open ended
Time adjusted for mastery	Understanding – not mastery – is the aim
Convergence is valued	Divergence/depth of views is encouraged
Feedback/correctives given	Creative/unique, "unanticipated" responses valued
Assessment through measurement procedures	Evaluation as descriptive-qualitative and complex, e.g. "if one follows these with these materials the effects will tend to be X"
"Objective" tests	Teacher as judge and action researcher
Training/instruction	Induction into forms/fields of knowledge
Uniformity/terminal behaviors forecasted	Different outcomes/divergence valued

is an outcomes-based education model while the former delineates an educational process. Moreover, Stenhouse's experiment with the Humanities Curriculum Project, sponsored by the Schools Council for Curriculum Reform and Examinations in Britain supported his claims. While the term "process" is used in many contexts, one feels obligation-bound to refer to the model as a process-research model since this was Stenhouse's choice of terminology to describe an educational experience led by key, guiding principles of procedure. A rather interesting account of curriculum as a "process," and somewhat different from that offered here, can be found in Kelly (1989).

The most fundamental criticism of the objectives model of planning by the specification of behavioral outcomes in advance of teaching is that it reduces the practice of teaching and educating to a form of instrumental engineering by seeing teaching and learning as an extrinsic activity – taking a means to an end. The truth of education is that it lies in the process itself. The educated mind will lead us to unanticipated destinations. Any reasonable form of inquiry has in-built standards, or "procedures" for conducting a search for knowledge. This chapter is concerned with a curriculum design grounded in these principles for procedure.

In the Tyler objectives model a curriculum is field tested as a product against a table of specifications outlining the outcomes it was designed to meet. Students are regarded as accumulating numerous educational or instructional objectives as results. It is very much a "banking" concept of education, as elucidated by Paulo Freire (1970). The process-inquiry model allows teachers to become artists rather than technicians in giving them a fair stake in qualitative judgment, classroom research and evaluation. It is also strongly linked with the belief that decision-making belongs to individual teachers and that curriculum development is the province of the local school. Such a model allows for a measure of continuous improvement and organic development.

Unlike the objectives model, in the process model the educational process and the values that it embraces become the standards to be judged. One welcomes variability and differentiated outcomes rather than predictable responses in this model. In the process model we are interested in growth and continuous organic improvement. On this view each school is autonomous, and with its own development plan engages in self-monitoring of its progress from year to year.

The process model is premised upon the belief that curriculum planning should not take an instrumental approach that is either based upon the nature of subject/discipline knowledge, or based upon a determination of the behavior a pupil is to exhibit, but rather, more crucially, it should be based on what counts as an educational procedure and the nature of the growth of that pupil. The translation then of this procedure into action constitutes a more improved theory for curriculum design.

In the objectives model the state plays a major role in setting goals and making decisions centrally and the problem is always seen as finding the correct curriculum and assessing the performances of students – this may be an American obsession, or at least an assumption that curriculum should not be the province of local communities, schools and teachers.

The process-inquiry model has three parts:

1 *Statement of the general aim*, for example to develop understanding of poverty.
2 *Statement of the principles of procedure* – these are the values underpinning the educational process, or procedures. In effect they are standards which an educator must observe in implementing the teaching strategy, and are the central values governing the pedagogy and interaction in the classroom.
3 *Statement of the criteria for assessing/judging student work.*

While the outcomes-based design is suitable for low-level rote learning, instruction and training programs, it is unsuited to pure induction into knowledge.

Rationale for a process model

Education must be a rational endeavor. All would agree that it cannot advocate irrational values, for example teaching children to commit burglary or murder. Yet rationality comes in different guises. Aristotle refers to two kinds of rationality in his work *Ethics*. First, Aristotle talks of making things as *"techne"* and doing things well as *"phronesis."* Technical rationality, or *techne*, is a form of reasoning suited to making products, while practical deliberation, the essence of curriculum, refers to acting well, or *phronesis*. These are contrasting views of rationality and what we must be able to determine is which one is driving a particular curriculum. As a consequence, we are left with two forms: a technical rationality and a practical-critical rationality. The former is important in training and instruction, the latter in education.

The curriculum is more than a body of knowledge. Knowledge is the persuasion of what is true on adequate evidence. But a subject does not rest alone on the facts. A collection of facts amounts to nothing more than an annual, or something akin to a railway timetable. It is the ordering of these facts in a constructivist fashion that is the business of the educated mind. It is one thing to know that certain rivers, oceans and mountains exist on earth but quite another to know the causes which have shaped and determined the topography of the land and seas, the effects of these entities on climate and so on. What I am driving at here is that the curriculum as practiced on the process model has its own internal logic, determined by its peculiar nature. Curriculum also has to do with questions of values, for example the value of respect for evidence, of taking care in drawing conclusions and the like. Consequently, some of these values are procedural – they guide us through our inquiries, and as such may be considered aims of education.

The process-inquiry model casts the curriculum developer in the role of researcher-investigator. In a strong sense this is a mandate for evaluation. Here I will outline what this model entails in terms of curriculum design. Our design model has three parts: the aim, principles of procedure and the teacher's role. The model is based upon the premise that a curriculum can count as rational planning by selecting values that are intrinsically worthwhile to the conduct of an educational process rather than ends, in the form of instructional objectives, which are external to that process. Yet one of the first considerations of the process model is to have criteria, or principles for selecting content, which do not depend upon the use of intended objectives. Several writers have attempted such a task (Raths, 1971; Hanley *et al.*, 1970) and I am aware of a number of curriculum projects that have advanced this principle of educational process, which do not depend upon the disciplines of knowledge – which do not require justification beyond their own in-built standards. The Humanities Curriculum Project in the United Kingdom, and Man: A Course of Study, connected with Jerome Bruner, along with the Schools Cultural Studies Project in Northern Ireland, showed that integrated curriculum (not discipline based) could be designed around educational procedures and a research pedagogy rather than educational objectives. We have always known that this was the case when teaching a pure discipline, but achieving implementation outside of the disciplines seems to me to be a great advance.

Which rationality – technical or practical?

The following represents some of the contrasting critical values underpinning product and process models of curriculum theory.

Table 5.2 Technical (social market) values versus practical science (hermeneutics) values

Technical		Practical science
Standards	vs.	Expression
Productivity	vs.	Excellence
Measurement	vs.	Understanding
Training	vs.	Education
Control	vs.	Freedom
Unity	vs.	Diversity
Objectivity	vs.	Subjectivity
Uniformity	vs.	Imagination

Source: after Jenkins, 1975.

Standards versus expression

On the one hand the practical science rationalist would stress the value of *expression* because it is an extremely individualist virtue wherein the educated mind struggles not to meet some pre-defined *standard* but for further growth. What the learner is to aspire to is clearly delineated in terms of outcomes and behaviors . . . what the student will "know and be able to do" is the usual phraseology of a *standards* value. It is also assumed that this notion of standards and performance levels and targets can be universally applied to all subjects across a curriculum. It may be worth asking whether some subjects, such as aesthetic activities, may have extreme difficulty in setting criteria by which performances can be subjected to standards.

Productivity versus excellence

An emphasis on productivity in the calls of "more for less" is endemic nowa-days in education. This is the spirit of accountability – that each person in the education equation is responsible for the results of their performance. Fewer professors and larger classes is the norm nowadays in universities. Costs are closely scrutinized and budgets are being cut back in the down-sized culture. On the other hand, true education requires the virtue of *excellence*. This concept leans towards the Greek concept of "*upbringing*," itself allied with socialization and education. Jenkins (1975) reminds us that historically, "excellence" emphasizes quality and reputation. There is ample evidence that the concept has increased currency since the "excellence" reform movement in education began in the USA and United Kingdom some thirty years ago.

Measurement versus understanding

The practical rationalist academic has favored the virtues of open-minded-ness tolerance, truth, respect for evidence, rigor in scholarship, honesty, cultural diversity, careful description and interpretation in the quest for *understanding*, which is perhaps the chief value in the search for truth. Measurement is emphasized by the forces of the technical rationalist position who demand objectivity, efficiency, productivity, control, measurement. At its crudest level "technical rationality" (TR) seeks simply to maximize its productivity and products through more "efficient" procedures so that outputs can be increased. This is all seen as a "competition" where resources are scarce and changes in the environment occur quickly. The purpose of the institution shifts subtly to that of a service provider; of getting students into employment and thus re-defining the purpose of education as being instru-mentalist and utilitarian in scope.

The measurement myth

One of the major problems with TR is the proclaimed belief that quality can be measured. Educational qualities and values are not always amenable to measurement. For example, when we think about measuring the effects of programs designed to increase sensitivity, tolerance and mutual under-standing among and between schoolchildren the measurement problems are considerable, if not insurmountable. Education has many purposes and values which make it susceptible to measurement.

Training versus education

At a simplistic level advocates of TR in schools and universities seek to set levels of performance as if they were targets. This view has been well presented above and reduces education to a production process rather than a creative and constructionist experience. Education implies the ability not to acquire skills and abilities but to go beyond these by using knowledge, skills and abilities in a creative and imaginative fashion.

Control versus freedom

Control emphasizes regulatory behavior; it conjures up the image of holding humans in restraint. In research control indicates the use of a standard of comparison for inferences. The TR group herald scientific management and the careful guiding of work towards the achievement of targets set. On the other hand, *freedom* implies the lack of restraint or regulation wherein educa-tion is unimpeded. Freedom comes from the Sanskrit *priya* meaning "to love." Allowing a person to not be subjected to bondage by a state or its institutions. The *OED* further indicates that freedom in Old English meant to act according to one's will or choice, and not be compelled by external direction or motivation. In short it is "the right to do."

Unity versus diversity

The Social Market Model (SMM) perspective advocates *unity* at the expense of *diversity.* The movement towards a national set of standards for teaching competencies is a case in point. We get simplistic prescriptions such as a "back to basics" or essentialist philosophy of reading, writing and mathe-matics along with allied conceptions of a common core or general studies program. This notion defies efforts at multiculturalism or pluralism of values and cultures. Rather than conducting exotic experiments we are requested to reach prescribed targets and goals within a narrowly defined curriculum.

Objectivity versus subjectivity

TR advocates would argue that *objectivity* is desirable in that it lays stress on what is external or independent of the human mind; just the opposite of what the rationalist philosopher would advocate. A more personal account of feelings and ideas would be subscribed to by the traditional academic rationalist. This perspective not only accepts subjective human interpretation but also exalts and prioritizes it. In education much of the present discussion can be understood in terms of the split between positivistic-objective empirical research paradigms and more subjective-qualitative understandings. There is indeed a two-culture position here between those prizing objective facts and those seeking subjective understandings.

Uniformity versus imagination

Imagination suggests creativity and expressiveness through the construction of images, plans and ideal models. Uniformity suggests representations of reality. Imagine my lad has two toy cars that he is playing with – one is a Jeep (we see plenty of representations in real road experiences of this model), the other is an ideal model – something called Chitty Chitty Bang Bang. Well we don't see many flying cars yet. Chitty Chitty Bang Bang is an ideal model – an expressive work of imagination.

My discussion here is also to do with conformity and getting things right, as in a uniform code of practice. Yet the educated mind is able to make enormous leaps in search of truth and meaning. The cultivation of imagination is our most precious product, if I may borrow from the behaviorists.

Principles for the selection of content

Here we are interested in establishing criteria that will assist with the selection of content. The following are offered in the literature:

1 All other things being equal, one activity is more worthwhile than another if it permits children to make informed choices in carrying out the activity and to reflect on the consequences of their choices.
2 All other things being equal, one activity is more worthwhile than another if it assigns to students active roles in the learning situation rather than passive ones.
3 All other things being equal, one activity is more worthwhile than another if it asks students to engage in inquiry into ideas, application of intellectual processes, or current problems, either personal or social.
4 All other things being equal, one activity is more worthwhile than another if it involves children with realia (i.e. real objects, materials and artifacts).

5 All other things being equal, one activity is more worthwhile than another if completion of the activity may be accomplished successfully by children at different levels of ability.

6 All other things being equal, one activity is more worthwhile than another if it asks students to examine in a new setting an idea, an application of an intellectual process, or a current problem which has been previously studied.

7 All other things being equal, one activity is more worthwhile than another if it requires students to examine topics or issues that citizens in our society do not normally examine – and that are typically ignored by the major communication media in the nation.

8 All other things being equal, one activity is more worthwhile than another if it involves students and faculty members in "risk"-taking – not a risk of life or limb, but a risk of success or failure.

9 All other things being equal one activity is more worthwhile than another if it requires students to rewrite, rehearse, and polish their initial efforts.

10 All other things being equal, one activity is more worthwhile than another if it involves students in the application and mastery of meaningful rules, standards, or disciplines.

11 All other things being equal, one activity is more worthwhile than another if it gives students a chance to share the planning, the carrying out of a plan, or the results of an activity with others.

12 All other things being equal, one activity is more worthwhile than another if it is relevant to the expressed purposes of the students.

(Raths, 1971: 716)

These criteria, or principles for selecting activities and content, set out by Louis Raths above, not only link to the well-established disciplines, but also clearly link with teaching principles and ethics. It seems acceptable to me that a curriculum can be adequately designed without using objectives.

Elements of a process-inquiry model

The model consists of an aim, a strategic teaching pedagogy and criteria for assessing its effectiveness. Monitoring can take the form of action inquiry. The following gives examples from the teaching of social studies.

Aim

To educate students in an understanding of multicultural traditions and "cultural pluralism" in society. This aim suggests that all ethnic groups and cultures are to be valued and celebrated through multicultural education/curriculum.

To encourage mutual understanding between and among students of different cultural traditions.

To promote tolerance and sensitivity in intercultural relations.

To work towards the elimination of prejudice and fear.

To help students to ask, and answer, research questions.

To assist students in clarifying personal values.

Principles of procedure

Principles of procedure are values that shape and form the basis of our pedagogy. By this I mean the "strategy" the teacher adopts to forward learning among students. These "principles" are the standards and values embedded in the very process of education. Some of these, for this unit, are:

1   that the teacher will help students to become aware of their beliefs, attitudes and values;
2   that we subject our values and beliefs to discussion in group sessions;
3   that controversial issues are identified (race relations, poverty, war, language usage etc.);
4   that knowledge of culture and ethnicity is offered to students in both traditional and experimental pedagogies;
5   that we help students to detect bias and prejudice;
6   that we enable students to understand racism and propaganda;
7   that we encourage a full and open discussion of the issues thrown up by the unit by all students;
8   that the chair protects divergence of opinion and subjects his or her authority to the criterion of "procedural neutrality" while discussing controversial value issues.

Role of the teacher

The teacher is a model of one who is open-minded and critical of prejudiced views. In short, he or she teaches to enhance multicultural understanding and acceptance of and respect for various groups in society. The idea here is to specify a teaching strategy that requests the teacher to subject his or her teaching and the effects of that teaching to research as the basis for evaluation and improvement.

What this asks of teachers is that they submit their own teaching as a chairperson to critical scrutiny in implementing the principles of procedure designed to achieve the overall aim of the curriculum. Thus with one stroke we marry the teacher as a rational agent and an action researcher in their own classroom. This also allows for curriculum and evaluation to become one rather than separate entities.

That the teacher adopts a pedagogy based upon discussion and monitors his or her role as a chairperson supporting student understanding, knowledge, tolerance and sensitivities.

This is a radical departure from teaching to pre-specified objectives. We are after depth of understanding in the process-inquiry model, not the recitation of trivial facts. The classroom strategy would be inquiry-based and need not begin with every teacher creating all the materials he or she will need. Traditional and well-written textbooks could be tapped as a source of knowledge. What is new is that in doing "history" or "chemistry" the student and teacher would pay close attention to the *principles and procedures* implicit as ways of doing these subjects. The paradigm of the discipline is honored. I have in mind certain criteria:

1   logical knowledge structure of the subject;
2   the key concepts which give the subject coherence and internal logic;
3   the tests of proof used in the subject (theorems in mathematics, experiments in chemistry);
4   learning the modes of inquiry in doing history or chemistry. What research skills permit new knowledge to be added to the subject?

Even the shift from traditional, fact-based teaching to one permitting inquiry and discussion will prove too demanding for some teachers. Teachers need to abandon this role of imparter of information. They will be asked to become a fellow historian or research chemist who is interested in gaining answers to the questions raised through the inquiry-discussion method. I have in mind a group seminar that is more than simply an exchange of ideas or views but is rather more finely tuned to the critical interpretation of data and evidence admitted to the discussion.

Evaluation is important in the process-inquiry model as it links teacher and student actions to research, and the teacher as researcher/evaluator of the curriculum work is key to the success of the model. The model recommends research-based teaching, which is exhorted often in the literature of the day. The curriculum becomes a means of researching, or studying the effects and problems thrown up by implementing some designed line of teaching. Every classroom is unique in its character and needs to be verified, tested and modified by each teacher. Our model suggests that teachers can improve their professional behavior by researching the problems raised by their teaching and curriculum. As Stenhouse remarked:

> It is not enough that teacher's work be studied: they need to study it themselves.
>
> (Stenhouse, 1975: 143)

This study of teachers' work by teachers constitutes educational action research.

Any curriculum is primarily concerned with content. The process model first implied a "teaching-learning" process embodying certain educational values rather than the specification of objectives. Stenhouse drew considerably upon the philosophy of R.S. Peters, who specified the nature of education and the process entailed in education. On Peters' thought (1959) our discourse about "aims" does not dictate that we are discussing extrinsic outcomes to that process but rather we are referring to principles of procedure for realizing educational values that are intrinsic to education itself. Aims refer then to educational criteria realized in rather than as a result of an educational process. Stenhouse moved to his process model on this very insight. So a curriculum should specify a worthwhile process of teaching and learning without determining what the outcomes would be. There is a practical rationality in the process model which is diametrically opposed to the ends-means rationality of the objectives model. We must never forget that debates about education are at root debates about political ideals, values and ideologies. Yet in a nation where "learning theory" has been the dominant voice this is a natural consequence of that thought.

Bruner has made the startling observation that whoever has undertaken the production of a curriculum has learned that it is more for teachers than it is for pupils:

> If it cannot change, move, perturb, and inform teachers it will have no effect on those whom they teach.
>
> (1966: xv)

The process-inquiry model and teacher education

Embodied within the process-inquiry model is a critical-practical action view of teacher education. This model is in direct opposition to both the Platonic and social market perspectives on teacher education. It is opposed to the technical rationality of the objectives model and it may be considered "practical" in that education is viewed as a worthwhile *activity* and *process*. It is a genuine *social practice*. It takes place in social situations of some complexity, requiring decision-making. The successful practitioner does not operate as if using a set of means to attain some ends but rather is engaged in intuitive and spontaneous direction and redirection of the educational process and learning enterprise guided by making professional judgments in critical incidents along the way. This is what I mean by saying that the curriculum requires a "reflexive" stance.

Championed by teacher-researcher advocates (Stenhouse, 1975; Elliott, 1991, 1993) the model has gained some currency in European, Australian and American contexts (McKernan, 1996). The emphasis is on understanding context, reflection and problem-solving, often in action-research scenarios (Elliott, 1993). The model is derived from Schon's 1983 account of reflective practice.

The essential principle is that good practice is bound up with interpretations of concrete situations as a whole and practice cannot be improved without first improving these situations. Good judgments cannot often be made in advance but must be made *in situ*. This is the aim of the teacher-researcher – development of greater "situational understanding." Personal knowledge and understandings are arrived at as a situation unfolds. Thus, teacher education ought to help students to develop those capacities for reflective thought and interpretation of situations as a basis for practical judgment.

The concept of education

An understanding of the concept of education may help us appreciate the process model over the popular product model. And while it may not solve our curriculum problem it may provide analytical lenses for critical reflection, understanding and human action. The roots of the word "education," as has been discussed, implies "leading out" or "rearing." In this sense education has to do with the development of the rational mind, and involves knowledge and intellectual processes for the individual. In "rearing" the notion of "parenting" comes to mind; as a parent cares for and rears the child, through education the student is raised and led to further growth. This parenting notion has a basis in law, given the acceptance of the principle of teachers acting *in loco parentis*, that is, in the place of the parent. In "leading out" one might contemplate the creative aspect and necessary response entailed in education; for we never know exactly where the educated mind will take one. Education has a great deal to do with the concepts of personal inquiry and the relationship between tutor and student is characterized by the twin concepts of "care" and "love" – concepts which are little written about by educationists. Thus we argue that education is philosophically about developments of the student which are achieved through learning and through the cultivation of the rational mind. This is not to say that education has only to do with intellectual development; it also has to do with aesthetic, physical, social, emotional, moral and vocational development. All of these forms of development involve elements of knowledge and cognitive development and involve rational understanding and powers of reason.

It is assumed nowadays by many students, parents and others that the primary purpose of education is to contribute to one's vocational and economic life. While this essentially narrow and instrumental or utilitarian purpose is indeed an argument made by those of the New Right, it is not the only reason, nor in our view the major reason for education; yet the social market advocates go further and stipulate that accountability is required because public funds are being expended on "investment spending." There is a more fundamental purpose of education – that of developing the individual as a *person*. This leads to the conviction that education must not be seen as merely an investment in the economy but also as a service to be judged by the contribution it makes to the well-being of the individual. This means simply that education is, in itself, a good thing. Education is *intrinsically* worthwhile and justifiable. Proponents of the social market perspective would argue that education is justifiable for its *extrinsic* utility; because it leads to jobs and economic wealth – the instrumentalist position. However, part of our problem is that there are alternative conceptions of education, as well as wrong conceptions, that are widely held.

Basically, education is under attack because the advocates of an objectives model have presented curriculum as a production package complete with input and output specifications for arriving at pre-determined goals or objectives. Objectives are satisfactory for training, and possibly instruction programs, but will not suffice for education. Behaviorist curriculum theorists, for example, have reduced education and curriculum to lists of behaviors, competencies and abilities that students need to achieve to be "educated." To transform education and curriculum into simple lists of outcomes is a gross distortion of knowledge and the epistemology of a subject (McKernan, 1993), rendering knowledge as instrumental when in fact true knowledge cannot be predicted in advance of an educational experience. How can I, for example, set, in advance of instruction, precise educational objectives stating what a student will know or be able to do as a result of reading *Hamlet*? To set the curriculum by objectives to be achieved conforms to some instrumentalist justification – because it leads to something, it is akin to taking a means to an end. In a sense, to have objectives is to set limits to human speculation and development. But an experience may be educational because of its *intrinsic value* – it can be justified simply because it is desirable and enjoyable for its own sake, as in the case of reading poetry or painting landscapes.

Criteria for education

On the process model view, several conditions, or criteria, are necessary for something to count as education. Something counts as *education* because it involves knowledge and understanding and has its own in-built standards of excellence immanent in it; rather than because it leads to an objective. Something can be picked out as *educational* also because it is desirable and permeates one's way of looking at things. A skilled and trained ballet dancer or mechanic is not necessarily educated because of their skill and performance abilities alone. What Hirst (1965) and Hirst and Peters (1970) have argued on this topic is that certain forms of knowledge, for example philosophy, mathematics and history, are educational because they are justifiable in terms of their own standards and worth. They have an organized structure and body of knowledge; they have key principles and concepts that give the particular discipline structure; they have respected methods of adding new knowledge to the subject; and finally some, such as mathematics, have tests of proof.

In his seminal work *Ethics and Education*, R.S. Peters (1966) posited that education implies the transmission of that which is worthwhile, possessing desirable qualities, and that it must involve knowledge and depth of understanding and some form of cognitive perspective. The concept of *education* is centrally connected with *induction into knowledge*, that is, with thought processes and intellectual cognitive activities which are not inert – this is what we are concerned with essentially in higher education. A second notion is that of *instruction*. Instruction is not an induction or initiation into knowledge. With instruction we are aiming at the acquisition and retention of information. Instruction seeks to impart information on the banking model of filling up students' heads with bits of data; the learning of the table of elements in chemistry for example. The thing about instruction is that it rests on the premise that the teacher is master of the knowledge which the student needs.

Finally, we speak of *training*. The concept of training, like that of instruction, is not equivalent to education. Training suggests the acquisition of skills, and excellent training results in heightened performances. An example would be a soldier who successfully completes "basic training" or an assault course; or a student handling scientific laboratory equipment skillfully. Training has to do with the enhancement of abilities and competencies.

I would argue that a great deal of what is being aimed at in education today, both in public schools and higher education, is not really education at all, but falls within the realm of *training and instruction*. When we examine the list of outcomes in school programs we discover concepts like competencies, intended learning outcomes, performance indicators, skills, techniques and abilities. Education implies careful use of knowledge to create new meanings, interpretations and understanding. An educated person is a *constructionist*; one who makes meaning. In educating students we are inducting them into the thought processes of the culture. The crucial element in education is that we can use it – to think and create.

A person who knows a lot of historical facts can be said to be *knowledgeable*, but we would not describe him or her as *educated* simply for this reason; while he or she may be able to give correct answers to history questions this might never affect the way in which the person looks at the architecture and institutions around him or her. He or she might never connect what he or she has learned about the Industrial Revolution with what he or she saw in the coalfields of West Virginia or the shipyards of New York. Education implies that one's outlook is transformed by what one knows. It is this transformational quality that makes mere living into a quality of life. It also becomes the basis for a more informed theory of action, as that advanced by Roy Bhaskar as "Transformational Social Action" with his advocacy for critical realism (Bhaskar, 1997). For how one lives ultimately depends upon one's education – what one knows and understands and how one uses that knowledge and understanding to illuminate and change one's life.

The lower level concepts of training and instruction do not provide the analytical, critical or interpretive capacities that are entailed in education, where the rational autonomous mind is at work. This "attack on rationalism" is embodied in the latest trend towards *Quality Management*, or QM, containing a language and rhetoric of students as *customers and clients*. "Continuous improvement" is its call: administrators and teachers are mandated to management and instruction by objectives, within cost-benefit analysis operations, which, along with the identification of performance indicators, goes hand in hand with an industrial jargon promoting a false conception of both *quality and education*. In the case of training and even at the level of instruction the QM movement provides reasonable fit – where product specifications are tight. However, this "technical model" breaks down where education comes into play. Stenhouse (1975: 82) argued that:

> Education as induction into knowledge is successful to the extent that it makes instructional objectives of students unpredictable.

This is so because in the nature of knowledge, as distinct from mere information, there is an epistemology and structure that sustains creative thought, thus providing the capacity for judgment and critique.

Rationalism holds to the view that good practice is ultimately determined from a theoretical understanding of educational principles; the sort of things that professors of the foundations of education aim at in their work. Rationality is in its primary sense a property of human thought, and of actions in so far as they are the product of human thought (Hare, 1981: 214). Rationality constitutes an action, desire or thought that has survived criticism by facts and logic. In our "education" of teachers we agree that one is able to teach if one not only has a firm grasp of the content one will teach but also the theoretical principles of education – the foundations upon which rational practices are based. Our goal is a professional and autonomous teacher who designs their further in-service development through reflective practice and self-regulation in the light of universal rationalist values and principles.

One of the major problems with curriculum and teacher education today is that teaching is seen to be largely a banking or depositional event; that is, education of teachers is the task of the college – or the "production unit" – and not principally a task of the teacher in training. For the reflective practitioner, however, the continuous professional development of the teacher becomes the responsibility of the self-autonomous rationalist mind. The division of labor between teachers and academics – between initial and in-service education – has led to a situation where the quality of teacher development has become the focus of the university and its total quality education program, or of local school administrators and central office, but not the responsibility of the practicing teacher. This must change if action

research and its flip side, action learning, are to be seen as modes of professional development.

Outcomes-based education (OBE) is one of the latest bandwagons to
come along in education under the banner of school "restructuring," "continuous educational improvement" and the development of "total quality"; a
trend unmistakably linked with technical rationality, process management
and the reforms of the conservative Right. The advent of technical rationality and OBE have been helped along by successive Republican and
Conservative coalitions and governments in Britain and the United States
since approximately the late 1970s. OBE has been derived from psycholog-
ical principles of *behaviorism* and tested in the industrial and corporate
sectors where terms like product specifications, costs, performance, standards
and, above all, quality are the new conceptual terms. Treating educational
institutions as if they were businesses or "production units" is highly
assumptive and dubious yet the concept of OBE has been recently introduced in education, including areas of administration, curriculum,
supervision, evaluation and testing; replete with performance indicators,
value-added quality, efficiency measures, upstream systems and process
inputs, all introduced to negate a rationalist belief in professional autonomous decision-making. Teacher educators are aware of these intrusive
attempts to negate professional autonomy which manifest themselves in
trends towards site-based management, standards and competency testing,
privatization, Charter Schools, educational vouchers and National Assessment of Educational Performance (NAEP) in the USA rankings on tests of
school subjects such as mathematics and science. It should be added that
much of the advocacy for objectives comes not from educators but rather
from external agents, such as politicians and/or administrators, not from
those ranks who are engaged in teaching and curriculum.

A major design problem of teacher education programs in the United
Kingdom and USA is that they are heavily resourced at the beginning of
initial teacher education and poorly resourced where it matters – at the
induction and in-service career education levels. We forget, at our peril, that
teacher education is a responsibility of the teacher, qua teacher, and not of
any institution.

The foundations of education are historically based largely upon rationalism and the development of teachers through the application of
educational principles and theories. This is the view that good teaching
practice derives from knowledge and critical understanding and interpretation of *knowledge and principles.* In addition to knowledge of subjects and
content that form the curriculum of public education, teacher education and
excellent teaching rests on this foundation or base of rational principles. Our
argument is that teachers and professors are rational-autonomous.

There are many misleading models of education being practiced. Instead
of seeing education in terms of rearing, learning or bringing up, most folk

equate it with formal schooling, which is not an inclusive notion, for one could be educated in military warfare without having attended any institution devoted to learning. Today the encroachment of narrow specialization and the increasingly instrumental view of knowledge and skills associated with technology have further eroded the pure concept of the educated person. A student becomes educated by engaging in processes of education which initiate their induction into worthwhile activities. Processes are not simple methods or strategies of teaching. They are procedures embodying values, a respect for the points of view offered in a discussion, a commitment to inquiry and so on. These are the "principles of procedure" discussed in this book.

Education as a social practice enables us to illuminate aspects of our lives. It would seem that knowledge gained through schooling transfers to problems and issues one faces outside of schooling. For John Dewey, education was:

> That reconstruction or reorganization of experience which adds to the meaning of experience, and which increases ability to direct the course of subsequent experience.
>
> (Dewey, 1966: 76)

The fact that Dewey conceptualized education as a process that would be further refined for growth indicates his belief that education would shed light on the student when school days were over. Education has norms or values built into it which in turn generate the aims teachers strive toward. These aims are intrinsic to the educational process. Many aims are therefore possible given worthwhileness. I am reminded that R.S. Peters made a brave attempt to sketch out what he felt were the general criteria for being educated:

> Criterion One: A commitment to what is internal to worth-while activity. That one takes delight in what one does for its own sake.

Richard Peters and others (Peters, Woods and Dray, 1973: 18) suggested:

> The first thing that must be said about the educated person is that (s)he must be one who not only pursues some particular activity such as science or cooking, but who is also capable of pursuing it for what there is in it as distinct from what it may lead on to or bring about.

Peters further suggested that the mark of a good school or good curriculum was the extent to which students possessed a desire to go on with the things into which they were initiated.

Criterion Two: Possession of a body of knowledge and some depth of knowledge and a conceptual scheme above the level of disconnected facts. That is, one understands the principles underlying what one does.

This implies some principles for the organization of facts; an understanding of "why" things are the way they are. Beyond this the educated mind would be able to link its knowledge to other areas of life. This knowledge permeates one's way of thinking so that one is "transformed" by what one knows.

Criterion Three: That one engages in many such pursuits and is therefore not narrowly specialized.

For example, a man committed to only mathematics and knowing little of other areas of life would be narrowly specialized and not considered as "educated."

Criterion Four: One's outlook and quality of life is transformed by being educated. That is that there is transfer of one's education to one's life and contemporary culture.

This is contrasted with the American passion for examination performance and results. This "meritocratic" factor has undesirable consequences, not least of which is the overemphasis on test results.

The duties entailed in curriculum improvement have a number of features. First, is the selection and ordering of principles for selection of the content of the course. Second, we must design and organize experiences for students that will enable them to be educationally involved. Third, we need a plan for researching the effects of our actions, and finally we need to organize our pattern of curriculum. Peters argued:

Education ... can have no ends beyond itself. Its value derives from principles and standards implicit in it. To be educated is not to have arrived at a destination; it is to travel with a different view. What is required is not feverish preparation for something that lies ahead, but to work with precision, passion and taste at worthwhile things that lie at hand.

(1964: 47)

Given the debilitating effects of most attempts to improve curriculum, schools need to implement the Process Model. Yet obstacles abound in requesting teachers to not only become researchers but simply become more reflective about their work. Research by Bennett (1993) argues that if teachers are to contribute to the betterment of schools and curriculum then they need to have proper support from both members of the school community and district office. Teachers cited that they needed greater skill and understanding of research methods to take on this task, something which Corey (1953) commented upon with the birth of action research in education. Bennett (1993: 69–70) found that:

1 teachers needed school and administrative support for research;
2 the definition and role of the teacher would have to be reconceptualized and refined to include a research brief;
3 teachers required staff development training for research, conference attendance and more research resources;
4 teachers need to test research findings in their own classrooms and settings.

In his book *How We Think* (1933) Dewey outlined what he believed to be the steps involved in the act of *reflective thinking*. The ultimate consequence for Dewey was to reach some definite conclusion or generalization. The role of *action* was central for Dewey:

Suggested inferences are tested in *thought* to see whether different elements in the suggestion are coherent with one another. They are also tested, after one has been adopted, by *action* to see whether the consequences that are anticipated in *thought* occur in *fact*.

Yet Dewey continues this discussion on the two methods by stating:

The two methods do not differ, however, in kind. Testing in thought for consistency involves acting in *imagination*. The other mode carries the imagined act out overtly.

(1933: 98)

For Dewey reflective thinking had five stages: suggestion, intellectualization, hypothesizing, reasoning and testing the hypothesis by overt action. He argued that the sequence of these stages was not necessarily fixed. The "aim of living is not perfection as a final goal, but the ever enduring process of perfecting, maturing refining" (Dewey, 1933: 98). The goal of education was not reaching some target by simply growing and more growth.

In *Education, Authority and Emancipation*, Stenhouse (1983: 185) argued that research counted as systematic self-critical inquiry made public. His idea was to shift the balance of power from the teacher as *an authority* to the students. The teacher could be *in authority* but in reflective and research-based teaching the teacher had to depreciate his or her claim to being *an authority* on a subject.

This type of systematic inquiry, which Stenhouse wished for students and teachers, was in essence a pattern of *action* learning through the thoughtful study of problems. This form of study becomes research when it is publicly disclosed, say through publication – the act of public acclamation evokes a critical response counting as new knowledge established through soundly based methods and being in some sense new. Teachers require prerequisites for this work. They need *imagination* to initiate projects and inquiries suitable for student involvement and they require sound *judgment* so as to discipline the inquiry.

These attributes very much operate as *principles of procedure*, or values, embodied in the process of education. We must commit to the view that the teacher, as a critic and scholar, can criticize the work of her or his pupils, so that they may learn together just as scholars who are critical of work in their field engage in discussion and dialogue with fellow scholars. Should not our students be treated with the same respect? Our curriculum needs to be knowledge based and we need to understand that a knowledge-based education is for everyone – not only scholars – and that the teaching profession is obligated to the great struggle with the immediate consequences of pursuing such an aspiration and ideal.

We must also accept that we can never be content with mastery of curriculum. Knowledge is provisional and static. We require the principle or belief that we need to *develop* and grow further in our understanding, knowledge and skill.

Our schools need to adopt the mission of the university, which is to extend our knowledge, not merely to transmit that which we hold in stewardship, and which was developed by previous generations of scholars. A number of scholars and curriculum workers are beginning to craft their own notions of "reflective practice." Reflection is in reality a form of specialized thinking arising from a troublesome or difficult concrete situation. It begins with a perceived problem.

Towards the development of situational understanding

Perhaps the most valuable tool available to the reflective practitioner is the development of a personal understanding of problematic educational situations; the improvement of one's practical reason and wisdom. What then is the upshot of this thinking about practical and ethical reasoning? From the hermeneutic and practicalist position the aim is arriving at a *situational understanding* and good judgment which is not deduced or prescribed by "grand theory," as Marxists, Platonists or Piagetians would have it. Theory is important, but it is subordinate to human intellect and free will and it takes a back seat to individual situational understanding of "grounded theory." The initial and some formal education of teachers takes place in universities or colleges. Higher education holds no secrets of life except through what Michael Oakeshott has called "arrests of experience" – those partial perspectives that alone give us some purchase on experience and the "possibility" of human understanding, which we call "knowledge." Most schools claim to have aims of advancing "knowledge." Teachers being committed to that aim must also grapple with the consequences of a theory of knowledge and this mighty ambition. In addition teachers are mandated to be moral agents.

Teaching and its counterpart, learning, are achieved in classrooms. Thus teachers must make the effects of their program accessible to research to understand if improvement is possible. This is the argument for each classroom being a "teacher-researcher" laboratory. As teachers we can pose as "experts" or "learners" along with our students. A Process Model favors the latter strategy.

Man: A Course of Study – an experimental Process Model

In advocating a process-inquiry model of education we are not without several good examples. During the 1970s Jerome Bruner helped to develop a social science curriculum for elementary level students titled Man: A Course of Study, in which a process of question-posing was paramount. It is not noteworthy that the US Congress attempted to sideline this course; what is significant is its design. The course attempted to focus upon those values which underpin a scientific structure of the disciplines approach to education. Man: A Course of Study (1970) (MACOS) stated pedagogical aims as "principles of procedure." These included:

1   To initiate and develop in youngsters a process of question-posing (the inquiry method);
2   To teach a research methodology where students can look for information to answer questions they have raised and use the framework developed in the course (e.g. the concept of the life cycle) and apply it to new areas;
3   To help youngsters develop the ability to use a variety of first-hand sources as evidence from which to develop hypotheses and draw conclusions;
4   To conduct classroom discussions in which youngsters learn to listen to others as well as express their own views;
5   To legitimize the search; that is, to give sanction and support to open-ended discussions where definitive answers to many questions are not found;
6   To encourage children to reflect on their own experiences;
7   To create a new role for the teacher, in which he/she becomes a resource rather than an authority.

(Bruner, in MACOS, 1970: 5)

Even a cursory glance at these pedagogical concerns reveals that they focus on the process of learning rather than some predigested content knowledge, or the outcomes or products of that experience.

With little doubt one can see the essence of these purposes as procedural. Lawrence Stenhouse has remarked that:

> I do not think that any curriculum innovation is likely substantially to improve intellectual power if it is not centrally concerned with the betterment of teaching.
>
> (1975: 39)

In my own curriculum development experiences I have tried to adopt such an approach, which is demonstrated in the following evidence from the Schools Cultural Studies Project, a five-year social studies program developed for Northern Ireland high schools in the mid 1970s, for which I served as a Curriculum Project Officer.

Summary of the process-inquiry model for curriculum

The central goal is that the educator subjects his or her teaching to a review of practice in light of the established teaching strategy adopted (whether Neutral Chair, Value Clarification agent etc.). One begins with broad aims, for example students will have an understanding of various arguments for why the USA went to war in Iraq. Thus the strategy is agreed and the educators introduce "content in the form of 'evidence'" for students to discuss. The group considers the "evidence" and airs their views on the subject. The teacher acts as a chairperson of the discussion. The goal is to forward student understanding of the issues raised. The teacher has the tasks of monitoring the quality of the discussion and also subjecting the entire process to critical action research. Thus curriculum, pedagogy and results are also researched through an action inquiry process where aims are contrasted with procedural criteria and judgment is rendered.

The aim of the process model of education is always understanding. Understanding cannot ever be achieved as a "final form of understanding." Understanding can only be deepened. I believe this is what Dewey had in mind when he spoke of the aim of education as being simply more "growth" of the learner. It is our most exciting challenge.

Part II

Democratic pedagogy

The practical

Chapter 6

The teacher as researcher

Action research as the basis for teaching and professional development

> We shall only teach better if we learn intelligently from the experience of shortfall; both in our grasp of the knowledge we offer and our knowledge of how to offer it. That is the case for research as the basis for teaching.
>
> Lawrence Stenhouse (1983: 193)

Quotations and definitions may not solve our research problems but they might provide spectacles for viewing them. Stenhouse (1981) argued that research is inquiry that is at once systematic, self-critical and open to public scrutiny; moreover it utilizes empirical tests where these are appropriate. Research can assist one in reasonably assessing local events accurately, thus improving our action and control, and it can help us to use our heads by throwing up explanatory concepts in which to ground our theories.

Trade in tradition, rhetoric and scholarship is the stock of most professors. Yet if we are to progress our understanding of the relationship of research with our own professional development and our practice as teachers we must appeal to reason, rationality and inquiry in order to engage in a serious debate about our direction as a community of discourse within this social milieu. My main point is that all teachers, wherever their location in the educational enterprise, have opportunities to learn and to develop professionally through research into their own practice. Moreover, if we are to take seriously the idea of teaching as a profession then this research dimension becomes crucial.

Present "technical" models of preparing teachers for professional careers are woefully inadequate. Eisner (2002) eloquently suggests that educational leadership is an art that is related to two other constructs: science and craft. I suggest that as teachers we live out a biography, a life career, characterized by three stages of professional development. First we learn our technical skills, the exercise of skills in pursuit of goals: to plan lessons, set assessments and so on. This is where the current outcomes-based education is stuck. Second, we develop our craft, which is the use of skilled technical knowledge in a masterly mode; we are "journeymen" and "journeywomen" now – no longer acolytes or apprentices. Finally, we work at becoming persons of intuitive wisdom and experience – artists using practical reason: the exercise of craft and technical knowledge in an intuitive way to produce original knowledge and unique outcomes and encounters. We have learned how to make "situational understanding" work in our favor.

Any concern to develop our professionalism must move beyond the mere exercise of technical know-how, which is the level where most Schools of Education are embedded, since that is merely the testing of our teaching and the pupils' learning against a blueprint of specifications. The artistic orientation demands the testing of our performance against an appeal to judgment. It is an evaluative response, a research action, into the educational process we have created for our students. I call this a "process-inquiry model" of educational practice. Good teachers are more akin to critics than markers of tests, just as the high-jumper does not improve by merely moving the bar up an inch higher, but by re-examining his or her performance: critiquing the approach and so on.

By objective criteria Picasso and Benjamin West would both get distinctions; yet the difference in excellence and quality between these painters is of fundamental importance in art and art criticism. This research-process model I put forward is committed to teacher development. It falls within the realm of what is increasingly being called "reflective practice"; the new professional role for teachers. If we, as professors or classroom teachers, are to extend our art and professionalism we must be able and have time and opportunity to inquire into our practice. Two of the most powerful constraints on teachers from engaging in action research of their own teaching are, first, that psychologically it is a very large threat to their own perceptions of their professional abilities; and second, that the school does not offer the resources and time to do research, or indeed offer rewards for teachers to engage in action research and share it with colleagues.

The conditions of teaching both in schools and in Colleges of Education at the present time make survival more urgent a concern than research or scholarship. There is also a tradition that teachers teach and professors do research. This traditional "division of labor" is steadfast and unchecked. Why do we grant sabbaticals to academics but not school teachers?

Elliott (1991) has argued that schools are unreflective cultures and that the task of making schools more effective is really bound up with making teachers more reflective: of creating an entirely new work ethic that places reflection in, and on, action at the center of the profession.

Education as a profession

One of the hallmarks of any profession is the use of research data and a knowledge base to solve problems and inform practice. I believe that the most distinguishing feature of a profession is the capacity for self-evaluation and improvement through inquiry into practice. A growing number of academics, yet only a handful of teachers, have discussed the implications of reflective, learning professionalism and the use of action research as a learning strategy (Altrichter *et al.*, 1993; Calderhead, 1988; Hoyle, 1984; Lomax, 1991; McKernan, 1996; McNiff, 1993; McNiff *et al.*, 1996; McNiff, 2000; McNiff and Whitehead, 2002; O'Hanlon, 1997; Reason and Bradbury, 2000; Revans, 1982; Schon, 1983, 1987; Winter, 1989; Zeichner and Liston, 1987). Education, I tell my students jokingly, is the second oldest profession.

One of the major problems with seeing education as a profession is that unlike other professions, for example Law or Medicine, there is no code of practice, or ethics, governing the educators (Sockett, 1983). However, that is only one criterion of a profession. I would define a profession as a body of individuals with qualifications for practice; possessing a theoretical and practical knowledge base; sharing a commitment to continuing education; service to the community; provision for self-autonomous decision-making; and a commitment to research and inquiry into practice which is shared by the community. On this definition we are thereabouts but have not quite arrived as a profession. The completion of this journey is urgently required.

There are daunting problems in stipulating the nature of research in education and in rendering those inquiries useful for cultural development. An ideological commitment to praxis and education as a moral enterprise might easily view schooling and curriculum as the legitimate object of cultural analysis and research as well as an area for social action. Thus our choice of a perspective may be seen to count as a political stance. Equally there are methodological consequences of adopting particular forms of inquiry. My orientation of teachers and schools as agents of cultural analysis and renewal is socially embedded and reverberates with the concerns of qualitative research – close-up studies in natural settings where interventions, improvement and self-evaluation are valued; this model lends legitimacy to the notion of educational action research.

My principal thesis in this chapter is that educational research belongs to the teacher qua teacher as much as the university professor as a democratic right.

The knowledge we teach in universities is won through research and I have come around to the belief that such knowledge cannot be taught correctly except through fidelity with the principles of procedure which produced it in the first place: this is the case for research-based teaching. I also believe that those who work in educational settings, the majority of them school teachers, have been largely disenfranchised from research and its findings; yet these individuals are asked to educate our youth for a future we cannot know or predict. The division of labor between the "researchers" and the "researched" is as unnecessary as it is unprofessional. All practitioners are in both a privileged and most advantageous position to benefit contemporary curriculum and instruction through the systematic exploration of their practice. Moreover, to adopt a research stance is, I shall argue, an act of cultural responsibility, for those who do are given opportunities to change, to reconstruct, not only curriculum and the culture of the school but, dare I say, the culture of society.

I wish to address an emerging style of research-based teaching, a critical pedagogy, within a conception of educational action research for both curriculum and cultural reconstruction. To view educational research and development in this way is to lay claim that schools are not only distributors of knowledge, but that teachers and pupils may be producers of knowledge. We need to begin to think of teaching as experiencing, creating, believing, planning, acting, inquiring into problematic actions and reflecting on action. It makes a lot of sense to talk about teachers as researchers.

Action research is a unique form of social inquiry since it is also carried out in such diverse fields as agriculture, industry, medicine and so on. I define action research as a form of collaborative and collective self-reflective inquiry that is conducted by participants in order to solve practical problems and to improve the quality of life in any social setting. Action research attempts to feed the judgment, and practical reasoning, of practitioners in concrete situations, and thus enable practitioners to improve the rationality and justice of those actions. Action research is a way of both learning and knowing about our practice.

The conduct of practical action research is not simply a matter of finding small problems to deal with in education for we are talking about wide-ranging cultural aspects of education, and not tiny bits of it. So, from this perspective it is equally important for the kindergarten teacher as it is for history and science teachers in the high schools as it is for university professors of education to see education within this cultural context. Culture is a word like curriculum – a portmanteau concept which can be used with many meanings. In employing the culture concept I am talking not about high culture but about beliefs, perceptions and most centrally values and meanings which offer patterns for behavior: a design for the way of life of a people. Education is mainly concerned with the communication of cultural values. It follows then that if schools are interested in values and the problems of communication then it is very appropriate for them to give resources to research these problems.

I also wish to draw a distinction between research *in* education, that is, inquiry that strengthens practice and theory in education, and research *on* education, for example that conducted from within the contributing foundation disciplines such as sociology, history and the psychology of education. It is my contention that research on education has contributed incidentally, if at all, to helping practitioners in classrooms. Educational research if it is to be at all helpful to classroom teachers or university lecturers requires that they test its implications for practice in their classrooms. Much educational research claims allegiance to the psycho-statistical model and is expressed in generalizations that cannot help in case-based particular circumstances.

The implications of school-based research and development for curriculum renewal was soon reinforced in a research assignment which addressed one of the most intractable problems of intergroup relations in Western Europe – the design of a curriculum in social and cultural studies embracing education for mutual understanding and tolerance among and between adolescents caught up in the civil and guerrilla war of 1970s Northern Ireland.

This was not a matter of updating social studies content but of designing a program that would enable pupils and teachers to reconstruct their culture in a time of crisis. It was an initiative of profound social reconstruction. The project asked schools to place some of these divisive controversial issues into the secondary school curriculum for discussion – the values for which young men and women were paying with their lives across the barricades of Northern Ireland.

I became interested in action research at this time and I noted the many action research projects carried out in the post-war social reconstructionist period in the USA by folk such as Hilda Taba, Kurt Lewin, Stephen Corey and others. These inquiries gave me heart – and these models sent a message to us in Northern Ireland which said intergroup harmony and the elimination of prejudice are the rightful concerns of the school community.

The relationship between research and effective teaching and learning is about as advanced as medicine at the time of Christ. I recall teaching political prisoners in Northern Ireland – the "terrorists" on both the Republican and Loyalist sides – and having it pointed out to me that we university types, for all our talk of problem-solving and social inquiry, hadn't done a very good job of finding solutions to Ireland's "Troubles." I had to agree with that young man, a political prisoner, who was formerly an undergraduate student at the university where I worked.

To call for more educational research may appear absurd at first sight. But that is what my aim is in this book – but it is not basic research but applied research which I am after. Research ought to be viewed as the basis for teaching. Traditionally, research has been the special preserve of the academic who works in the contemplative culture of the university, or the external research agency. The theory widely received is that the university exists to pass on culture, to conduct research and to train novice researchers. The university, and more particularly, Schools of Education, exist to advance and disseminate knowledge, and to provide professional training and skills. This model has been the root cause of much dissatisfaction in recent years as practitioners in first and second level institutions have not been the general beneficiaries of the knowledge and research on education.

How can we do things better and more effectively? The "effective schools" research suggests several possibilities. Effective schools are responsive to pupils. The teachers have a good pastoral care system and seek to involve pupils in the total school culture. In my rambling about schools in

Ireland and the United Kingdom I have found that it is a combination of pressure and support that characterizes the good school. Yet there are varieties of the demanding school. First, there is the demanding school that is unresponsive to pupils – it serves to alienate them. There is the school that is unresponsive and undemanding – where it serves to be anomic. I have questioned this exclusive research focus on the school as a unit; it has ignored the classroom, the teachers, pupils and community. A study by Pauly (1991) argues that success or failure of schools depends on daily life in classrooms, and the author points alarmingly to the fact that educational policy has paid scant attention to the influence of classrooms per se on education. The effective schools literature uses "the school" as the basic unit for analysis. It is culturally naive. This presents an abstract picture – it is like the Rand McNally Road Atlas map of North Carolina, when we really need an Ordnance Survey map of the bends and potholes in this or that road.

School-based research is trying to counteract the history of educational research: an epoch characterized by much mindless number crunching. As a young researcher on the killing fields of Northern Ireland in the early 1970s I was inspired by the radical and innovatory approaches to ethnographic research in classrooms (Smith and Geoffrey, 1968) and qualitative program evaluation and naturalistic research that helped us to see, feel and understand our project effects – as opposed to merely controlling, measuring and attempting to predict events. The work of David Jenkins, Malcolm Parlett, David Hamilton, Robert Stake and Elliot Eisner is instructive of that genre of qualitative design. We had gone "Beyond the Numbers Game," as my colleague David Jenkins concluded.

Qualitative or naturalistic research places a premium bunting on description, understanding, interpretation and, in the special case of action research, problem solving. These values I personally prefer to the goals of measurement, correlation of variables and the myth of control and prediction as primary virtues in quantitative inquiry.

Over the past thirty-five years I have been seeking the possibility of extending research to the school community and of arguing that this is an act of enormous social and cultural responsibility. Thus, I intend to describe the kind of responsibility that is the special remit of the university. That is, those who work in the university and enjoy the rights of academic freedom must also extend that general right, in a democracy, to those who work in elementary and secondary education. Teachers, students and others in the community are entitled to the same rights of freedom of inquiry, autonomy, speech and publication as university/college professors. Yet as noted in Chapter 2, academic freedom is quite different for primary and secondary teachers as compared with tertiary level faculty. Intellectual freedom is granted to the society and not exclusively to the university. What counts as a general right for me, as an individual, is also a right for all other educators.

Yet problems abound. The most important problem is shortage of time available to those who work in schools. In a recent survey of action researchers in the USA, United Kingdom and Ireland (McKernan, 1992) it was found that *lack of time* was mentioned unanimously by all respondents as the most difficult constraint connected with doing teacher-research. Simply put, we must firstly address the political agenda that teacher-researchers hold. *Time* must be found for some, not all, teachers, to engage in fruitful school-based inquiries.

Second, there is the problem of access to research training, and results. I know of few schools where current educational research and scholarly journals are available to staff and students. The test of good research is that it is made public – chiefly to other scholar-researchers. There are models that describe action inquiry but few examples of how to teach action inquiry in the literature. I would question the limitations of this model and argue that it might be even more valid to translate this research in a courteous manner so that all members of the community can have access to and understand it: perhaps publish it in the local town newspaper or screen discussions on community television. Is it accepted that we do not see this principle as part of our professional responsibility? This might lead us into the great challenge of the "demystification of educational research" for in the end the public have a right to information and knowledge as an accountability measure – let alone the fact that most universities are supported from public funds. In fact over the past few decades teachers working at action research have shown the way forward (Elliott, 1991; McKernan, 1996).

Third, there is the problem of creating partnerships with other elements in the culture – families, corporations and central office administrators – and of making our results available to these audiences.

Fourth, it has been argued that educational ideas as expressed in books and academic journal writing are not easily taken on board by teachers. However, if those ideas were presented in the vernacular as exciting hypotheses or proposals then I believe greater numbers of teachers would come forward to research their effects for practice in schools. This curriculum would count as being intelligent – not correct or dogmatic, as so many specifications present themselves.

In the same way that inquiry in mathematics or philosophy can provide a foundation for teaching and understanding those disciplines, research in education can provide a platform for pedagogy and learning about teaching. The classroom is the teacher's laboratory and, as Dewey suggested, the contribution that teachers can make to research in education is an un-worked mine (Dewey, 1929).

Curriculum, be it in the academy, or the Greenville NC public schools, is thus a hypothesis, or proposal, that invites the critical and reflective response of the practitioner. Thus, research becomes the basis for teaching, or administrating. What we need to put on offer is a curriculum conceived not as a final and prescriptive solution, but as a set of hypotheses and procedural principles that teachers can test and effectively translate into reflexive social practice. My work in school-based curriculum development has rested upon two principles. The first is that the teacher and school as a center of inquiry and development (Schaefer, 1967) is primarily linked to strengthening the reflective judgment of teachers and, as a consequence, to the self-directed improvement of practice. Second, it is my belief that the most important area for educational research is the curriculum because that is the medium through which knowledge is communicated. Our slogan was, and remains, "no curriculum development without teacher development."

Through self-reflection, the teacher or university professor becomes a conscious artist, and through the practice of his or her art, the teacher is able to employ personal judgment as a tool for inquiry. Nothing that is offered by way of mandate by Colleges of Education, state departments or teacher educators ought to be accepted uncritically – those who deny this assertion would do well to study the infamous case of Sir Cyril Burt who cooked his results to match his model-building, regrettably with disastrous policy results for schools in Britain that were divided into three types – Grammar, Technical and Comprehensive – to coincide with his "results" about human intelligence.

We must attempt to avoid the acceptance of a "rhetoric of results." The purpose of research is to supplement, enrich and extend our powers of judgment, not to supplant them with dogma. Research-grounded teaching is definitely more demanding than teaching rooted in the rhetoric of result-conclusions.

Stenhouse (1975) argued that to request that we all become research-based teachers is to ask us to share with our colleagues and students the fundamental process of inquiry – of learning the wisdom which we do not at this moment possess so that our students can get into critical perspective the knowledge and learning which we trust is ours. Yet as a teacher-educator it is comfortable to accept a rhetoric of conclusions idea of teaching. It is safe and secure in that it does not ask us to create knowledge. Professional schools are reluctant to appear as models for inquiry – better that they cling to the reassurance of past models, texts and results to ease the agony of their collective cultural responsibility.

True education in the disciplines or other worthwhile activities has an in-built standard of excellence – and thus it can be evaluated on the basis of the ideals and values immanent in the "doing" of the subject itself, rather than because of some minimal outcome. For example, there are certain principles of procedure for doing mathematics, such as understanding the tests of truth for the discipline; understanding the internal logic of the subject; its epistemology and its related concepts; and knowing how to conduct further inquiry in the subject. These principles of procedure should be our "objectives."

The question posed by Professor John Elliott (1993) is this: "Do we want our education to be like a manufacturing or training process, or like an educational process?" The idea of education makes sense only in the context of the latter as a reflective social practice. I must confess to feeling uncomfortable with all of the renewed talk about outcomes-based education and assessment – it is a technical response, not an artistic or educational response which, I suspect, if left unchecked will ultimately lead to the technologization of human reason. Teachers up and down Britain, and throughout Western Europe, have rebelled against this curriculum where children are tested at ages seven, nine, eleven, thirteen and sixteen. Performance levels have been specified for the ten subjects in the United Kingdom curriculum and teachers are frustrated with the amount of time taken up with assessment. In North Carolina pupils have major tests at end of grades three through eight and during later high school years. The problem with the subject curriculum is that it is knowledge based.

A second potent query to pose is "How does one get the gallon curriculum into the pint timetable?" The curriculum in the USA, as in Europe, is like the library where books are continuously added to the shelf, but none are ever withdrawn. At present some sixty subjects, on average, are offered at the high school level alone.

We must be careful to distinguish education from mere training or instruction. Education enhances the freedom of the student by inducting him or her into the knowledge of his or her culture as a living, thinking process. Knowledge allows us to think creatively. Outcomes-based assessment weakens standards of quality and renders knowledge as instrumental.

Curriculum would include the activities and experiences that contribute to the growth of the pupil. Remember that coherence is in the eye of the beholder – the pupil. Curriculum is made up largely of experiences designed for learning – we must not forget it is always a selection from culture. The hard question is "What aspects of culture will be selected?" Understanding, and indeed knowledge, is always provisional and fraught with difficulties – even for philosophers. As educators we are for social action and freedom of inquiry, but far too often we restrict the precincts of our understanding to the campus. Let me offer a concrete case of an educational institution that engages in socially responsible action – the Open University television programs screened on BBC TV are some of the most popular programs in Western Europe. A premise of the Open University is to make knowledge, research and skills available to the community and thus they have got round the problem of accessibility.

Another problem I would see in establishing research-based teaching is that of the academic culture of Colleges and Schools of Education resisting such a brief. Educational research is big business in the USA and increasingly so in Europe. Philanthropic and government agencies control the purse strings and therefore define the research agenda: we must define precisely how far this is a serious problem for our social responsibility.

Research, it is argued, should be conducted by "objective" experts,

usually trained in quasi-physical science methodology with a bent for empirical inquiry rooted in positivist traditions. Yet pure objectivity in social
research is not attainable. Our objectivity is always fallible as we are part of
the social facts we seek to explain. We as researchers affect the situations we
inquire into. I say research belongs to the practitioner as much as the
external expert. External researchers often define the school problems they
wish to research when it ought to be the practitioners who identify research
concerns. Practitioners are still, in the main, treated as clients and not
collaborators in research. A most fundamental task is to train teachers and
administrators in the art of researching their work. We need to work at
deriving practical theory, not imposing grand theory on practitioners. Even
action researchers are being asked to genuflect to the grand theories of
Habermas, Adorno and others. I have noted a recent trend for critical theorists to impose the grand theory of the Frankfurt School on the action
research movement – this amounts to the hijacking of the movement. This
is where I feel a new partnership might be created between universities and
schools. We should not take for granted the notion that somehow schools
have an in-built capacity for research and evaluation work. Our teachers need
new and imaginative courses in qualitative inquiry and educational action
research.

A most interesting partnership is that between politicians and school
persons. It is my contention that during the Thatcher–Reagan years the
profession was devalued, de-funded and, indeed, mistrusted. The accountability movement has served to strip and streamline school budgets of
needed resources. Successive governments have attempted to strip what little
political power teacher organizations possessed – to wit, the demise of the
Schools Council for Curriculum and Examinations in Britain in 1986 – with
major decision-making now returned to the Minister for Education and the
Department of Education and Science. During Thatcher's reign an edict was
telegraphed to the provinces that those in initial teacher training would
spend something in the region of 60 percent of their time in schools and 40
percent in teacher training institutions. Whether one agrees with this idea
or not the fact remains that teacher educators had no say in this policy. The
implications for teacher education are frightening for the profession.

Never before in history has the profession of teaching called for so much
commitment, skill and creative exercise of craft and art than it does at this
time. If politicians do not come good on their promises of excellence
through imaginative partnerships then the entire exercise of recent reforms,
whether through teacher action research, professional development schools
or the National Curriculum, will be for nought.

I argue the case for school–university partnership in research and development well knowing that it is unfashionable in many quarters, yet I present it
without embarrassment or apology since good schools already have established this concept of partnership – between teachers and pupils, teachers

and parents and teachers and educational authorities in the community. Schools of Education and public schools both already have a purchase on what counts as effectiveness and good research. While lecturers and professors keep a close eye on research they largely ignore school staff. We need to pool our results; make them truly the subject of self-critical and systematic public inquiry if they are to count as "research." One project that I would like to see undertaken would be the study of a "bad" or ineffective school, under the leadership of a new principal and in partnership with university researchers and supervisors/practitioners as the basis for making that school more effective. All of us would, I think, learn much from that study.

One of the major weaknesses of the teacher-researcher movement is the almost total neglect of the politics of action/school research. We need to be very clear that school-sited research by practitioners has a political agenda since it will demand resources, localized forms of decision-making and power to produce changes: the political struggle of practical action. Many unanswered queries remain: "How can we get teacher-research institutionalized as a professional work ethic?" "What are the political and conceptual challenges facing teacher-research?" We need to ask, "What role can teacher-research play in teacher initial and in-service education?" "What benefits might accrue from a policy in which local school boards and central offices hire educational action researchers who in turn induct scores of school staff into the methodology of research-based reflective practice?" These are crucial questions that require answering. What I can say in commenting on the teacher-researcher movement by way of answering is that in Ireland, Britain and several other European nations teacher-research is making a difference to the quality of life in schools and that this is being tried with some excellent results. Some schools have hired staff to teach half-time and to research their own schools half-time. In my tenure in University College Dublin I demanded that postgraduate students on in-service courses, many of them with long years of experience, spend considerable time in schools doing action research in an attempt to develop and improve curriculum and teaching. Several others (Lomax, 1991; McNiff, 2000) report similar programs for in-service education in the United Kingdom. The students have responded well – they remark that these "practical inquiries" are far more satisfying than their traditional foundation studies for higher degrees.

What ideals do I have to offer? Let us turn to our social action agenda. First, I have argued that all educators have a responsibility for research. This could be realized by providing courses for initial and in-service teachers to conduct practical research. The sort of naive traditional quantitative-statistically based educational research courses do not serve school educators well. Very few undergraduate programs teach education students how to do classroom research and development work. We must begin. We need action research courses on all award-bearing programs. For example, in respect of the accessibility argument we allow students to learn about research by researching priority problems in their school community and giving them responsibility for disseminating these results to their colleagues, parents and pupils.

Second, we can offer our professional skills of doing research to others in schools and elsewhere in ways that develop styles of teaching that promote rather than demote inquiry, and that advance styles of teacher-administrator self-development and evaluation. Universities in kind can consider establishment of courses in research-based teaching that promote university–school partnerships and the recognition of school staff as honorary lecturers who will share their private, practical, professional knowledge in ways heretofore unexplored.

The curriculum, if it is worthy, is expressed in the form of a pedagogy that places a premium on the process of inquiry and education; based on a conception of knowledge, an epistemology, that argues that knowledge is merely provisional, the base camp for our next attack. And while curriculum planning may be argued to be a rational activity, we might consider the issue of which rationality is on offer: technical or practical? (MacIntyre, 1988).

The vital thing about the curriculum is that it invites all teachers to improve their knowledge of their craft and how to get knowledge by the exercise of that craft and art. Personally, I find it both worrying and arrogant that the traditional form of educational research is not tolerant of experimentation with modes of inquiry, particularly at a time when curriculum research is very fertile with a plethora of new emerging forms of inquiry (Short, 1991).

Another area where action research is making an important contribution is in the field of teacher and program evaluation. Democratic empowerment evaluation is now being revived (Fetterman, 2001; MacDonald and Walker, 1976). Small naturalistic evaluation studies are becoming a cottage industry – there is a ready and receptive market in schools for second order facilitators of action research and evaluation. World class evaluators including Barry MacDonald, Stephen Kemmis and John Elliott have demonstrated that action research and democratic evaluation can mix in with the best of the traditional evaluation models and teams. Yet, most school systems have not responded generously with research proposals coming up from grass roots level, and further little pressure has been applied to administrators and supervisors to re-create in-service opportunities which take account of practitioner research. In fairness, since the middle 1990s there has been some public state funding for teachers doing action research – for example in North Carolina the state offers some funding in specialist areas such as music education for teacher-based action research.

We need both degree and non-degree credit for practitioner research. One colleague commented, "teachers go to in-service workshops and researchers go to conferences . . . sometimes!" Do we need this professional split? It is time for us to pay closer attention to the forms of institutional structures that will weld together Colleges of Teacher Education with local school systems.

Constraints on action research in schools and colleges

Barriers, or constraints on teacher-research, abound (McKernan, 1992). Because of their isolation and concomitant subordination as functionaries in a complex bureaucracy the organization of schools in the Western world militates against research-based teaching and cultural analysis. Teachers' workloads help to maintain this isolation and the division of labor between the researchers and the researched. Most of my postgraduate teachers say they just do not have any time to conduct action research. It needs pointing out that teaching, and curriculum in general, has a long history of subordination to academics, school officials and not least to educational publishers. The teacher-researcher movement is now trying to counteract that history. The worst enemy is lack of "time to do research." John Dewey mentioned this fact in that splendid volume *The Sources of a Science of Education* (Dewey, 1929) when he discussed the possible role of the teacher as an "investigator." Another problem is the lack of research skills and resources by potential teacher-researchers.

Because practitioner research has a political agenda it grants power and authority and a decision-making status to practitioners. It thus poses a threat to traditional decision-makers and researchers. It is a direct challenge to the empirical mode of inquiry conducted in Schools of Education. Since it is still very much a minority pursuit it has not yet been granted the Good Housekeeping Stamp of Approval for teacher release time.

Conclusions

The days ahead demand curriculum and an education system which is responsive to the public, and one in which educators may also submit "report cards" and evaluations on their situation. The system needs to be flexible, accountable and professionally rewarding. I think of education and teaching as a professional vocation, a career, although I am aware that disunity marks the profession. One of the elements missing from teaching which is a criterion of other professions is a code of ethics to govern practice. Any rightful notion of the teacher as a researcher must surely include:

1   a commitment to teaching and research as part of the occupational work;
2   a commitment to the development of reflection as the means for improving practice;
3   a commitment to the development of a community of discourse sharing

theoretical and practical knowledge and understanding within common valued goals;
4   a commitment to the dissemination of practical wisdom and research results.

These are the things that we must be mainly about to meet the challenge of change and to fulfill our collective research roles for improved teaching and self-professional development.

Chapter 7

Action research and philosophy

Origins, nature and conduct of inquiry

> Every art and every inquiry, and similarly every action and pursuit, is
> thought to aim at some good . . . therefore if there is an end for all that we
> do, this will be the good achievable by action, and if there are more than
> one, these will be the goods achievable by action.
>
> Aristotle, *Nichomachean Ethics*, Bk 1: 1,094–97

One would not be wrong to think that the basis for the *good* on Aristotle's
view is *action*. The questions raised in this chapter are those concerned with
practical reason or wisdom – an answer to the question "What do I need to
do now as a practitioner?" In this chapter I wish to present an argument that
supports a form of critical inquiry which has emerged during the last fifty
years and the processes which underpin that form of praxis and its philosophical justification as an argument for the superiority of action research
over the flawed virtues of objectivist positivism. Action research aims at
improving the quality of choices and human action in social settings and
therefore improving a practical situation.

While several noted writers have addressed "linguistic" turns in theory
(Gadamer, 1981), stipulating that all the ways of interpreting day-to-day
lived life are through *language*, this chapter will seek to explore *action* turns
as the basis for a more grounded theory of action inquiry and to describe
something of the method and conduct of action inquiry.

Theoretical origins of action research

There are many arguments relating to the origins of action research. Herbert
Altrichter has argued that action research was first conceived by Moreno
while working with European prostitutes around 1913 (Altrichter *et al.*,
1993; Moreno, 1934). It is probably the case that the process of action
research, or action inquiry, as I, and many practitioners, prefer, originated
somewhere in the desires of American Pragmatism, principally John

Dewey's theoretical musings on the concept of reflective thinking and problem-solving (Dewey, 1910).

Another conceivable theory is that of using social research to address social problems in late-nineteenth-century England with the proposals of G.B. Shaw, and Sidney and Beatrice Webb, who along with other Fabian socialists established the London School of Economics with the specific desire to solve some of the pressing social problems of the day, that is, poverty, prostitution and illegal rents (McKernan, 2004).

In a chapter titled "The Teacher as Investigator" in *The Sources of a Science of Education* (1929) Dewey argued that the classroom teacher had a ready-made laboratory that was an "un-worked mine" of opportunities to learn from research. Early examples include US public policy field work with Native American Indians' housing problems (Collier, 1945) as well as the most often cited field theory experiments of Kurt Lewin (Lewin, 1946, 1951) in social psychology. Regardless of the source, what is apposite is that what counts as action research nowadays is a paradigm with a logic contrary to that of the positivist hypothetico-deductive tradition of research, the scientific positivist tradition being concerned with representation of the world and interpretational theory construction rather than the more immediate practical business of improved action within it (Greenwood and Levin, 2001).

Since all practitioners are actors in social settings, surely the aim of research is not merely to describe, interpret or even to collect knowledge about the world but to develop a more profound situational understanding and knowledge with which to reason about and guide us in choosing appropriate and improved behavior for action in social settings. It is a theory of action we are after.

Processes of education are tried and tested ways, paradigms for conduct if you will, by which persons become some way or another – it is an "initiation" into a form of life. Not only is there a process of action research but there is a process of "action learning" involved. If a person is to learn to think ethically or sociologically the learning experiences must include some kinds of moral or social issue.

When action research was first widely promoted as a practical problem-solving methodology and concept in the 1940s (Lewin, 1946) it was conceived, from within social psychology and social research fields, as a cyclical model of reconnaissance of a problematic human action series and the application of human action in an effort to resolve the conflict situation. But simple problem-solving is not sufficient as a basis for praxis.

Field theory and action research 1930–

It has been suggested that action research first began with Collier's pragmatic solutions to Indian housing in 1930s USA (Collier, 1945). Yet it is Kurt Lewin and his idea of field theory that is the most well-documented basis for the idea of action research. He viewed it as "change experiments" that would lead to laws of social life, that is, practical action would be led by scientific laws by understanding the forces in the field, or natural-social environment (Lewin, 1948: 205).

To understand behavior one needs to understand the social surround of facts, or the "field." For Lewin theory alone was useless unless grounded in facts and empirical data. These experiments in field theory, or topography as Lewin also referred to them, led to his work in changing behavior: the Group Dynamics movement begun at the National Training Laboratory or "T-Group" strategies implemented at MIT and other behavior therapy institutes. Indeed much of the work of the Tavistock Institute of Human Relations in London grew out of this collaborative group action research tradition (Wallace, 1987).

However, Richard Rorty, the pragmatist philosopher, has argued that Dewey's logic of inquiry yielded a great influence:

> Pragmatists favor problem solving (Dewey, 1910) and hope to break with the picture which, in Wittgenstein's words, "holds us captive" – the Cartesian-Lockean picture of a mind seeking to get in touch with a reality outside itself. So they start with a Darwinian account of human beings as animals doing their best to cope with the environment – doing their best to develop tools which will enable them to enjoy more pleasure and less pain. Words are among the tools which these clever animals have developed.
>
> (1999: xxii–xxiii)

Action research attempted to begin from a social science vantage and adopted some of the accoutrements of field psychology science. In 1957, Hodgkinson wrote a provocative paper critical of action research as the social science community adopted the then in vogue Research, Development and Dissemination model (RD&D) so as to enable "scientific" style inquiry for purposes of preferred fund granting. Simple social setting, practical problem-solving forms of action research almost completely disappeared. Some of this work was applied to problems of anti-Semitism and race relations training for school personnel in the 1950s (Taba and Noel, 1957). The USA was experiencing increased enmity and prejudice directed towards minority groups, especially Jews and African Americans. This led to action research for improved intergroup relations in schools and communities (Taba and Noel, 1957).

Stephen Corey of Columbia's Teachers College encouraged teachers to adopt hypothesis testing of solutions to practical problems to improve practice. In the United Kingdom the Tavistock Institute of Human Relations advanced action research as part of human relations issues and management concerns with actors as clients.

School improvements and practical action research 1950–

Action research in education began in a spirit of improving school practices in mid-twentieth-century USA (Corey, 1953; Taba and Noel, 1957) and centering human relations through curriculum. This approach was cast as a quasi-scientific style of problem-solving with hypothesis-testing language. After a decline in the 1960s action research re-emerged as a result of the curriculum development movement in the UK during the late 1960s and early 70s. Not only were classroom teachers at the fore of many of the curriculum projects, for example the work of the Schools Council Humanities Curriculum Project, directed by Lawrence Stenhouse, but these teachers understood the link between theory and practice or, more specifically, between curriculum and research.

Committed to a concept of self-improvement, the "teacher-researcher" movement made bold strides in this phase which I shall call the "Practical Science" period. New approaches and developments in curriculum theory, notably the work of Joseph Schwab and his well-known lectures on "The Practical," broke new ground and language for curriculum, but the demand that curriculum projects have in-built evaluation controls led to a Stenhousian renaissance for action research as part of a Process Model for curriculum design. Sadly, Lawrence Stenhouse died before his Research Model could be more fully developed. Yet the curriculum reform movement and school-based experimentation gave a new epistemological basis for an expanded theory of action research in schools.

Some of this "extended professional" perspective has found its way into action research as a management strategy (Mayo, 1949; Wallace, 1987). This "collaborative action research" style came out of work by Lewin at the National Training Laboratory and at the Tavistock Institute as a part of human relations training for managers and the moral obligations of management through collaborative action.

Critical theory and educational action research

In 1986 Wilfred Carr and Stephen Kemmis published their ideas on action research in a well-received book, *Becoming Critical: Education, Knowledge and Action Research*, as a critical-emancipatory response to injustices in human settings based upon the critical philosophy of Jurgen Habermas (Habermas, 1972). This work signaled a breakthrough in that it couched action inquiry in Habermas' critical theory and began the critical action research discourse. I suspect Carr and Kemmis had in mind the inequalities and politically incorrect or unjust decisions that are made in schools and colleges. In fact, Carr and Kemmis define action research in such terms:

Action research is simply a form of self-reflective enquiry undertaken by participants in social situations in order to improve the rationality and justice of their own practices, their understanding of these practices, and the situations in which the practices are carried out.

(1986: 162)

Habermas (1972) claimed that knowledge reflected constitutive interests in both prediction and control. For example the early scientific action research work in education and management was masking a concern with power and top-down strategies of control. One of its shortcomings was that Habermas has not elucidated an account of what a critical social science would look like – he only dealt with an abstracted theory of communication.

Recently, there have been a number of new books that have adopted a critical perspective aimed at assisting students, teachers and faculty to use action research for social justice, peace and humanistic ends. The work of Carson and Sumara in Canada (1997), Bill Atweh, Stephen Kemmis and Patricia Weeks in Australia (Atweh *et al.*, 1998) and Susan Noffke in the USA (1995) have all promoted the idea of cultivating critical communities in schools, colleges and community settings using participatory action inquiry to achieve greater social justice and equality.

To be honest, before this time not much attention was devoted to a rigorous philosophical analysis treatment of action inquiry. Action research, reared on Pragmatism, has retained a flavor of commonsense problem-solving. But these simple actions of making choices and knowing what and how to choose are the bases of practical reasoning.

It had seemed moribund, with most publications re-iterating some wooden series of pragmatic problem-solving steps. Frameworks that developed as a response to postmodernism – to wit the critical theory of Habermas; the practical science hermeneutic constructs of Gadamer; and the application of a more rigorous discussion by curricularists, such as John Elliott – gave action research a more sophisticated theory and epistemology. Action research is growing theoretically. It has been countering the grandiose claims of positivism and hermeneutics (Winter, 2001).

To be educated is to use a process that results in desirable qualities such as the development of mind and sound use of reasoning in the production of human action. It is a combination of understanding, reason and action. Some values embedded in praxis are procedural, such as careful collection of evidence; checking and not falsely presenting data; clarity and communication; protecting divergence of opinion on issues under discussion; and so forth. This observation led John Dewey to conclude that the virtues embodied in living and acting are no different from those involved in education, for both the learner and the liver exhibit virtues of critical, disciplined and reasoned inquiry.

The major development of action research in education has come from teachers "trying out" various ideas and evaluating these. Thus the educational values which are held to be important in student learning – such as making reasoned arguments in a discussion, or discoveries – should also be matched by values embedded in teaching procedures such as teachers helping to facilitate good discussion work.

The improvement of human action in a problematic social situation is at base a practical event. It requires a rational process of reflective inquiry and choosing of alternative possible actions that will ultimately lead to improvement. This is the quality of practical reasoning which leads to practical knowledge. It is knowing "what to do" in the situation. Situational analysis is a primary goal for action inquiry. It does not have as a primary goal the elucidation of explanatory theories but at base improved human action. As eloquently expressed by Rorty:

> We cannot regard truth as a goal of inquiry. The purpose of inquiry is to achieve agreement among human beings about what to do, to bring consensus on the end to be achieved and the means to be used to achieve those ends. Inquiry that does not achieve co-ordination of behavior is not inquiry but simply wordplay.
>
> (1999: xxv)

Action research has always been relegated to the second division of the research league table (Hodgkinson, 1957; Sanford, 1970). One criticism of action inquiry is that the results of studies are not generalizable. Stenhouse (1983) suggested, to the contrary, that if one builds up a number of case files of similar action researches, then sampling of this universe can count as a valid basis for generalization.

Action inquiry, rightful intention and human action

The goal of practical knowledge, on Aristotle's view, is rightful action caused by moral good intention. The most wonderful outcome of education is to use speculative reason operating upon curiosity or doubt as a way of arriving at truth or good knowledge. Thus inquiry, reason and good intention – or ethics – are all involved. Education is a form of freedom always. The freedom to inquire, to speculate, to establish answers – with Gramsci it asserts that the purpose of the school is to formulate "humanism," human intellectual discipline and the ability of "moral independence." Schools mostly seem to operate as distributors of knowledge. Through a concerted program of teacher and student inquiry schools can be centers for inquiry and the creation of knowledge (Schaefer, 1967). This is what universities aspire to through faculty and students pursuing research. It should be the same with the schools, especially at the secondary level where students have absorbed research methods and project work.

Critical realism as a philosophical base

Critical realism asserts that we have no option but to assume the existence of an objective reality. However, in doing so, our knowledge of it is always subject to error and imperfection – it is "fallible" (Collier, 1994: 16, 50). The critical researcher-observer is never detached and independent as positivism would have it, but always part of the situation, as Roy Bhaskar, the English social theorist and chief advocate for critical realism, argues (1986: 160).

We forge our explanations as cases and tales as narratives. This critical inquiry, or research, is thus never perfect or complete, argue critical realists, and constitutes a program of practical work and practical reasoning about the world. Yet despite this imperfection and the non-exact nature of our inquiries, critical realism is useful in that it plays up the notion that we can make choices that lead to improvement in practice and understanding. This is critical realism's possibility: the idea that we can identify factors so as to explain the situation. In making these decisions, based on critical observation by a reflective thinking agent, we are involved in a transformative change process. This is why Bhaskar calls his critical realism a "transformational model." Through action research as critical inquiry we can avoid the inadequacies of positivism.

Richard Winter (2001) argues that, although critical realism is a model for inquiry in general, it also seems to be entirely compatible with the values and processes of action research. Indeed, as indicated below, in some ways action research offers a more complete realization of the principles of critical realism than is usually possible within the parameters of conventional "academic" social science.

Bhaskar's philosophy of critical realism (1979, 1986) emerged first as a reaction against positivism and hermeneutics as adequate theories (Kaboub, 2001). The proposition is that something is real if it brings about visible consequences. Things are as they are but knowledge of them may change as personal awareness grows. He began (1979) with the question "To what extent can society be studied in the same way nature is studied?" Positivists say society, schools and curriculum can be studied according to the Humean notion of law (Naturalism). Contrary to this hermeneutics argues that society cannot be studied using a naturalist methodology as deep meanings are hidden. We must deconstruct these meanings – in doing so total objectivity may be lost. Naturalism is defined as the unity of method between the social and natural sciences.

Critical realism asserts reality exists independent of people and our knowledge of it; that people do not create society – it pre-exists, but social actors can "transform" it. The two grand theories of society and behavior are Model 1 (Weber), that society determines human behavior (voluntarism) and action; and Model 2 (Durkheim), that individuals create society (reification).

A third model – that of Berger – argues that society is the objectification or externalization of human beings and humans are the internalization of consciousness of society.

For Bhaskar this is confusing and wrong. Bhaskar disagrees with all three models and argues for a transformational theory – which makes possible also individual autonomy in changing schools and curriculum. Model 4, then (the transformational model of social action – for critical realists Model 1), has actions but no conditions; Model 2 has conditions but no actions. Model 3 confuses action and condition, but Model 4 emphasizes material continuity and thus accounts for change and history.

Bhaskar's model advocates that:

> People do not create society. For it always pre-exists them and is a necessary condition for their activity. Rather, society must be regarded as an ensemble of structures, practices and conventions which individuals reproduce or transform, but which would not exist unless they did so. Society does not exist independently of human activity (the error of reification). But it is not the product of it (the error of voluntarism).
>
> (1998: 36)

Action research has become much more sophisticated as philosophers have expanded upon its nature and purpose since 1980. From the practical, cyclical ends-means rationality of Lewin and Corey in the 1950s action research has moved to a practical science through teacher-researcher efforts (Elliott, 1991; Levin and Rock, 2003; Noffke, 1995; Mills, 2003; Sagor, 2000; Stenhouse, 1975), to a more full-blown theory of social action and inquiry (Winter, 2001). We must trust that our quest for practical wisdom and knowledge shall only continue and that the excesses of defunct theories of behaviorism and naive claims of positivist traditions can be set aside in favor of a living philosophy of critical choice and action.

The conduct of action research: towards situational understanding

There is a growing body of literature on the methodology for doing action research (Altrichter et al., 1993; Carson and Sumara, 1997; Elliott, 1981; Hendricks, 2006; Hopkins, 1985; Hustler et al., 1985; McKernan, 1996). Established methods of ethnographic and social research are the stock in trade of action research. Action research permits a wide range of obtrusive and unobtrusive measures from participant observation to case study and triangulation. There is no preference for qualitative over quantitative methods. Often the research problem will dictate the appropriate research methods and at times new methods can be created to fit the research design.

Procedures for doing action research

As a process, action inquiry (McKernan, 1991, 1996), or studied enactment, comports with a series of rational action steps in its process. As with all inquiry action research begins with the realization of a problematic situation or difficulty one wishes to improve.

1. Recognizing the difficulty or problem

John Dewey, in his classic book *How We Think* (1910), argued that the first stage of the reflective thought process was to recognize the nature of the unsatisfactory situation and try to conceptualize the problem or difficulty. At this initial stage one realizes there is a concrete difficulty and one seeks to get clear about the dimensions of this difficulty. This is the first stage of reflection on practice. For example, in my graduate education class we recognized that student understanding of controversial issues and having an assertive voice on issues like poverty constituted issues we needed to better understand how to help with. We further felt that not all students were participating in discussion work and this was a major issue requiring an action intervention. We recognized that discussion would be a beneficial strategy for enhancing understanding but we also needed "evidence" in the form of materials for injection into our discussions about poverty in North Carolina.

2. Clarifying the problem

I noted that not all of the graduate students would join in the discussions and devised a list of queries about the problem:

- Who does and does not speak in seminar discussion work?
- What is the character/nature of the professor's comments in discussions? Are questions put to students divergent or convergent in nature?
- Why aren't some students participating?
- What role should I (the instructor) take in discussion work?
- What evidence can be provided to students to prepare them for discussion?

I concluded that my first action research question or problem was "How do I mount discussions that lead to deepened student understanding of the issue of poverty?"

3. Conducting a situational analysis

Here the practitioner would gather data that might help answer some of the queries posed above. To do this I would have to use some methods of classroom observation. I did this through video-taping my seminars with the class, asking questions, handing out short questionnaires and interviewing some of the students. I also kept a diary with field notes from the sessions. This is basically a needs assessment exercise.

4. Creating action proposals/possible solutions

These proposal ideas included, but were not limited to, the following:

1   The professor needs to help students with value clarification – not be a moral expert. To this end I outlined a process for value/issue clarification but would not, even when pressed by students, commit to an authoritative moral line myself.
2   I believed that student involvement might increase in the discussions if I treated them as equals and gave respect to their "voice."
3   I believed that discussion quality would be advanced if we changed the furniture in the traditional classroom to that of a circular group and I announced that students would be expected to have a view at some stage on the work being discussed.
4   I set out several rules for the conduct of the discussion groups, for example no one is to offer ridicule to another. Students would see me as a "chairperson" whose role was to facilitate the discussion and record the sessions.
5   That group size is a significant factor inhibiting discussion work – the larger the group the less likely the students will all participate.
6   Students need "evidence" or handouts/data giving them some information and knowledge of the issues under discussion. This was seen not as my problem as the chair but that students should contribute data as well.

5. Developing an action research plan and timeline

After examination of data a full semester-length action plan was developed to research the problems and effects of teaching about poverty in the class.

We conceptualized the research process as a series of cycles of action, reflection, data gathering and redefinition. It looked something like the events described in the timeline below (see Table 7.1).

We were able to identify a practical problem: getting students involved in discussion of controversial issues, for example poverty and schooling. One of the outcomes, which I had not planned on, was a rather full unit of resource materials, submitted by graduate students, on the theme of poverty, for example US Census statistical data, statistics for North Carolina by county regions, readings, and so on. These were fed into the ongoing discussions and greatly clarified needed facts at times.

Table 7.1 Cycles of inquiry, data gathering and analytic judgment

Week	Activity	Methodology	Time	Analysis
1	Meet students Define seminar rules/syllabus	Diary, VCR	2hrs	Self-observation of data View video of Ford T-Project (Elliott and Adelman, 1973)
2–4	Action plan with students	Class video Work in groups	6hrs	View video Interviews/students
5–7	Implement plan	Class video	6hrs	Blackboard discussion with all students
8–10	Collect data	Interviews, BB chat	6hrs	Quadrangulation
11–13	Follow plan	Class recordings	6hrs	Discuss with students
14–16	Write-up	Discuss report	6hrs	Circulate report

6. Implementing and reflecting on the plan

The action plan was implemented over the sixteen weeks of the semester as per the cycle chart above. Its practice is validated by the classroom tapes. It was one thing to collect data but quite a separate matter to analyze and reflect on the action taken. Eight practicing teachers were enrolled on the course "action research and curriculum development." Their reflections made this a collaborative project of nine participants including myself.

7. Collecting the data

A key step is the collection of data in the research setting. A number of methods are available for action researchers (McKernan, 1996). I have described briefly some of these research methods below. A researcher may choose to video-tape his new action proposal and interview students as a follow-up. He may also invite a second order action researcher to conduct non-participant observation in the classroom or take field notes while in the setting. Care needs to be taken in keeping data organized for later analysis.

8. Gaining situational insight and understanding: explaining the data

There is planning and acting but the most significant part of action research is the quest for wisdom through practical reasoning and reflection on the action of the project. "What is my situational understanding of what I have experienced through the intervention?" "What have I learned?" Here one needs to stop and reflect on the action. What have the students learned from the experience? A good deal of time was devoted to writing up the personal experiences of each participant and understanding these unique perceptions. We observed and viewed the video tapes and looked for insights and conclusions. In this activity one becomes familiar with support resources and constraints on action. For example, can we develop this course while under pressure to meet other examination system requirements? I learned that the project required more resource support than I thought. The use of a teaching aid or technician would have greatly aided the data collection stages for example.

One exhumes underlying causes and issues and seeks to explain these in light of emergent solutions and ongoing difficulties. By allowing for democratic involvement the actors may speak through these results.

9. Disseminating the results

Stenhouse (1981) believed that inquiry did not count as research unless it was publicly disclosed and critiqued. Furthermore, each graduate teacher has agreed to make a copy of the report available to their fellow faculty members at schools where they labor. We feel this is an honest way of opening up further discussion and to share what we have learned from the action research process. For inquiry to count as legitimate research there must be a written record of the project's activities and findings which is made "public" by being accessible to participants and interested stakeholders. Too often researchers do research "on" teachers and school settings and walk away without sharing the data. This is unethical on this account of research. There is a commitment to share and disseminate the research so that others may learn and grow. Unless we study, describe and disseminate our "action enactments" we cannot move forward systematically.

Some action research methods

I have previously written at length about how to conduct action research and the variety of methods available (McKernan, 1996), both obtrusive and unobtrusive. Data needs to be collected in a systematic fashion. A sample of some of the research techniques available are:

1 *Participant observation*: where the researcher takes an active participant role with the population he or she is studying and lives equally among the group. For example, a college professor who may take on a role of an elementary school teacher to better understand the work of teachers. The researcher has to not only act in fidelity with the group but be devoted to researching the setting and actors (Spradley, 1980).

2 *Non-participant observation*: an example would be a researcher who might sit at the back of a classroom but not engage in the work of the group other than to record what is happening.

3 *Use of video records*: using a video camera and audio technology to record the actual events related to the research problem in the setting.

4 *Document analysis*: examination of official records, statements, letters, lesson plans, mission statements, attendance records and so on related to the research topic.

5 *Case study*: a written report of actions, interpretations, of actors, conducted *in situ*, containing a conclusive account of the evidence collected. Such an account might include illustrations, statistical data, narrative verbatim recollections and so on. It is a crafting of a story in a real sense. Case records and case data would make up the records for a case study. Many techniques feed case study work: document analysis, observations of behavior, possibly interviewing and keeping field notes.

6 *Diary*: a personal journal which records actions, descriptive accounts, interpretations, questions and explanations kept on a day-to-day basis while doing fieldwork. Keep notes relating to day-to-day progress and difficulties.

7 *Dialogue journal*: a unique personal journal in which a student and teacher carry on a running dialogue, in writing, on topics and issues of importance. These are confidential – for the eyes of teacher and student alone.

8 *Field notes*: the running account of data collected in the field. Records, usually written after the event, based on naturalistic observation. Favored by anthropologists and ethnographers, field notes may be simply descriptive in describing facts of a social setting such as how many students are present, or they may be "conceptual" in suggesting categories for understanding behavior and speculating about theory.

9 *Shadow studies*: a particular form of a case study in which a key informant or actor is "followed" for a specified period of time to better understand his or her life and culture. A classic is *One Boy's Day* by Barker and Wright (1951) in which a mid-western seven-year-old boy was studied from 7 a.m. until 9 p.m. Sometimes referred to as stream of behavior chronicles (McKernan, 1996).

10 *Questionnaires*: self-report instruments, usually paper based, which are completed by a respondent and in which a series of questions are either closed or open-ended. Perhaps the most popular method of data collection in the social sciences. Essentially, an interview by proxy. The questionnaire method is often disadvantaged by low completion/return rates.

11 *Interviews*: may be structured questions, like the questionnaire, or unstructured, where the respondent is given free rein to discuss ideas or opinions to a prompt. Usually done in a face-to face situation but

sometimes done via internet or telephone conversation. A variation is the Key Informant Interview which is held with a key "gatekeeper," that is, a union president or school superintendent.

12 *Checklists and rating scales*: these instruments ask respondents to check if behavior is present or not. Rating scales ask the respondent to make a rating or evaluation – a form of making an assessment along a continuum or scale from high to low, good or bad and so on. They ask one to make an evaluation of an object or behavior in terms of an estimated value.

13 *Content analysis*: a method for analyzing and deconstructing the meaning of a message or communication. Content analyses have been performed on literary works and the speeches of figures such as John Dewey or Adolph Hitler.

14 *Life/career history*: narrative written accounts of the biographical or career history data of a person, written by the person. For example, early frontier teachers sometimes wrote about their careers over the years. These are subjective accounts but often very insightful and readable histories.

15 *Physical trace data*: are related to real objects – either erosion data or accretion data. An erosion measure might be used to see the wear and usage of a textbook. An accretion measure might be seen in terms of deposits: graffiti left by students on the walls of the school or desks. An unobtrusive method.

16 *Quadrangulation*: an adaptation of the method of "triangulation" (Denzin, 1970) put forward by McKernan (1996). Triangulation is an old nautical term which means plotting one's navigational position by reference to several other reference points. In research it means collecting data from several corroborative perspectives: multiple actors, concepts and research methods are used to verify the conclusions reached. There are two types of use. First, "multiple participant-actor": a second order action researcher working with a practitioner in a collaborative relationship represents the first part. The second part is the second order facilitator with the classroom pupils as they discuss the ongoing action inquiry project. The third part represents the second order action researcher with other project participants, say colleague teachers at the school or administrators. The final stage is when all the data – film, questionnaires, interviews – are made available to all the project actors. There is also a second style or mode of quadrangulation. In action research we should look at employing multiple styles: research methods; key concepts; theories; and actors. Looking for corroboration in and among these methods, actors and theoretical constructs will enhance validity, a persistent issue in all human social inquiry.

Chapter 8

The action research seminar and democratic pedagogy

> Teaching which accepts fidelity to knowledge as a criterion can never be judged adequate and rest content. Teachers must be educated to develop their art, not to master it, for the claim to mastery merely signals the abandoning of aspiration.
>
> Lawrence Stenhouse (1983: 189)

This chapter describes, and critically examines, a form of reflective teaching – the *action research seminar* – for the implementation of democratic values and pedagogy in a university social foundations of education class. The argument is advanced that teacher education programs emphasizing reflective and democratic principles and theory must also utilize a democratic and critically reflective pedagogy rather than authoritarian teaching styles, as demonstrated by over-reliance upon the formal lecture, didactic classroom presentation and demonstration teaching methods so commonly found in the everyday contemplative culture of the college and university.

Embedded in this concept of education is the notion of the teacher-researcher; the view that certain principles of procedure lead to the realization of our valued aims in practice. To this end criteria in the form of pedagogical principles are discussed as an alternative to the behaviorist domination of curriculum through outcomes and targets. As such this chapter contributes to the development of a democratic *process model* of curriculum. Further, it is argued that how we teach ultimately has a strong effect upon the way our students will teach in the future. Finally, some research effects of using teacher action research in education are presented.

Perhaps the most fundamental value and role of schooling is the education of youth for reflective democratic citizenship. If we accept that education implies the transmission of something that is intrinsically worthwhile in a manner that is morally acceptable (Peters, 1966), then the question of teaching method, or pedagogy, becomes a central issue for teachers everywhere.

Given that most educators subscribe to this democratic rhetoric, it is ironic to find that teaching styles in higher education fall, at least arguably, within the realm of teaching styles which are deemed highly autocratic and authoritarian. Authoritarian styles and pedagogies include lectures, class-room presentations, teacher-tutorials, expert demonstrations and allied didactic modes of instructor-directed teaching where knowledge is deposited with students according to the concept of "banking education" as elucidated by Freire (1972). In authoritarian teaching students are often treated as passive spectators, rather than as active and equal participants.

The notion of active student participation – that of experience – is a crucial ingredient for democracy and education (Dewey, 1969), as intelligently directed development of individuals and is central to the teaching strategies discussed in this chapter. Experience in this sense involves the actual life experience of the student. An increasing number of Schools and Colleges of Education have instituted "reflective practice programs" but as yet there is little consensus precisely on what this term means.

This chapter is in two parts. In the first part the action research seminar is described whereby student-led action research projects are offered and conceptualized within a model of reflective graduate-level education. In the second, some research evidence related to the use of action research in higher education is offered.

I would endorse the Deweyan view that practical inquiry implies reflection upon means and ends simultaneously. In connection with teaching this suggests that educators both develop and clarify their conceptions of education and learning by inquiring into and being reflective on activity created by the teaching strategies they engage in in their own classrooms. As such, this counts as a significant attempt at producing a professional development theory of democratic teaching.

These strategies of democratic teaching are thus rooted in logic for values such as equality, rationality, open-mindedness, multiculturalism, tolerance, acceptance, respect for inquiry and evidence, reflective and critical thinking, and discussion for understanding key issues in the foundations of education. Philosophers, psychologists and educationalists (Dewey, 1933, 1969; Lewin, 1951; Stenhouse, 1975; Elliott, 1991) have suggested that experience, coupled with reflection, results in personal growth. Critical pedagogy linked with personal action research and cooperative forms of teaching and learning not only support democratic values but include a structure and form of teaching embodied in *key principles of procedure* which is a model for pre-service education students in higher education. Students should not be expected to teach democratically if their professors do not. In short, one learns to teach the way one has been taught to teach.

While it is mainly the case that foundation courses "cover" issues like race, social class, gender and poverty inequalities, few programs go beyond simple discussion. It is argued here that we need programs that link student understanding of concepts and principles with purposeful student social action. There is some evidence of an increase in "service learning" elements not only in teacher education classrooms but in public schools themselves.

The action research seminar

Action research is systematic inquiry conducted by practitioners to improve the quality of action in a social setting (Elliott, 1991; McKernan, 1996). In recent years action research has emerged as a major form of teacher professional development (Elliott, 1991; Noffke and Stevenson, 1995) and as a collaborative research enterprise involving professors with teachers and students in schools. Action research has been considered by some critical theorists to be a "form of self-reflective enquiry undertaken by participants in social situations in order to improve the rationality and justice of their own practices, their understanding of these practices, and the situations in which these practices are carried out" (Carr and Kemmis, 1986: 162). In this sense it aims at securing equality and justice in social institutions and practices and eradicating the encroachment of authoritarian behavior. A distinction needs to be made between "doing" action research and "teaching" action research. Interestingly, far less attention has been paid to the latter (Altrichter, 1991; McKernan, 1994) than to the former. The "teaching," or pedagogical face, of action research has not been well-developed. By this I mean "How can I, as a professor, teach through action research?" Altrichter (1991: 21) argues that teaching action research under institutionalized conditions is impossible. I have field tested this question in three universities and have found it possible and necessary to introduce students to action research through award bearing courses.

In teacher education, action research has been implemented in order to achieve a number of goals including: problem-solving; reflective thinking and teaching; curriculum development; and research. An overlooked and implicit outcome of action research in educational settings has been that of developing a democratic classroom based upon democratic values. Action research does not treat those with the problem as clients but as collaborative researchers. As such, action research affords a voice to students (Noffke, 1995). A teacher's voice is essential for action research. As a tool for empowerment this teacher voice refers to what Noddings (1984, 1992) calls an ethic of caring, or the provision of pastoral care by a humane tutor (McKernan et al., 1985). Students and in-service teachers require a voice in both oral and written presentations in higher education in a democratic society.

The use of the action inquiry/research seminar (McKernan, 1994, 1996) constitutes an attempt to not only provide students with a voice that is to be recognized, but to test a theory of curriculum realized through a process of education as opposed to the achievement of specific pre-determined objectives as products of education. Students and teachers seem more comfortable with the term inquiry rather than research, thus the term action inquiry has often been adopted in place of action research.

At Columbia University's Teachers College, Abraham Shumsky (1958) outlined an experimental in-service course based upon action research for "action learning" in college teaching during the late 1950s. Action research was a major tool in the curriculum development movement of mid-century America in the promotion of human relations education and intergroup education (Taba and Noel, 1957) and used extensively to promote student understanding of controversial value issues in humanities curriculum during the 1960s and 70s in the halcyon days of British curriculum reform (Elliott, 1991; Stenhouse, 1975).

The use of action research in higher education and the provision of courses that describe the process of doing action research have been increasing dramatically in recent years (Elliott and Sarland, 1995; Lomax, 1994; McKernan, 1994, 1996) and other examples of teaching action research can be found in Altrichter (1991); Elliott (1991); and Noffke and Stevenson (1995).

McKernan (1994, 1996) instituted a graduate action research seminar as the basis for teaching Education 6424 "Foundations and Curriculum Development" at East Carolina University in the fall term, 1994, and has made continuous refinements to the course in successive semesters. Experiments in using action research to create democratic classrooms in college education courses have been reported by Noffke (1995) and others (Stevenson et al., 1995).

Utilizing and teaching action research in schools and graduate/postgraduate education has been an enduring interest of the author (McKernan, 1988, 1994, 1995, 1996) particularly in terms of introducing both initial and in-service education teachers to action research for curriculum improvement. The major vehicle driving this work has been the action research seminar. In Education 6424 the graduate students select a practical school problem and seek, through action research, to solve and understand that problem. The seminar is the teaching method par excellence in graduate level education. In brief, it is a small, democratically managed and self-directed strategy for learning.

Features of the action research seminar

The action research seminar holds at least the following features:

- that problems that affect the professional work of the member become the basis for action research/learning;
- that the mode of inquiry has discussion work at its core;
- that the chair has responsibility for standards, and limits, of the inquiry;
- that it is characterized by group collaboration and sharing as distinct from authority-expert models of teaching;

- that documented evidence is presented through a formal report as a means of leading the seminar by a member of the group;
- that the course leader is not a lecturer, but rather one who guides and facilitates student understanding. The role of the professor is one of facilitation and guidance;
- that the group adopts a critical stance towards the topic under discussion;
- that there is a shared community of discourse which seeks to commit to inquiry as opposed to voices of authority;
- that there is a commitment to cooperative deliberation on a common problem.

Principles of procedure for the seminar

The seminar, ideally, should be composed of a small group of between six and a dozen members. During the fall semester enrollment was large, with twenty-one students. One of the constraints of university teaching is that graduate classes are invariably larger, it seems, each year. The seminar meets weekly, with the first named author, for three hours, after the seventh week of term. Presenters prepare a paper and speak for about thirty minutes, which includes delivery and discussion of issues and problems.

The action research seminar is a small, democratic forum whereby student-led presentations relating to their action research projects are presented, discussed and further disseminated. These often take the shape of case studies written up in a narrative tradition. Often multi-media presentations are used that avail themselves of computer assisted technology, overheads, slides, photographic data and curriculum materials.

One useful guideline is to begin with problems and issues in the curriculum that are faced by the postgraduate students. These would be practical problems that the postgraduate teachers encounter in their daily work. Sharing these concerns in the graduate seminar is an act of courage and professionalism that results in respect from all. There is, in a sense, a group concern to share the problem and to engage in "action learning" (Revans, 1982). Another aspect of this is that by allowing the students to define the research agenda the course validates their experience and gives credence to their work. In order that the seminar proceeds smoothly, some guidelines for running the seminar have been established.

First, the professor acts as an impartial chairperson in the sense of seeking to forward human understanding of the issues that become the focus of the seminar without using his or her authority to influence outcomes or values. Presentations can be styled around short synopses of similar research work or what the student has read on the topic. Second, a critical view can be adopted towards a policy position and research evidence presented to support that line of thought.

Principles of procedure for discussion pedagogy

Experience of successful seminars seems to happen when the chair keeps the following procedures and principles in mind. The chair should endeavor to:

1   set limits to the discussions;
2   ensure that students follow the action research cycle of Plan, Act, Observe, Reflect and Disseminate Findings;
3   carefully summarize arguments and evidence;
4   ensure that group members have built upon each other's ideas;
5   attempt, through careful questioning, to provide an intellectual climate for research and self-reflective critique;
6   introduce new evidence and points of view not considered by the group;
7   keep a research brief on the ongoing work of the group.

The adoption of the role of "impartial chairperson" may not be acceptable to all professors. It is offered as an alternative pedagogy. Yet students inevitably look to their professors for authoritative positions when the values underpinning this course seek to empower students. The role of impartiality allows a conservative or liberal for example, to put his or her views in their strongest light. The chair can make inputs without taking sides, thus encouraging a critical attitude to evidence, texts or ideas. Students have a redefined role too. As they begin to take part in the teaching strategies of the action research seminar, they are not relinquishing control – but sharing it. By casting off their passive role they put on the cloaks of autonomy and accountability through becoming participants. The students shift from seeing professors as authority figures to viewing themselves as architects of knowledge and sources of authority. Professors can now evaluate a whole new set of procedural values such as students' respect for evidence, sources, rigor in research and so on, thus adopting a teacher-researcher stance.

Students thus prepare "cases" of their experiments with solutions to practical school problems at the seminar. Action research is very much a personal and practical inquiry aimed at improving the quality of life in a social setting. In advance of the action research seminar, some students engage in an action research project, which may take a number of weeks to complete. What is significant about action research is that there exists no division of labor between insiders (teachers) and outsiders (expert researchers). The research belongs to the teacher and students, and rightly so, in a democratic classroom. Above all else it is a form of democratic inquiry in which the participants learn from their actions and share their learnings.

Students are encouraged to present their action research project presentations by adopting the model of action research outlined below. As a first step, they describe their research problem in a one-page summary statement. Next, they develop a research plan. They then record the actions they take to solve their problem. This stage is followed by careful observations of the effects of their actions in trying to solve the problem. Then they must reflect upon their outcomes, and where they now stand. Finally, and this is a missing ingredient in most other action research, they need to disseminate and critically evaluate the results of their action research efforts. The researcher tables a report to the students and involved colleagues, administrators or parents given the nature of involvement by others. The seminar fulfills, in part, this dissemination obligation.

The activities of action research: a structure for the seminar

Students often have trouble getting started with action research. They often find it helpful to break their seminar down into discrete parts so that there is continuity, coherence and structure in their presentation.

1. Identifying and clarifying the general idea and plan of action

The general idea is a statement which links an idea to action. It is vital to describe and explain the facts relating to the problematic situation and link this with a critical analysis. It is framed in Education 6424 as a personal inquiry question:

- How can students' biology test scores be improved?
- How can a teacher work to raise self-image and esteem through art?
- What can be done to do away with disruptive lunchroom behavior?
- How can the elderly be used as valued human resources in the school?

In short, the idea refers to a situation, or the quality of action within a setting one wishes to improve.

2. Initiating the action

Here we draft a list of the "hunches" that we will employ as "problem solutions." For example, the teacher may hypothesize that by changing teaching methods and using peer tutors in enrichment activities with low achieving students test scores may improve.

3. Observe and research the action

During this phase one monitors the action hunches in action. Systematic observation is linked with record keeping. One member of the seminar used a diary and had pupils keep a diary as well as utilizing photographs to capture a rich slice of life in the project. Other research methods include: interviews, field notes, video-audio devices, questionnaires, tests, triangulation, peer observation, document analysis and content analysis (McKernan, 1996).

4. Reflect on the action

One must employ self-evaluation at this stage. "How am I doing?" "What have I/we learned thus far with the inquiry?" These answers will help us to understand where we have to go from here. Reflection on the action is the vehicle for understanding.

5. Disseminate the results

Such inquiry does not count as research unless it is disseminated. There needs to be a community of discourse. Every practitioner thus becomes a member of this community. Students are encouraged to share their findings with central office, other teachers, parents and other audiences. Stenhouse (1975) believed that research was systematic, self-critical inquiry made public. Therefore dissemination is a critical component of the research act.

There is of course no guarantee that our research problem will be solved. Yet we can be sure that we will better understand that problem, and perhaps a few others, by engaging in action research. We should never forget that the knowledge that we teach in universities has been won through research; and that such knowledge cannot be taught correctly except through some form of research-based teaching.

Jennifer's project

Jennifer has been teaching high school science for six years and is completing her Master of Arts in education. Jennifer selected the following research question: "How can students' end-of-chapter test scores in Biology be improved?" She wrote a qualitative case study of her action research project which contained the following features:

1   Many of her students were failing and had to repeat biology.
2   Her "hunches" for solving the problem included involving students in more "hands-on" science; small cooperative learning groups.
3   Her main hypothesis was: Through action research students' grades will improve because of more active student roles; students will make note cards in cooperative learning groups so as to review the material in a four-week period. She also increased contact with parents.

After observing students for two weeks she reflected on the slightly positive increases in scores. A journal was kept each day by the teacher and the students. Jennifer employed "triangulation" so that she could observe herself at work. In triangulation a teacher is observed and recorded by another colleague; some students are interviewed by the observer; and finally, the observer and teacher reflect on these data – thus perspectives on teaching are gained from the observer, teacher and students. Three students in five different classes were monitored throughout the project. After some thirteen quizzes and tests the students were on target for scoring at the seventieth percentile level.

Principles of procedure for chairing the action research seminar

What is asked of the chair of an action research seminar is:

1 to accept the desirability of mounting open-ended and free discussions of project issues;
2 to abandon the role of being an "authority" on all matters, in particular those that are value-laden. Students do look to the professor for authoritative answers. They wrongly assume that professors know the right answers and that the professor is simply setting up the conditions for them to learn these through a hidden agenda format. Yet the autonomy of inquiry demands that both the professor and the student be learners. Understanding is a critical aim in the course;
3 to adopt the criterion of value impartiality when dealing with contentious issues;
4 to use discussion as the major strategy for ensuring understanding;
5 to protect divergence of opinion within the group seminar;
6 to assume responsibility for quality and standards in learning through research;
7 to create conditions conducive to full and free discussion work;
8 to clarify the issues under discussion;
9 to keep under review the topic of discussion and round off discussions with a cogent summary organizing various positions;
10 to introduce relevant "evidence" when required;
11 to ensure that the above principles of procedure are observed.

These rules of engagement are circulated and discussed in advance of formal seminar meetings. In short, the chair is responsible for both the conditions of the seminar-discussions and the standards of judgment. By being faithful to these principles the chair is teaching the principles of procedure for discussion and inquiry. These principles thus become important evaluative criteria for the professor.

At the outset of our courses we speak at length about collaborative learning experiences, higher level reasoning and reflective practice. One should not expect that prospective teachers be prepared to practice these approaches unless they have personal knowledge and experience with them.

These activities provide students with the opportunity to adjust successfully to a major redefinition of their roles as students and the role of the professor. These are only a sample of the teaching strategies which can be incorporated into the collaborative learning classroom; the possibilities of other activities are limited only by the instructor's imagination. Just as with the action research seminar criteria, the form of "principles of procedure" function as criteria for the assessment of students' work. To what extent can students use knowledge and key concepts to explore issues in reflective discussion groups? To what extent do students examine a wide variety of views and evidence on an issue under discussion? It seems irresponsible to state pre-determined outcomes in the form of objectives in advance of instruction that seeks to elicit creative responses from students. Thus, we implement our curriculum not with a view to assessing objectives framed as "outcomes," but, rather, by examining the internal processes by which education is conducted. This allows us to postulate a "process model" of curriculum versus the traditional "objectives model" for the design of our work. By working with principles of procedure we are forced to adopt a research stance towards our teaching which requests self-evaluation of our teaching and professional development through judgment. A style of pedagogy which rests on action research and student reflection for human understanding places the onus for professional development on the individual professor and student rather than the School of Education as the unit of development.

Some research evidence

There is some research evidence (Stevenson et al., 1995) that teaching action research leads to the creation of "democratic communities." In a case study of teaching action research at the State University of New York, Buffalo, Stevenson and colleagues found that their effort had became one of promoting "multiple democratic communities" rather than a single class community. In an evaluation of the course students were asked "To what extent do you feel that the groups that have been formed in this class are becoming democratic communities?" In response to this question most conveyed a feeling that the groups were becoming democratic communities, with two students arguing that they had experienced a democratic community from the start. Groups were most commonly perceived as democratic communities because of members' respect for each person and his or her views, the effort to give each project an equal share of time and attention, and the capacity for each member to be sincere without offending the others.

At the University of Wisconsin at Madison, the pre-service teacher education program has successfully employed action research within a social reconstructionist ideology for the past decade (Liston and Zeichner, 1990) to develop reflective practitioners.

In the United Kingdom, one survey connected with the Teachers as Researchers Project found that the University of East Anglia was named by most respondents as the leading center for action research excellence, followed by the University of Bath, and Cambridge Institute of Education (Elliott and Sarland, 1995).

Most action researchers are introduced to action research through award bearing courses taught at universities. The teaching of action research has not received enough attention over the years and this would be a profitable area for funding and further research (Altrichter, 1991; McKernan, 1994). While some clearly visible centers of action research excellence exist, such as the Centre for Applied Research in Education at the University of East Anglia, Norwich, England, and at the University of Bath, where Peter Reason directs a PhD program in action research, many more courses in action research need to be made available as required units on Master's and Doctoral degree programs in the United Kingdom and USA.

Conclusions

Researchers of democratic teaching and action research as reflective practice (Noffke, 1995; Stevenson *et al.*, 1995; Zeichner and Gore, 1995) believe that action research and forms of critical pedagogy promote democratic classrooms and reflective thinking, whether these classrooms be in higher education or the nation's public and private schools. Reflective thought consists in active, careful and persistent examination of any belief, or purported form of knowledge, in light of the grounds that support it and the further conclusions towards which it tends, according to Dewey's theory of reflective teaching (1933), which he justified on the grounds of the democratic ethic.

At base this ethic argues that learning is the result of an experiment – the process of education in the classroom where students solve problems and learn how to think. The school in a democratic state becomes a vital institution in improving the quality of life in the culture. On this view schools become agencies for cultural change through a critical pedagogy (Giroux, 1985, 1988) by providing students with critical thinking tools to reconstruct society. Thus, the school – through its experimentalist teachers using action research and collaborative learning and group discussion – is a working model of democracy. Regrettably, teacher education often fails to maximize opportunities to prepare aspiring teachers for democratic pedagogy; in particular in developing reflective powers or research skills. From a rationalist perspective, the individual teacher, in our view, has a responsibility for autonomous professional self-development too. Tools such as journal writing, group discussion and seminar presentations permit collective growth based upon the knowledge, experience and research work of the students. For too long the social market perspective of the School of Education, viewed as a "production unit," along with its technical-rational ideology, has claimed responsibility for teacher development. As has been noted, this pattern of professional training is heavily resourced at the front end of teacher initial training and weakly resourced during the crucial years of service to the profession. Teachers have been reclaiming their right to professional development through democratically empowering teaching styles and pedagogies. This counts as a promising start.

Chapter 9

Controversial issues, evidence and pedagogy

> And truly I too speak as one who knows not – only guesses. But that there is a difference in kind between right opinion and knowledge, this, it seems to me, I do *not* guess; but of the few things, if any, that I would claim to know, this is one.
>
> Plato, *Meno*, 98b

Lawrence Stenhouse reminded us that:

> Educational prophets may teach private wisdom but educators must deal in public knowledge and value-laden issues.
>
> (Stenhouse, 1975: 6)

As civil servants, teachers are held accountable for their actions and performance. Moreover, the profession is committed to employing an interpretive and critical perspective to assist students in their understandings. Yet simple knowledge, or indeed the development of persuasive theories, is not the goal of our pedagogy. The aim of teaching is to have students recognize the relationship between knowledge and action and its consequences for good through a joint inquiry in the classroom. Understanding culture and the controversial issues raised by the clash of values seems to me to be the overarching point of education. I shall address this in connection with my own work within the teaching of a foundations of education class to initial teacher education students.

This chapter addresses a pedagogical strategy for teaching for human understanding and for handling the controversial issues and values that arise in any such exploration into the human condition. This is a process-inquiry model for pedagogy and action research. I believe there is a sense of urgency about this aspect of our professional life and contemplative university culture that demands a practical response to values education. Contentious issues arise in college courses over which some people are prepared to fight and kill one another; and it may well be that if we do not find some way to deal with these issues through rational discussion and with the hope of promoting tolerance and mutual understanding, then conflict and violence will continue to escalate.

The rationale for dealing with value issues is explicitly addressed by the Council of Learned Societies (USA) under section 2, normative perspectives:

> Foundational studies encourage students to develop their own value positions regarding education on the basis of critical study and their own reflections.

This notion of students developing their own *values* forms a central plank of this chapter.

In 1973, I accepted a doctoral studentship, and subsequently a post as a curriculum development officer, addressing cultural studies and peace education in Northern Ireland. The project central team, and local teachers, experimented with school-based curriculum development in social and cultural studies using social reconstructionist action research and novel teaching methods to promote tolerance, rationality and mutual understanding in intergroup relations. It is of some comfort to note that, as a direct result of our Schools Cultural Studies Project work, the project aim – "the development of education for mutual understanding" (EMU) – was incorporated into the work of all teachers in Northern Ireland and the United Kingdom as part of the statutory Great Education Reform Bill (GERBIL) of the Thatcher Conservative government. Ironically, GERBIL demolished much of the autonomy and empowerment of United Kingdom schools and teachers regarding curriculum reform. In further policy directives it is now the case that all teachers in the United Kingdom have a responsibility for the implementation of education for mutual understanding under current curriculum guidelines. Indeed, it was just such a purpose which led the "founding father" of action research, Kurt Lewin (1946), to design action research for solving unjust social practices of prejudice and intergroup relations. He called his book on the topic *Resolving Social Conflicts*. In teaching, we work with a curriculum. By the concept of "curriculum" I refer not to a "syllabus" – a mere list of content topics – nor to what the Germans call a *Lehrplan* and the Norwegians forbiddingly call a "Monsterplan" – a prescription of aims, methods and content. Such initiatives equate curriculum with outcomes and objectives – an outputs model. I understand by "curriculum" the offering of valued knowledge, skills and *dispositions* (such as affective and value development) through a variety of experiences and arrangements while students are in education.

Education is a process and not a product. Moreover, a curriculum has intentions, transactions and effects. Believing that teachers are accountable for their results, the curriculum invites a research response on the part of the teacher and students. I am more concerned with the process of education and the values realized through that process than with specific low-level outcomes such as instructional objectives defined in behavioral terms. For me a curriculum can be developed by a logic other than the pre-specification of objectives – it can be derived from explicating the values embedded in the process of attempting to communicate the essential principles of and educational proposal in such a form that it is open to critical scrutiny and capable of effective translation into practice. To adopt this perspective is to submit our teaching to research so that we shall know the effects of our practice. Teaching on this view is a form of "action research": inquiry by practitioners to solve their own practical problems. A social foundations curriculum ought, at a minimum, to provide a basis for planning a course and researching it empirically, including its justification.

R.S. Peters, the noted British philosopher of education, has argued for the intrinsic justification of curriculum content – not simply justification because the content leads to some objective. He suggested (1966) that education implies the transmission of what is worthwhile to those committed to it – and that it must involve knowledge, understanding and some form of cognitive perspective, which are not inert. Peters speaks to activities that have their own in-built standards of excellence, and thus can be appraised because of the standards immanent in them rather than because of what they lead to. What Peters is driving at is that certain forms of knowledge, such as philosophy and history, are justifiable within the curriculum because of their own intrinsic worth. This "Process Model," developed later by Lawrence Stenhouse, poses a powerful challenge to the behavioral-technical model of curriculum design through objectives.

Towards a pedagogy for controversial issues

Here I wish to describe a pedagogical strategy that I use in two of my current courses: Education 3200, An Introduction to American Education, and Education 6424, Action Research and Curriculum Development, a graduate-level course, given at East Carolina University. The strategy discussed here is what I call "The Impartial Chairperson" or "Neutral Chairperson" in value-laden discussion.

There is no doubt that foundations courses are rife with controversial value issues, for example prayer in schools, proliferating school violence episodes, contraceptives in school programs of health education, the use of corporal punishment, the use of educational voucher aid for private schooling and so on. In her book *Deciding What to Teach*, Dorothy Fraser suggests a definition:

> A controversial issue involves a problem about which different individuals and groups urge conflicting courses of action. It is an issue for which society has not found a solution that can be universally accepted.
>
> (1963, cited in Stenhouse, 1983: 120)

In short, a controversial issue cannot be settled by recourse to factual evidence because it involves values. As teachers, we must deal with values in the classroom. This chapter is exploratory in the sense of offering a model, subjected to some empirical research, that shows how a professor, along with interested students, might operate value-based discussions. In both of the courses mentioned above students lead seminars on topics they have researched (the action research seminar is employed for the graduate students).

Value issues and procedural neutrality

Let me endeavor to construct an example. It is a commonplace that if education does not raise value issues which are controversial, or as I prefer, contentious issues, then the professor is not being faithful to the standards set out for academic instruction in foundational studies by the Council for Learned Societies in Education; or, there is total consensus or unanimity in the American culture, or the classroom, on these issues – a situation which is quite inconceivable in reality.

I take as my definition of the concept of "value": "an enduring belief that a certain object, mode of behavior or some ideal end-state of existence is supremely preferable to alternatives, and this belief is held worthwhile by an individual" (Rokeach, 1973: 5). Teaching, learning and curriculum are inextricably entwined in problems of facts and values. Milton Rokeach (1973) has given a thorough review of the nature of human values. It seems to me that while considerable attention is paid to values by psychologists and that while teachers have been preoccupied with student outcomes in terms of behavior, knowledge acquisition and so on, little is paid to their moral or spiritual/value development in higher education or to the processes of teaching which bring these changes about. We are aware of certain undesirable teaching behaviors, such as indoctrination, preaching (moralizing) and propagandizing in the classroom, by small numbers of professors. Yet most new teaching strategies and methods are defended on little more than hunches or personal prejudices. What has to be going on to count as good teaching? Teaching of course can take many forms – lying down on the classroom floor could count as teaching in a specific context. Solving problems, cleaning the blackboard and other classroom duties are all work. Looked at one way teaching can take so many different forms of working that, like making love, suggest there seems pretty well no limit to the activities it can involve. The thing about education is that it leads to unanticipated outcomes because it is education, and not training or indoctrination. In fact, on my reasoning, education is successful to the extent that it leads the students to unanticipated outcomes and behaviors by creating new meanings, which are unpredictable in advance of teaching.

Education is at least a three-headed monster. First, there is "training," which suggests the acquisition of skills: the heightening of one's performance or ability. Second, we have "instruction," by which I mean simply learning new information – the results of retention. Third, there is "induction," which is concerned with thought processes and intellectual activities and knowledge. Education as induction into knowledge is what we are concerned with in higher education foundations courses. Here we induct students into the epistemologies and thought systems of the culture. The vital thing about education as induction is that we can use it – we can think with it. This is the essential feature of knowledge as distinct from information. As such, it provides a framework for judgment, including value judgments – and by employing certain principles of procedure which might, in a loose sense, look like aims is at once a purposeful activity. We are planning our work rationally by adopting ends, albeit as broad aims, but we do so in the absence of some narrow ends-means linear behavioral sense. We are curriculum planning by a logic other than the use of the objectives model – we are being faithful to the implementation of critical principles of procedure within a discipline.

The action research seminar

In Chapter 8 we examined in some detail the action research seminar, which holds at least the following features:

1   It is characterized by group collaboration and sharing as distinct from authority-expert models of teaching.
2   Documented evidence is presented as a means of leading the seminar, by a member of the group.
3   The tutor is not a lecturer, but rather one who guides and facilitates student understanding. Thus, the role of the professor is one of facilitation and guidance.
4   The group adopts a critical stance towards the topic under discussion.
5   There is a shared community of discourse which seeks to commit to inquiry as opposed to voices of authority.

Pedagogical procedures

The seminar, ideally, should be a small group – say six to twelve members. Our seminar meets weekly, after the seventh week of term. Presenters prepare a paper and speak for between twenty minutes and one hour. While a postgraduate student working under the direction of Professor Malcolm Skilbeck and Professor H.T. Sockett I joined a group of caring and concerned university scientists, educationalists and others in a seminar on "Cultural Studies" in Northern Ireland. Our foundational papers laid the basis for the largest ever social-cultural studies curriculum development project in

Ireland. From that experience, I believe it best to organize the seminar around problems in culture, or what we called the "upside-down core curriculum." That is, to focus on the negatives in the culture such as discrimination, prejudice and violence in an attempt to develop mutual understanding and tolerance between and among ethnic groups.

Students thus prepare "cases" of their experiments with solutions to practical school problems at the seminar. Action research is very much personal and practical inquiry aimed at improving the quality of life in a social setting. One of my postgraduate students, Sybil, is an art teacher and teacher of disruptive teenagers in rehabilitative "alternative programs," believing that art can help improve the self-image of disruptive students. She is an extraordinary humanist and self-actualized person. She would draw each member of the university seminar while we worked through the semester. She also drew her teenage students and had them draw themselves in class. All research begins with a question. Her action research question was "How can I, as an art teacher, improve the self-image of my students through art therapy?"

The value-neutral/impartial chairperson

What I am asking of myself, as the chair of the action research seminar, or the Eduction 3200 undergraduate seminar sessions, and not always the seminar leader, is first to accept the desirability of mounting open-ended and free discussions of value issues. Second, the chair needs to abandon the role of being an "authority" on value-laden matters. Students do look to the professor for authoritative answers. Yet the autonomy of inquiry demands that both the professor and the student be learners. Understanding is a concept that still baffles not only philosophers but also others. Thus, understanding is a problematic concept for educators. Let me explore an example here. Can it be said that there is a correct understanding of the Vietnam War? Shortly after returning from Vietnam, I was asked if I understood that war. My reply is now as it was then: "It is not that I do not understand the Vietnam War but that I do not understand war . . . period." Perhaps this may count as a new category of understanding?

Third, the professor as a chairperson may wish to not exert his or her authority role and to adopt the criterion of neutrality when dealing with contentious issues. Fourth, discussion is the major strategy for ensuring understanding. Fifth, that divergence of opinion within the group seminar needs to be protected. Sixth, that the chair has responsibility for quality and standards in learning through research. Seventh, that the chair creates conditions conducive to full and free discussion work. Eighth, that the chair clarifies the issues under discussion. Ninth that the chair keeps under review the topic of discussion and rounds off discussions with a cogent summary organizing various positions. Tenth, to introduce relevant "evidence" when required. Finally, ensure that the above principles of procedure are observed. These rules of engagement are circulated and discussed in advance of formal seminar meetings. In short, the Chair is responsible for both the conditions of the seminar-discussions and the standards of judgment. By being faithful to these principles the Chair is teaching the principles of procedure for research work.

Principles of pedagogical procedure

In my experience, the seminars that have been successful are ones where the Chair:

1 Has set limits to the discussions.
2 Questioned sources and resources.
3 Carefully summarized arguments and evidence.
4 Ensured that group members have built upon one another's ideas.
5 Attempted through careful questioning, to provide an intellectual climate for action research and self-reflective critique.
6 Provides members of the seminar with "evidence"; readings, handouts, charts, data, any content that will help provide perspective for the students. We cannot assume that students have knowledge of the issue under discussion. The concept of "evidence" is crucial here. We cannot simply expect all students to have formulated critical views on a topic and therefore we need to supply them with fact and resource sheets in advance of the seminars and discussion work.

The adoption of the role of neutral chairperson may not be acceptable to all professors. It has been criticized for its neutrality on issues regarding questions of racism, or poverty, where teachers are not expected to be neutral. However, this does not mean that the teacher does not hold a value position – only that he or she is unwilling to use their authority to intimidate student thinking. For example, a teacher might be expected to be against racism, say the case of the holocaust, or blatant gender bias. On the other hand, while teaching in Northern Ireland I had the children of British Army soldiers, terrorists and pacifists in the same classroom. In that situation consensus was not possible and it would have been divisive and irresponsible, on my view, to lay down some moral line for all to accept. In addition, the role of neutrality allows an agnostic or atheist to help a fundamentalist Christian, for example, to put his or her views in their strongest light. The chair can make inputs without taking sides, thus encouraging a critical attitude to evidence, texts or ideas.

The role of the teacher on controversial value issues

This raises for me a serious query: What roles are available for one wishing to involve students in value-laden explorations? First, one might conceivably attempt allowing the professor to give his or her sincerely held point of view. Yet, the professor is in an inescapable authority position in the classroom, one which leaves him or her open to the charge of using the classroom as a public platform to promote his or her own values and views. In the face of such criticism, the profession would find itself committed to defending the professor who advocates pacifism to regular army students or abortion to students who are "right to lifers." This position scarcely seems tenable but it is attractive to many at first view. I believe that adopting this view leads to the problems of moralizing *on* value issues. At worst, this is simply indoctrination. This traditional stance is only successful where all parties are in agreement. It does seem illogical given the lack of consensus in a democratic classroom.

Second, the teacher might aspire to value avoidance, a role that is drastically different from value neutrality. However, doing nothing is in the end to adopt a strategy after all. Third, one could be convinced that the best stance would be to teach students the skills of value analysis – a school of thought which is aimed at teaching students the logic of analyzing value statements; separating facts from value statements and so on. It is a worthwhile approach but so technically orchestrated that the procedure obscures the discussion for understanding. A fourth role might be to act as the introducer of various moral dilemmas after the work of Lawrence Kohlberg, suggesting opposing positions. Fifth, one could adopt the position of "values clarification" as proposed by Sidney Simon and his colleagues (Simon *et al.*, 1972) through their humanistic education pedagogies, which built upon the idea of "valuing" offered by Dewey. In this stance, the teacher attempts to teach the process of valuing rather than some end values. It is a position commanding some following but one in which the professor asserts the authority of his or her personally held values. Moreover, it is a stance that some have argued is guilty of ethical relativism. For example, a student might adopt an irrational value and declare that this was chosen freely after thoughtfully searching the alternatives. I once taught an Irish Republican Army prisoner who had killed soldiers because he believed he was a "freedom fighter."

If we follow logically the process of values clarification, all values are legitimate if they are chosen after following the seven-stage valuing process, as outlined by Simon *et al.* (1972). Finally, the value-neutral chairperson role is a method of teaching which, if executed properly, will ensure tutors and professors do not taint students with their own biases – while at the same time advancing the understanding of the student. I believe this could lead to the basis for a professional ethic for dealing with contentious issues in higher education. This is not a value-free role. The decision to include controversial issues in class discussions is itself a value position.

In conclusion, the adoption of procedural neutrality does not mean that the chairperson does not hold a value stance on the issue in question, but rather that the chair should not use his or her position as the course leader/ professor and its authority to unnecessarily influence students on issues that cannot be settled by recourse to data or evidence. The chair is deeply committed to values education – a misconception of this position. Procedural neutrality on value issues seems to me to represent a position deep within moral philosophy – that is, that there is a distinction between "substantive" and "procedural" (methodological) values. Neutral chairing advocates a strategy which asks students to review cases and evidence under the chairing of a tutor who represents "educative values" – rationality, logical procedures, evidence, truth, critical standards and so on – but who maintains neutrality on "substantive" value issues. After R.S. Peters (1966) we are attempting to teach students rational principles of procedure for arriving at substantive value positions. It also demands that students and teachers inquire into their own work. As an action research process it does not claim to be correct – or a blueprint for success – it merely invites our critical response.

Students learn most of the time in and out of classrooms. Schools take public responsibility for planning, implementing and evaluating pupil learning. I take the concept of "pedagogy" to denote the art of teaching since it seems more than simple instructing, or teaching as contemporaneously understood. A pedagogy is a strategy for promoting student learning which uses strategies to lead students from ignorance in the classic Silver Latin definition of *educare*. In doing this, a great judgmental weight is afforded to educators in the process model.

Teachers need to be included in policy-making, not treated as mere functionaries in a state-mandated bureaucracy. Things will not really progress until educators have reclaimed their policy-making power in a true democratic Schools Council idea where the local school has power to decide on content, aims and pedagogy as well as a remit to research the effects of their actions.

Chapter 10

Ethics, inquiry and practical reason

Towards an improved pedagogy

> For through doubting we come to inquiry, and through
> Inquiry we perceive the truth.
>
> Peter Abelard, *Sic et Non* (1904)

Towards a constructivist critical pedagogy

This work seeks to further explore some principles of procedure for a critical pedagogy for understanding controversial issues such as poverty, war and violence and related controversial value issues by educators and students. Such a pedagogy would count as a critical theory of action and embodies at least four elements:

1 a consideration of ethics and ethical principles of procedure in discussion-based work;
2 a commitment to the development of situational understanding, or practical reason;
3 a commitment to inquiry and teacher action research;
4 principles for the selection of evidence and curriculum content.

The gist of what has been established thus far is that the concept of education, after the conception sketched by R.S. Peters, is associated with those activities, skills, values and knowledge worth achieving, transmitted and implemented in a morally acceptable manner while being open to reason. Education is ultimately about working with knowledge and values and with some degree of passion about things at hand for intrinsic enjoyment. In its true sense education is constructionist – making meaning through the use of imagination, knowledge and values. Very little direct attention has been devoted to the pedagogy of imagination or creational imagining. Like critical thinking, imagination is a quality most are for, but it seems few know anything of its successful execution in classroom settings. In the United Kingdom the thought of the philosopher Mary Warnock on human imagination (1976) and, in Canada, that of Kieran Egan have been notable (Egan, 1990, 1992, 2005).

Curriculum has subdued, and not advanced, human imagination. Unanticipated outcomes are signs of the true thinker yet too often the curriculum values regurgitated results. Thus, this chapter takes as its subject matter three essential elements for curriculum: ethics in curriculum work; the conduct of inquiry as a central principle in curriculum improvement; and finally some notes on the development of practical reason through curriculum. This form of curriculum will cast the teacher in the role of one with an idea that is tested in practice in the classroom. This teacher-as-researcher role will lead to better pedagogical knowledge through trial and error.

When one chooses through one's free will to live according to some moral, honorable standard in accordance with law, one can reasonably be thought to live a good, or virtuous, moral life. This is a precept advanced by the three great Greek philosophers: Socrates, Plato and Aristotle. Yet how do we know what is right or moral? A second, and perhaps more crucial, question is "Why should I be moral?" Furthermore, how do we know what is true? These questions can be understood by understanding the relationship of morality with what Thomas Aquinas called "prudence." Plato, in his *Republic*, established that it was perhaps in our best interests to live morally; that is, it would be prudent. Rational justifications for living morally have to be, when all is said and done, prudential.

This brings me to the point that the educator may have higher moral standards than he or she is fitted for. I mean, we may try to be more courageous than we really are capable of being and lead those in our charge to fatal consequences – for example by leading a group of schoolboys up a treacherous mountainside when we have little knowledge of climbing. This is very like Aristotle's point that principles have to be suited to those who have to follow them. It would indeed be sad if our attempts at moral education produced casualties and fatalities. Yet to educate to a disposition towards war or terrorism is to bring the child or student to have a moral disposition or professional attitude. Yet it may be that to bring up the child in some moral code will in fact increase the student's chances of being happy, for those who live morally have perhaps the best chance at happiness (Hare, 1981: 205).

Ethics

Ethics is concerned with matters of right and wrong, proper conduct versus misconduct. Ethical claims tell us how things ought to or should be, they do not describe factually how reality is. If I said "the world is round" it is a true statement because this can be verified empirically through data and sensory observations – and it is a fact. Ethical claims like "she is a good woman" make a prescriptive versus a descriptive claim. There is still another question to consider. Ethical claims are not the same as simple value judgments. I could say "He is a good embezzler" which makes a normative value claim (he is competent/good) but it doesn't tell us that we accept or morally approve of embezzlement or stealing. So, we need some sense of principles for ethical conduct in our educational work.

Taking responsibility for creativity is a trait that needs promotion. Education, to count as proper virtuous activity, must seek to develop what has long been called "practical reason" and virtues like prudence, which is the ability to choose wisely the good and avoid evil. Immanuel Kant, who had much to say about practical reason, was of the view that all the good in the world arises out of education (Kant, 1960, cited in Schubert, 1986: 1). Since the goal of practical reason is action, not knowledge, the truth attained by the intellect must be caused by its conformity to right purpose and intention. There can be no necessary science of practical reason, since virtuous activity allows for variety. If we are to have any curriculum of practical reason at all, we must be content to apply the principles to various conclusions and proceed from rough arguments which demonstrate truth in a general way. A curriculum, to be worthwhile, should help the student think and learn throughout life.

This chapter, first, seeks to explain issues concerned with ethical and moral questions of curriculum as the basis for theory and design. Second, it argues that there must be a concern to develop the imaginative faculty of the student and help with the intent to live according to practical reason, a logic that places virtue and the desire to act in a lawful and morally acceptable manner. Any new design requires the play of creative imagination. Can we visualize a curriculum without predetermined objectives? Can we allow our imagination to generate a whole new way of thinking about the implementation of our educational proposals? For example, when I was an undergraduate student in the 1960s a popular pedagogical work (Postman and Weingartner, 1969) took inquiry learning to extreme lengths, as evidenced by the provocative title *Teaching as a Subversive Activity*. The book outlined a plan to base all education around the questions that students brought to school – a true inquiry model which actually was put in practice in New York City. Not making any appraisal of that particular plan it was born out of imagination to engage students more practicably in research.

Can a curriculum then be produced by another means than reaching objectives? This was my initial starting idea for this book. Why must every public school curriculum conform to this simplistic ends-means ideology of linear technical rationality? Surely there are good arguments for experimenting with alternative designs? Planning curriculum is the roadmap for that education to be experienced. Education, being value driven, has obvious connections with ethics, or moral philosophy. Education then is concerned with answers to questions relating to the justification of choices involving practical matters. Practical questions are the heart of educational practice when we consider "what is the case" or "what should be the case" with curriculum. Indeed, education is about "worthwhile activities." On this view education involves judgments of value about worthwhile things. We need to be quite clear in our discussion of such concepts – and that is a principal task of philosophy of education: to examine words and concepts, say "education," as distinct from "training." A theory that will include the educator as a researcher/scholar (critical action inquiry) and possessing skills of practical reason and situational understanding is at the heart of this professional "ethical model." This chapter will attempt to begin this discussion.

After Aristotle (1998) in his *Nichomachean Ethics Book 1*, one might decide: The goal of practical knowledge is rightful action caused by moral good intention. The most wonderful outcome of education is to use speculative reason operating upon curiosity or doubt as a way of arriving at truth or good knowledge. Thus inquiry, reason and good intention – or ethics – are all involved. Education is a form of freedom always. The freedom to inquire, to speculate, to establish answers – as Antonio Gramsci asserts, the purpose of the school is to formulate "humanism"; that human intellectual discipline and the ability of "moral independence." Schools mostly seem to operate as distributors of knowledge. Through a concerted program of teacher and student inquiry schools can be centers for inquiry and the creation of knowledge. This is what universities aspire to through faculty and students pursuing research. It should be the same with schools, especially at the secondary level, where students have absorbed research methods and project work.

What then is the upshot of this thinking about practical and ethical reasoning? From the critical-hermeneutic and practicalist position the aim is arriving at a situational understanding and good judgment which is not deduced or prescribed. Theory is important but it is subordinate to human intellect and free will and it takes a back seat to individual situational understanding of "grounded theory." To rely rigidly on book theories is to not allow the possibility of a volitional thinking synthesis to occur – a wholly unanticipated, born-out-of-the-educator's-imagination type of response. The initial and some formal education of teachers take place in universities or colleges. Higher education holds no secrets of life except through what Michael Oakeshott (1933) has called "arrests of experience" – those partial perspectives that alone give us some purchase on experience and the "possibility" of human understanding, which we call "knowledge." Most schools claim to have aims of advancing "knowledge." Teachers committed to that aim must also grapple with the consequences of a theory of knowledge and this mighty ambition. In addition, teachers are mandated to be moral agents.

Some principles of procedure

What are some of the principles of procedure, or "aims," of an inquiry-based curriculum? This is a crucial prong in the argument for a process model of curriculum design. I am arguing that at least eight criteria must be borne in mind as principles of procedure:

1   respect for persons;
2   teaching students a research methodology;
3   discussion as the main pedagogical strategy;
4   teacher being "impartial chairperson" of discussion work;
5   discussion of controversial value issues;
6   involving students in research-based work;
7   encouraging students to clarify human values through personal choosing from among alternative courses of action;
8   being fair – treating all students equally.

These principles of procedure guide my work as a classroom educator. First, there must be *respect for persons*. In all discussion-based work, diversity of opinion is always valued. Second, *teaching a research methodology* is a major pedagogical aim – to teach to ask the right questions is more important than furnishing pre-digested answers. Third, to *organize classroom-based discussion* so that students have empowerment – the ability to listen as well as make points. Fourth, to create *a role in which the educator is another voice, but having special responsibility for chairing discussion and lesson work*. Fifth, to *examine the "upside down" core issues* – not normally examined, yet playing a part in culture (war, poverty, terrorism, sexuality, work). Sixth, to *engage the curiosity of students' concerns through research work*. Seventh, to *allow students the opportunities to make choices* – after considering reflectively the consequences of their choices – that is, engage students in the process of valuing (Dewey, 1938). Finally, *always strive for equality and fairness in discussion-based teaching*. Through observing these principles of procedure the educator and students are acting on values that are instrumental in the creation of desired ends-in-view – tolerance in the classroom, respect for "evidence," democratic cooperation, honesty and justice.

Teaching about teachers as researchers, ethics and the development of "practical reason" is on the rise. This was a necessary reaction to the moribund state of ends-means planning that the technical engineers since Bobbitt have promoted. In the aftermath of 9/11, the unethical business procedures in Enron and stock market world in the past years have made ethicists welcome. Over the past decades a whole host of new centers in academia have devoted themselves to the study of practical ethics. For example, the Kennedy Center at Georgetown University opened in 1972 with a four-prong set of principles to guide ethical behavior: individual autonomy, non-malfeasance, beneficence and justice. More than ever before it is necessary for ethics to keep pace with technology and science as new ethical dilemmas emerge. Students of all disciplines, including education, require knowledge and understanding of the "normative" – including the spiritual – and should be able to express their moral understandings and to develop "education of self" so that their own moral and ethical identity of self can grow.

Elliott (1993) suggests that professional development once initiated in a manner that leads to autonomy through self-understanding will itself perpetuate new ways of understanding and social acting. However, even more importantly, it is crucial that practitioners have this discussion and share their experiences of professional action in an ever-changing school culture. The shared consciousness will be vital for the continued improvement of professional practice – which is owned by educators to begin with. It seems however that school culture is organized to deprive and not encourage such a collective shared consciousness and that this is a major problem for administration. A task of critical action research has been to examine, understand and reduce the injustices in social/educational settings through problem-solving applied to day-to-day inequities in our professional lives (Carr and Kemmis, 1986). Elliott (1993) concludes that good reflective practitioners employ practical reason and science, as a hermeneutic, in making on-the-spot intuitive decisions that result in improved professional performance. Such an art is what is referred to as situational understanding.

Practical reasoning has not received much attention in teacher education programs, yet there are signs of a growing literature relating to education (Dunne, 1997). Good and wise decisions rest on the judgments of teachers and the situational understandings they exhibit. Good professional practice then is manifest through an "ethical model" of practical wisdom and reason – the ability to come up with a wise response in the face of a difficult problem that poses great uncertainty. Reflective practitioners do not espouse theoretical guidelines when faced with problems, rather they intuitively contemplate and compare their actions with actions that warrant good results in their experience.

Logical thought and, perhaps, philosophic procedures ought to help us think better about moral issues and curriculum. I surmise that any "improvement" in our thinking will be in terms of situational understandings and practical reasoning – indeed in improving *rationality*. Durkheim, for example, believed in the power of inductive reason in ethics to understand all that was in our world – he labeled this "uncompromising rationality," the idea that nothing in reality was beyond the scope of reason. But is there a rational modality to answering moral questions? The first step towards answering a question is to *understand* it; which when all is said and done entails a complete clarity about the words contained in the question. So, analytical philosophy may prove to be a powerful ally in our quest. This is because words and concepts owe their meaning to their logical properties. The enormous value in practical reason (*ratio practica*) is a mine that public school curriculum has not worked.

Curriculum theory needs new models to allow educators to experiment with the improvement of human understanding. This is not just a technical problem – it is a moral and ethical problem of great importance. There is a great need for imagination in not only design but as a pupil aim (Egan, 1990) and variety in curriculum theory, since education, like politics, is a practice much subscribed to. It also needs to be clear that curriculum theory is a subset of the larger educational theory field. Practical reasoning is crucial here as opposed to theoretic reasoning. Practical reason leads to actions that are good as distinct from mere knowledge about ends or action. *Phronesis* is the Greek notion that captures this idea – a combination of action and reason. There has been a revival of interest in "practical reason."

We need to apply ethical concerns to the selection of content. For example, which subjects should be included in curriculum because of knowledge and ethical/moral development? Education is ordinarily concerned with different "forms of knowledge and thought," for example mathematics and science. There are also issues about how these forms of knowledge are related to learning and the psychology of educational experiences.

This author sets forward the notion that instructional objectives, as instrumental ends, are destructive to the epistemic character of forms of knowledge. However, we first require principles of procedure for the selection of content. We need to be justified in teaching algebra rather than marbles or bingo. Moreover, we require a common teaching strategy to implement the curriculum. How is the curriculum to be taught?

Of concern for educators is the notion that inquiry will gain knowledge and that this will really only have great value if students use this knowledge in their lives. Of great import is the notion of using knowledge as an interpretive tool. For teachers, to move the boundaries of curriculum theory farther they will have to harness the knowledge hard won through experimentation in schools in a sort of situational sense; that is, when faced with perplexing and messy situations, one doesn't call upon "grand theory" to solve problems, but rather one's intuition, experience and skill – one's knowledge is used as a form of sorting out the mess. It is this "situational theorizing" that I have in mind when I think of teachers as researchers. I believe this is what Schwab had in mind when he eschewed curriculum theory and argued for the "practical" in curriculum development.

Curriculum selection principles

Furthermore, we require principles relating to the sequence and articulation of concepts, facts and content and finally principles that throw up evidence about the evaluative nature of student performance. If it is correct to say that the curriculum is a mind-altering device then we had better take the selection and inclusion of its content in a serious way.

In addition to the content there are major considerations requiring the role of the teacher as a researcher/evaluator. Since the model is a process and research one the theory articulated here needs to set up:

1   principles on which to research the action;
2   principles on which to judge students;
3   principles of ethical value in student development;
4   principles for the selection of content;
5   principles to assess our adherence to our teaching strategy.

Ethical principles of procedure

It seems fair and just that teachers abide by ethical principles in the conduct of teaching. The National Education Association (NEA) Code of Conduct is useful as a document attempting to outline a code for public school teachers in the USA and is apposite here.

In the USA the NEA, which is not a trade union but a professional association of educators numbering 2.8 million (Ornstein and Levine, 2005), signals two areas of commitment: One to students by teachers and one to the profession. I would build upon the NEA Code and include several other concerns.

Educators will respect principles concerning:

1   equity in treatment of students, colleagues and parents;
2   intellectual freedom (never constrain a student from inquiry);
3   due process and punishment;
4   a commitment to reflection, research and the development of the profession;
5   a commitment to sound moral conduct;
6   a commitment to extend the range of teaching so that students are not constrained in their freedom to learn;
7   a commitment to confidentiality;
8   a commitment to honesty (not falsifying, for example, their resumes to gain advantage in recruitment to a professional post);
9   acting with dignity – never embarrassing or abusing a student, teacher or other person through their actions and work.

The educator, in taking an ethical position, must be prepared to face some of the most crucial and profound questions concerning conduct. Education and curriculum have principles implied as improvement, worth and so on. The way in which the curriculum is composed – its content – and the manner of pedagogy – or how it is implemented – are serious ethical issues. Here we need to enter the realm of moral philosophy. We must understand why slavery and murder are reprehensible yet content treating divorce, gambling and the like may not be palpably so. We need to understand that burglars may have excellent skills of thievery but that to behave accordingly is unlawful and unethical.

Yet there are values and moral principles such as "being fair," "respect for views," "protecting diversity of opinion" and so on which are clearly desired aims of curriculum work. Yet questions are rarely raised about the justification of these values at all. They are unexamined. Furthermore, no basis has emerged in ethical theories for claiming that any of these theories is justified. We need a rational basis for the justification of content and teaching. We cannot abandon this argument. I am arguing that certain "principles of procedure" are necessary conditions for a form of curriculum transaction to have meaning. I have to demonstrate this procedure being followed by a teacher committed to it that uses it seriously. So, if it can be shown that such principles are necessary would this then be a strong argument for its usage and the justification of the principles under scrutiny? We must have justification in education, for what every educator must ask and answer is: "What ought I do in the class?"

That education has been confused with instruction and even training shows clearly how so many wrongly perceive the concept of education. Michael Oakeshott makes a wonderfully telling distinction between the concepts of *work* and *play*, intimating that education belongs to the play category and poetic imagination. Work signifies mastering the world to secure human wants, while play comes from the idea of the Greek and Roman notion of *liberalia studium*, or liberal studies, which are enjoyed for their own sake.

A curriculum must be morally justified. Advocacy for pillaging in war or rape of citizens would not be acceptable. Thus, curriculum policies are driven by *ethical* considerations. These are ultimately considerations that concern doing good. I have not seen any rigorous examination of all the universe of values that the curriculum is going for anywhere in my career of thirty years in Europe or the USA. Yet the primary aim of educational practice is to get students to acquire especially democratic values. Thus, it would appear that for students to act wisely they will have to know a great deal about democratic behavior in a variety of contexts. It is not a question of how much content or knowledge one has acquired but the notion that an individual can think in the form of knowledge.

Central to education and the development of mind must be a pedagogy that improves teaching: a research-based program of professional self-development, led by those who are the practitioners, if you will. There is no curriculum development without teacher development. The teacher-researcher movement is providing a research base for this idea. Inquiry is at the core of teacher development as much as it is at the core of intellectual advancement. Thus a pedagogy based in the inductive inquiry process of reflective thought (Dewey, 1910) underpins this pedagogy. Such a teaching style is more of an art form. Indeed the European notion of "pedagogy" deliberately is chosen because it is more than mere instruction. This book's model requires a pedagogy that is creative, artful and critical. A critical art induces imagination and demands reflection, contemplative thought, rumination, of the relationship between teacher and taught; it would be deliberately open to various accounts as a matter of ethics. It would choose controversial subjects and seek to exhume the irrational and unjust practices found in the classroom, school and relationships therein, community and society. The teacher acts as a sort of facilitator of discussion. This raises a rather serious issue of the teacher's authority status. I believe, after much experience and experimentation, that the best role for the teacher in critical pedagogy is that of a neutral chairperson. The teacher is not neutral in seeing that the content is selected but in the furtherance of the student's understanding of the controversial value issues that come into the classroom discussion. Since teachers have positions of authority that weighting may have a negative influence on their ability to prevent pure student learning.

Imagination and creativity

Teachers hoping to develop creative imagination need to observe certain values and procedures. However, one word of sharp criticism may put the lid on an open mind so that it stays closed. Sympathetic engagement may be a way forward: not scolding but supportive. Professor Kieran Egan (1990, 1992, 2005) is actively engaged in practical projects that seek to help teachers engage the student's imagination. The establishment of the International Educational Research Group based on Egan's work at Simon Fraser University is a sound example. The group is channeling their efforts into curriculum research and exemplar materials production in this endeavor.

I think that one of the virtues not well highlighted in teaching is that of prudence. After Thomas Aquinas it was held that it was not enough to be good – one had to know and be prudent in making decisions, rather than enjoying good results with poor intentions. One might ask a teacher "why should I be moral?" – a question asked in Plato's *Republic* – yet Plato may have been misguided in arguing that to live morally is in our best interests; that is, in accord with *prudence*. It is not the case that to do what we morally ought to do is always in our prudential interest (Hare, 1981: 191). What Professor Hare suggests is that we develop what he terms "prudential principles"; these are like what Aristotle refers to as moral virtues – being courageous, having self-control, perseverance. They are "instrumental" values in that they signify a virtue as a mode of behaving, or desirable conduct, on Hare's account, but one can see that they would clearly influence the discipline and habit of practicing intrinsic values such as a concern for justice and equality (more terminal virtues). So, it seems that some of the important principles of procedure are indeed virtues that will help realize the desired ends we seek: being honest and fair will help promote the end of peace, wisdom and so on. Having *respect for students* and being *fair to all* of them are priority instrumental virtues in my day-to-day teaching. This is where, then, prudence and morality intersect. One is unlikely to be a successful purse snatcher without perseverance and courage.

The poverty curriculum project

In North Carolina, poverty deeply affects educational participation. I am working at present on a research strategy with my graduate class (Education 6424), Action Research and Curriculum Development, to have students engage in both inquiry and curriculum improvement, that will develop curriculum materials for teacher education on the problems and effects of teaching about poverty. Certainly, materials are needed but that is not the most important product here. We also need to be rational – that is, education cannot be pointless, or aimless, so to speak. We must have rational intent.

Stenhouse (1975) argued that a curriculum must, as a minimum, provide the basis for planning a course and studying its effects empirically and further considering the grounds for its justification. In terms of its aim, it requires the formulation of its intention which is accessible to critical scrutiny. To be educated on this view is not to have arrived at a destination; it is to travel with a different view. What is required is not feverish preparation for something that lies ahead, but working with precision, passion and taste at worthwhile things that lie at hand. Traveling is not about the end result, say arriving in New York City, more about the journey, the process, and the encounters that make up the experience. This is, I think, what Stenhouse was driving at.

The rage nowadays is all for objectives, or intended learning outcomes, when in yesteryear it was about having an aim or purpose. Aims specify a rational cause or direction – for example: To enable students to conduct research; or, to educate students in a deep understanding of controversial issues relating to war, gender inequalities, poverty and its effects on children as learners and by encouraging opportunities to assist children affected by poverty while adopting a role of leader of inquiries and facilitator of student inquiry into the problems and effects of poverty. Thus, we are attempting to elicit responses from students but not to predetermine and define the outcome of that response. The procedural values that help each student to reach their own perspective is the purpose – to do anything else would be to either teach a rhetoric of conclusions or to indoctrinate students. The aims of the poverty project are as follows:

1   to assist students to become aware of poverty in North Carolina;
2   to identify attitudes to poverty by groups in society;
3   to understand the "culture of poverty" and its many faces;
4   to provide evidence in the shape of demographic and scientific facts regarding poverty;
5   to analyze the problems that stem from poverty that affect learning;
6   to organize students to combat poverty;
7   to help students design research projects that provide factual evidence of poverty in their community.

Pedagogically, the principles of procedure would aim at:

1   getting the students to pose research questions about poverty. This would become a hypothesis-based strategy of inquiry which would need to be adopted as a general pedagogical strategy within an inquiry learning classroom;
2   teaching this research method to students in the class;
3   conducting classroom discussions in which all students listen and contribute based upon facts and evidence;
4   pointing out that some questions contain "controversial value positions" which cannot be settled by recourse to "evidence" but rather embody value judgments;
5   adopting a new pedagogical role of teacher as discussion leader who is neutral. He or she is not "an authority" but acts "in authority" on value issues;
6   watching the data generated by students as to its quality. Good students using the procedures of research will inevitably come up with good data.

The teaching strategy would be as follows:

1   Adopt a role of chair of discussion.
2   Be critical of dogmatic/prejudiced views.
3   Offer opportunities to explore a wide range of views in the classroom.
4   Provide "evidence" or data upon which students may be informed of the issue.
5   Encourage inquiry learning as opposed to didactic teaching.
6   Implement both a teaching and teacher-as-researcher brief.
7   Protect the differences of opinion offered by students.
8   Inject new "evidence" for students to consider.

Thus an educator, teaching a unit on a controversial value issue or topic, for example poverty or violence, will see this as an educational experience of some value. It is so because it now gives teachers the power of curriculum development and a strategy through action research to inquire and research the effects of their own teaching. This is a strategy where some experience has already been garnered (I think of the Humanities Curriculum Project, sponsored by the UK School Council 1967–72; and our own work with the Schools Cultural Studies Project, based at Ulster University, Northern Ireland from 1973–80). This is because underpinning this approach is a belief that students who understand the social and cultural milieu and the constraints on human action and change will adopt an educational theory in the social-reconstructionist tradition, to work for improved social change and social justice in society. By understanding poverty students may be able to take actions that will reduce or eliminate poverty – even if they cannot take such action they will understand the cultural surround of poverty which will enable them to assist students trapped in poverty.

Thomas Aquinas (1225–74)

This concern for ethical behavior for reason and inquiry summon up a dual concept of pedagogy and scholarship not unlike that espoused by Thomas Aquinas, the thirteenth-century Parisian Scholastic. Aquinas did not view teaching as merely a career or livelihood. He was severe in his judgment also of university teachers who were motivated by vanity and glorious self-aggrandizement with their own pedagogical performances. For Aquinas teaching and scholarship was service to God as a way of loving God by serving students. He saw teaching as combining elements of the contemplative life (cloisters at that time for monks and hermits – the eremitic tradition) with the secular life of the university and town. This was because the teacher on Aquinas' view must be committed to the content that she or he teaches and the students who receive this instruction. While Aquinas did not dwell on educational practice or theory he did make two important contributions. He was the eminent scholar of his day and his intellectual achievement was staggering; as is the impact that Thomism had during the period 1848 to the close of the Second World War.

In North America, this revival was led by men like Mortimer Adler, Robert Hutchins, Jacques Maritain and Etienne Gilson. Thomism was mainly, but not exclusively, a theory discussed by Catholics for private education. Yet there seems to be something recommending the virtues of Thomism worth exploring in our reconstructed curriculum perspective for a more universal audience. While Thomism is not much discussed nowadays, the principle of truth for Aquinas – practical action that is also moral – should be exhumed for curriculum planners as a principle.

In his discourse on Aristotle's *Nicomachean Ethics*, Aquinas expounded on Aristotle's two modes of intelligent action. Practical action he found in the arts and sciences, holding that in practical matters one reasons about the means for achievement of the goal and then one transforms that specific decision into action to achieve the goal. Aquinas argued, after Aristotle, that the *truth* of our reasoning depended largely upon whether the means achieved the results of the intention. Aquinas further argued that this pragmatic intelligence also has a moral dimension intrinsic to such action and the action cannot claim to be true unless it is also ethical/moral. Yet it is time to set out in more precise detail how moral concepts can help us educate students to use moral arguments. In short, we need a format for teaching critical thinking about ethical/value issues.

The term "practical reason" is a special type of reasoning, which is related to the deductions of speculative logic. To know what to do in this or that situation is to have some license over practical reason. Practical reason is fed through the use of "situational understanding" as discussed earlier. Aquinas argued, after Aristotle, for two ways of doing intellectual work: that directed at understanding the world and that ordered towards changing it (Donohue, 1968: 87). Aquinas divides these as perfect speculative thinking and practical thinking and reason. Practical reason aims at change. A teacher who knows how to decline Latin verbs or to write lyrics or compose Haiku poems is performing practical arts. There is a right way to calculate taxes and a wrong way just as there is a right way to chart a navigational course, or bake a cake, and a wrong way. The success of the sailor, cook or poet consistently is no accident – it is the result of intelligence controlling materials. Aquinas argues that the arts are "the right way of making things"; in *Summa Theologiae*, he grounded his theory of correct reasoning on the human ability to discover an underlying order in any field of inquiry.

With practical reason one begins with the principle that all human acts are directed to an end and then the individual will come to recognize the fundamental element of ethics to be "do good and avoid evil." The composer and carpenter will consistently turn out fine tunes and furniture because they have this practical reason as an applied human art. Moral philosophy then seemed to diverge in two directions – one moral concerns and reasons, the other theoretical and scientific. The variety and differences among the will's acts lead Aquinas to use the term *"ratio practica"* specifically to distinguish the method of moral reasoning from that of strictly scientific knowledge.

Aristotle was of the belief that the end of practical reason was truth of right action and desire for the good. He believed this was possible through human reason alone. Aquinas argued that practical reason was directly attributable to eternal law, and God, which makes reason possible. Indeed, it is curious that Aquinas is similar to Aristotle in his description of human action and yet is so faithful theologically. Practical reason requires a foundation more secure than the accepted practice of human actions. In the search for that basis, Aquinas and other Scholastics attempt to construct a theory of practical reason that becomes an account of the nature of moral goodness itself.

While he says little of curriculum proper, Aquinas had several interesting notions on the subject of learning. He refers to these in his writings as, first, *inventio*, that is, learning by oneself through discovery (long before child-centered theorists such as Rousseau, Pestalozzi and Froebel), which he regarded as the highest form of learning and which can be seen to be related to "research" or notions of "inquiry." Second, Aquinas uses the concept *disciplina*, which refers to learning with instruction through the disciplines – aided by a teacher, since most people do not have the courage or perseverance to learn alone. *Disciplina* eventuates in forms of knowledge we now refer to as the "disciplines of knowledge," the seven liberal arts which consisted of the *Trivium* (language arts) of rhetoric, logic and grammar, and the *Quadrivium* (mathematics, ethics, music and physics (natural philosophy)). It is sad that Aquinas, perhaps the most learned man of the thirteenth century, with so much to say on education, had little to say about the nature of curriculum. If we understand Aquinas to mean that "invention" is similar to inquiry then we can consider both the student and the teacher as learners through a commitment to research.

It is worth noting that Aquinas, like Aristotle, shared a deep skepticism about Plato's notion that virtue could be taught. Aquinas reasoned that while teachers could help lead students to understand the concept of truthfulness, this was no guarantee that the student would be an honest person. The best one can do, he suggested, was to put students in front of moral positions and to help people to act virtuously so that they would develop good habits of character through the exercise of their own free will. This is akin to what the principal of a primary school in Dublin once said to me: "Morals are caught, not taught, Jim." He later explained that there were four Rs in education: Reading, Riting, Rithmetic and Rugby. Even today education often avoids the moral dimensions, especially in state schools.

Teachers need to know about moral education and how to help students with moral choices, dilemmas and the clarification of beliefs that will guide their choosing and acting. For these reasons all teachers are moral educators and they should have a familiarity with philosophies of education and the many theories so that they can build their own "situational understanding" of knowledge, truth and morals.

From the early Christian period, moral reasoning was linked with Christian thought: firstly through the writings of Augustine and then later the brilliance of Peter Abelard and Thomas Aquinas at Paris. Perhaps this linkage with Christianity is a major constraint on state schools handling moral issues, as state schools, at least in the USA, are directed to not aid religious groups or thought under the First Amendment "Establishment Clause" of the Constitution.

The religious factor and the institution of the Church was the most dominant agency in the medieval period. The good teacher, said Aquinas, had faith and love for his students as much as for his scholarship and he tried to evoke that "care" in his work as a model of the "good." Aquinas stood for the teacher as a role model of virtues. In being an appropriate model an educator is a moral agent. Notwithstanding deductive reasoning, which has been all but abandoned in our Modern World in favor of inductive reasoning, there is still great value in the scholarly logic warranted by Thomist ideas and theory of education as Scholasticism.

Peter Abelard (1079–1142)

Lawrence Stenhouse (1983) suggests that Peter Abelard may have been the first genuine humanist and researcher during the medieval period. He was a critical theorist in that he made institutions and persons the object of his critiques. He is regarded as the founding figure of rational speculation in Western universities – even though he lived before the universities of Europe and of Paris were founded. Abelard lectured in Paris, indeed in the college where the University of Paris came to be based later. He established a great tradition and was followed some years later by Thomas Aquinas, the Scholastic and moral philosopher. Paris was to be the intellectual center of European university education for centuries. It was Abelard who set the tone – and he paid a high price for his critical theories, including castration by fellow student clerics due to his love for Heloise, a niece of a Bishop in France who was outraged by the affair between them.

Abelard was a brilliant dialectician and legendary lecturer (Marenbon, 1997), being, by repute, a charismatic teacher with a wonderful elocution and strong voice. In his ethics, Abelard stressed the subjective nature of morality. For him the goodness of an act is not determined by its results but by its *motivation or intent*. He wrote:

> It is one thing to inquire into truth by deliberation, but quite another to make ostentation the end of all disputation, for while the first is devoted study which strives to edify, the second is but the mere impulse of pride which seeks only for self-glory. By the one we set out to learn the wisdom which we do not possess; by the other we parade the learning which we trust is ours.
>
> (Sikes, 1961: 55)

Abelard situated education then as a provisional base camp – never a finality but merely a staging post for more inquiry. This concern for knowledge won through inquiry is the heart of rational and practical reason. Research-based teaching was eminently preferable, for Abelard, over instruction through what Lawrence Stenhouse describes as teaching "a rhetoric of conclusions" (1983: 178).

Teaching which accepts trusted knowledge is an inadequate notion. Teachers must be committed to testing knowledge and establishing new knowledge claims, always clinging to the belief that inquiry will yield more. It is a certainty in a world of uncertainty. If we are faithful to our belief that education differs markedly from instruction and/or training then we must eschew the pre-specification of outcomes in the form of behavioral objectives. We are not after a "rhetoric of results" but the development of the educated person.

Part III

Teacher values and teacher education

Chapter 11

Teachers' human values and ideologies

> Every community, like every action, is aimed at some good. Good in individual actions is traced back to virtues which are sources of action and have a natural basis in the psychological faculties of man.
>
> Aristotle, *Politics*

This chapter presents the results of a cross-cultural inquiry into the values held by teachers in the USA, Costa Rica, Palestine and the Republic of Ireland. This work seeks to discuss these values in relation to ideological preferences and the curriculum. If we are to engage in models of critical inquiry into educational issues and ground our work in a theory of education, whether Essentialism or Critical Realism, we should hold some evidence about teachers' desired values. The surveys were completed using the terminal and instrumental value systems of teacher education students and practicing teachers utilizing the Rokeach Value Survey (Rokeach, 1973) Form D in the Republic of Ireland (N = 302), Palestine (N = 147), Costa Rica (N = 27) and the USA (N = 194). The data were subjected to six hypotheses related to value perspectives identified in the curriculum thought of Chapter 1 and a cluster analysis of the thirty-six values in the survey: educational, caring, religious, political, social and personal model types emerged as significant.

Results suggest, with the exception of the Palestinians, that teachers do not aspire, surprisingly one would think, towards educational values – the intellectual-epistemological dimensions of their careers – which may have negative effects for critical theorists aspiring towards transformative intellectualism and social change. Irish students were absolutely "social" in typology and placed a premium on caring/personal values in orientation while Arabs were educational-intellectual and also aspired highest towards freedom and peace. Americans valued highly religious ends and Costa Ricans, like the Irish, held the social factor in high regard.

The results suggest that subjects within cultures enduring conflict express desire for specific values such as equal rights, freedom and peace, thus providing a population of teachers that are loving, responsible and honest in their instrumental value systems while seeking family security and respect as ideal end-states of existence. Thus personal values are prioritized by educators who view themselves as dependable and reliable in the execution of duties.

A second important development is the testing of the six value orientations, or ideological preferences, outlined. A Cumulative Value Index was created for each of these perspectives. That is, values in the survey which clustered together in terms of the six concepts tell us more about how each of the national cohorts compare in terms of each value orientation.

Finally, the issue of values in teaching and education is addressed. The clash of values now prominent in the technical rational world versus the academic rational hermeneutic perspective represents a new and special conflict particularly acute within the academy for those in higher education.

It should be indicated at the outset that I, along with others, believe philosophy, social science and education to have a very practical relevance. Plato divided academic subjects into those which are good in themselves, those instrumental for achieving ulterior purposes and those which are both. I hold that philosophy and education fall into the latter and best class of subjects. If these subjects fell only into the first classification of academic subjects then they would be worth pursuing for their intrinsic value alone.

Culture impinges upon education and teaching in many ways. The teacher is unavoidably a bearer of human values and meanings which are mediated through teaching and curriculum. My main search has been to determine those values which are central in teachers' human belief systems for it is my contention that values more than any other concept are the best indicators of understanding not only culture but human behavior.

As a beginning postgraduate research student of culture, values and education in Northern Ireland I first read the value research ideas of Allport, Vernon and Lindzey, A Study of Values (Allport et al., 1960), based on a theory of value and six "types of man," along with the empirical value inquiries of Milton Rokeach (1973). I wished to obtain some measure of the values of students caught up in a culture in crisis. While some value work was done with high school students (McKernan and Russell, 1980) I did not have the opportunity until later to survey groups of teacher education students I had contact with in several cultures. These teacher data are presented in this chapter.

It is my intention here to argue that while most policy-makers, but few philosophers in education, view education as a production technology governed by product specifications and objective targets, and that while some philosophers argue for rejuvenated forms of rationality, the human values underpinning teachers' belief systems fall within what I have loosely labeled the domains of the educational, caring, religious, political, social and personal ideologies. Teacher values embody a caring and humanistic rather than a technical or critical-intellectual perspective. These are the categories that catch the eye of students and teachers and our education system should reflect these beliefs.

R.S. Peters (1966) has remarked that the concept of education implies the transmission of something that is intrinsically worthwhile in a morally acceptable manner by those who are committed to it. On this view education is, indeed, a normative and value-laden enterprise. The question does arise as to what values educators ascribe to and if these teachers have a lasting effect on the values of their students. The latter part of this question is regrettably outside the scope of this study. Moreover, one might ask if these values are shared cross-culturally by similar educators. Whilst there have been considerable studies of educators' attitudes there have been relatively few studies of their values. This is in my view due to the fact that psychologists have provided more sophisticated methods for measuring attitudes than values due to the work of measurement psychologists such as Likert, Bogardus and Guttman. Rokeach (1973) argued that values, rather than attitudes, are the chief determinants of behavior and the antecedents of values can be traced to culture, society, institutions and personality factors. Virtually all writers point to the "oughtness" character of values, therefore indicating a moral or ethical dimension to behavior.

Are there value clusters or orientations which characterize teachers as a group? For example, do teachers give primacy more to personal, rationalist, technical, aesthetic or utilitarian preferences in their value hierarchies? Recent forays by critical theorists have set forth technical, scientific-positivist and critical interpretive models of the professional educator.

This book implies that good education is grounded in good interpretations of practical situations as a whole and cannot be improved without improving these interpretations. It embodies a system of practical culture, that is, a system of values conditioned by practical concerns and decisions made *in situ*. Teacher education needs to focus on helping pre-service and in-service teachers, and their pupils, to develop capacities for *situational understanding* as a basis for wise action.

The study is exploratory and merely descriptive – and in one sense, longitudinal, insofar as data has been collected from "convenience" samples of students the author has interacted with during his academic career in Ireland, Palestine, Central America and the United States.

It is concerned with the analysis of values as social indicators in the profession and of the quality and range of human beliefs in a number of cultures and for viewing human values as social indicators for programs of education. Just as unemployment figures are social indicators of the health of the economy, value rankings may be regarded as normative aspirations or conceptions of the desirable; in short, the respondents' values. As such they count as qualitative indicators for culture and especially for education. Social indicators are more than just some measure of a social variable. Such indicators count as a measure of where we are compared with some theoretical conception of where we ought to be. These value data point to gaps in the quality of life for teachers and teacher education students on three continents.

Finally, I argue for curriculum to be grounded in procedural values rather than arguing for curriculum specified in behavioral targets. This is the basis for the process-inquiry theory of curriculum discussed in Chapter 5. Such a view of teachers' values is embedded in promoting students' situational understandings which we have hardly begun to explore and promote in teacher education. We need to be about this work, and about it with some conviction and passion if we are to compete against the "social market" and craft-like rationality of the production-minded Behaviorists. If the social-market perspective becomes the alternative to a now fading Platonic rationalism then we can effectively write off any contribution that the *critical-reflective practitioner* view can make in modern American higher education. Our values will have been made redundant in the educational marketplace.

The USA and Irish respondents were students in foundations of education courses taught by the author between 1983 and 2004. The data from Ireland were collected systematically from Higher Diploma in Education students at University College Dublin during the period 1983–91. The Costa Rican data were collected in 1998. Palestinian data were collected while conducting curriculum development work during 1994 and 2000.

First, I shall present empirical survey data relating to the ranking of human values by teachers in the Republic of Ireland, Costa Rica, Palestine and the USA. Students at East Carolina University represent USA data. Next, I discuss the Cumulative Value Indexes for the six ideologies discovered in the data. These data are presented here for the first time. I shall conclude with a discussion of the significance of the findings for the curriculum.

The nature of values and the Value Survey instrument

In stating that one has a value one is suggesting that certain beliefs are held worthwhile or are desired by an individual or group. Some philosophers have referred to ideal ends (terminal/substantive) or values as modes of behavior (instrumental values/procedural). This distinction between ends and means has been worked by social scientists and philosophers.

More than any other concept, the "problem of values" appears in all fields of the social sciences, and value elements are potentially important as variables to be analyzed in all major areas of investigation. For the purposes of this work the concept of value, aside from the worth ascribed to *objects*, is a belief which refers to beliefs concerning desirable *modes of conduct* or desirable *end-states of existence*. Rokeach (1973) refers to these two types as *instrumental values* and *terminal values*, encompassing an ends-means conceptualization. Thus, a value is defined as "an enduring belief that a specific mode of conduct or end-state of existence is personally or socially preferable to an opposite or converse mode of conductor end-state of existence." A "value system" is "an enduring organization of beliefs concerning preferable modes of conduct or end-states of existence along a continuum of relative importance" (Rokeach 1973: 5).

The Value Survey

Tables 11.1 and 11.2 reveal two lists of eighteen alphabetically arranged terminal (end-state ideals) and instrumental (modes of conduct) values, using the Rokeach Value Survey (Form E). The author was present to administer the survey, which was presented as a survey of human values. The instruction to the respondent is "rank each value in order of importance to you; the most important being ranked '1' and least important ranked '18'." The rank order method suggests that it is not the absence or presence of a value, but their relative ordering, that is of interest. The survey is simple and efficient to administer – the average completion time is around fifteen minutes. Respondents report that they find the exercise thought-provoking and many ask for a blank copy to take away for further study. It is a projective test in the sense that it elicits responses in the form of rankings that come from internal demands rather than independent external sources. The test–re-test reliabilities for Form E are 0.74 for terminal and 0.70 for instrumental values (Feather, 1971).

The cross-cultural survey of human values

Early on in my career, while working as a curriculum development officer with a large cultural studies/peace education project in Northern Ireland, I became interested in the values of adolescents and teachers in a society in conflict. I was also extremely interested in understanding how these values might reflect broad patterns of culture and evoke educational responses from schools and teachers. This is a question which still intrigues to this day.

While systematic cross-cultural value studies may still be in the future, data are available from a number of investigators (Rokeach, 1973). It is possible to identify specific values that distinguish sub-groups within the present study. In this study six ideological models, or teacher value orientations, have been analyzed: Educational, Caring, Religious, Social, Political and Personal Models. These orientations also bear a close resemblance to curriculum ideologies discussed by theorists in Chapter 3.

Table 11.1 Terminal value medians (as composite rank orders) for cross-cultural groups of American, Costa Rican, Palestinian and Irish students and teachers

	USA (UG) N = 140	USA (G) 54	COSTA RICAN 27	PALES. (UG) 147	REP. IRE (G) 302
A COMFORTABLE LIFE (a prosperous life)	(13)	(13)	(14)	(13)	(13)
AN EXCITING LIFE (a stimulating, active life)	(16)	(15)	(13)	(17)	(12)
A SENSE OF ACCOMPLISHMENT (to make a lasting contribution)	(11)	(6)	(9)	(15)	(9)
A WORLD AT PEACE (free of war and conflict)	(7)	(9)	(10)	(5)	(7)
A WORLD OF BEAUTY (beauty of nature and the arts)	(18)	(17)	(15)	(18)	(15)
EQUALITY (brotherhood, equal opportunity for all)	(9)	(12)	(11)	(10)	(11)
FAMILY SECURITY (taking care of loved ones)	(4)	(1)	(2)	(3)	(6)
FREEDOM (independence, free choice)	(6)	(7)	(3)	(2)	(5)
HAPPINESS (contentedness)	(3)	(8)	(5)	(9)	(1)
INNER HARMONY (freedom from inner conflict)	(8)	(4)	(4)	(6)	(2)
MATURE LOVE (sexual and spiritual intimacy)	(12)	(11)	(6)	(12)	(8)
NATIONAL SECURITY (protection from attack)	(15)	(14)	(18)	(11)	(18)
PLEASURE (an enjoyable, leisurely life)	(14)	(16)	(17)	(16)	(14)
SALVATION (saved, eternal life)	(1)	(3)	(12)	(14)	(17)
SELF-RESPECT (self-esteem)	(2)	(2)	(1)	(1)	(4)
SOCIAL RECOGNITION (respect, admiration)	(17)	(18)	(16)	(7)	(16)
TRUE FRIENDSHIP (close companionship)	(5)	(10)	(8)	(8)	(3)
WISDOM (a mature understanding of life)	(10)	(5)	(7)	(4)	(10)

Note: Figures shown are the composite rank orders for the median statistic.

Table 11.2 Instrumental value medians (as composite rank orders) for cross-cultural groups of American, Costa Rican, Palestinian and Irish students and teachers

	USA (UG) N = 140	USA (G) 54	COSTA RICAN 27	PALES. (UG) 147	REP. IRE (GRAD.) 302
AMBITIOUS (hard-working, aspiring)	(6)	(10)	(17)	(2)	(12)
BROADMINDED (open-minded)	(8)	(8)	(6)	(5)	(4)
CAPABLE (competent, effective)	(11)	(7)	(5)	(14)	(10)
CHEERFUL (light-hearted, joyful)	(12)	(11)	(7)	(13)	(5)
CLEAN (neat, tidy)	(17)	(17)	(13)	(15)	(17)
COURAGEOUS (standing up for one's beliefs)	(13)	(12)	(8)	(10)	(9)
FORGIVING (willing to pardon others)	(4)	(4)	(9)	(12)	(6)
HELPFUL (work for others' welfare)	(5)	(9)	(12)	(16)	(7)
HONEST (sincere, truthful)	(1)	(1)	(1)	(4)	(1)
IMAGINATIVE (daring, creative)	(18)	(14)	(16)	(18)	(14)
INDEPENDENT (self-reliant, self-sufficient)	(9)	(5)	(15)	(6)	(8)
INTELLECTUAL (intelligent, reflective)	(14)	(6)	(10)	(1)	(15)
LOGICAL (consistent, rational)	(15)	(16)	(11)	(3)	(16)
LOVING (affectionate, tender)	(2)	(3)	(3)	(8)	(2)
OBEDIENT (dutiful, respectful)	(16)	(18)	(18)	(17)	(18)
POLITE (courteous, well-mannered)	(7)	(15)	(14)	(11)	(13)
RESPONSIBLE (dependable, reliable)	(3)	(2)	(2)	(7)	(3)
SELF-CONTROLLED (restrained, self-disciplined)	(10)	(13)	(4)	(9)	(11)

Note: Figures shown are composite rank orders for the median statistic.

The six ideologies and Cumulative Value Indexes

From the thirty-six values of the survey some six value factors (educational, caring, religious, political, social and personal) were identified after submitting all data to an intercorrelation matrix where cluster analysis derived six major factors: To understand how the six ideologies, or value orientations, compared cross-nationally, a Cumulative Value Index was created for each orientation. Median rankings were determined for each value, then the sum of the medians for values representing that particular value orientation were summed, giving us a Cumulative Value Index.

The educational ideology

For each national group the median ranking on each of the values was ascertained and then summed across the five values making up the "educational value perspective" (see Table 11.3). In the educational model it was expected that student teachers and practicing teachers would choose the "educational values" broadly indicating selected academic-cognitive traits – broadminded, imaginative, intellectual, logical, wise – near the top of their value hierarchy insofar as they represent the rational, scholarly and cognitive dimensions of the educated teacher. If the call of critical theorists for "transformative intellectuals" is to be realized then this model is on a road to nowhere. Our findings indicate that undergraduate students of education, with the sole exception of our Arab respondents, do not value very highly the monolithic-universal set of common "educational values." The instrumental value *Imaginative* comes last or near the bottom for all groups surveyed. The value *Broadminded* is ranked eighth by Americans and sixth and fifth by Costa Ricans and Palestinians. Irish graduate students ranked it highest at fourth on their list. Similarly the terminal value *Wise* received a medium rank of tenth by American and Irish respondents and seventh by Costa Ricans. American graduate students did show some preference for the

Table 11.3 The cumulative educational index

	USA (ug) N = 140	USA (g) 54	C.R. 27	PAL. 147	IRE. 302
Broadminded	(8)	(8)	(6)	(5)	(4)
Imaginative	(18)	(14)	(16)	(18)	(14)
Intellectual	(14)	(6)	(10)	(1)	(16)
Logical	(15)	(16)	(11)	(3)	(16)
Wise	(10)	(5)	(7)	(4)	(10)
Cumulative index	65	49	50	31	60

Note: Numbers in parentheses represent the median ranking for each group.

"educational values," ranking *Wise* fifth and *Intellectual* sixth. What is of most interest regarding the educational values is the split between Western teachers and the Palestinians. The Palestinians ranked the instrumental values *Intellectual* and *Logical* first and third and the terminal value *Wise* fourth overall, differing significantly from the Western teachers by placing a higher rank on each of the four educational values.

All too often the notion that teaching is a profession characterized by rationality, open-mindedness and contemplative intellectualism may be the great myth of modern education. The question is, rather, are university programs and traditional conceptions of teaching in the tradition of *Goodbye Mr. Chips* a rude fiction which has transformed the conception of teaching into a form that enables policy-makers and professors to manipulate and control students' thinking in order to reproduce the central assumptions underpinning a contemplative academic-teaching culture and educational model which is detached from the reality of school teachers?

Above all groups the Palestinian university students revered the values embodied in the educational model.

The caring ideology

Some students have defined successful teachers as displaying values of "caring" and "fairness." It is quite surprising that, despite the legal notion of the teacher as a parent substitute, concepts of care, love, nurture, helper are not made more of in the literature of teacher education, research and, of course, in day-to-day life in our schools. In the present study it is argued that the two values that correlate with this model are *Loving* and *Helpful* (see Table 11.4). Teaching is a "labor of love," argue equality-educationalists (see Lynch, 1990). Of all groups the Americans valued *Loving* and *Helpful* highest – which might have implications for the pastoral effects of teaching. In Britain and Ireland there has been considerable interest in implementing programs of "pastoral" care and guidance in schools, programs aimed at increasing the effectiveness of the "caring role" of teachers as "tutors," partic-ularly at the high school levels. The notion there is that each teacher acts as a

Table 11.4 The cumulative caring index

| | USA (ug) | USA (g) | C.R. | PAL. | IRE. |
	N = 140	54	27	147	302
Loving	(2)	(3)	(3)	(8)	(2)
Helpful	(5)	(9)	(12)	(16)	(7)
Cumulative index	7	12	15	24	9

Note: Numbers in parentheses represent the median ranking for each group.

"tutor" or mentor to a class of students who have access to her or him on a one-on-one basis should they need it. The role permits personal and vocational guidance and works not as a "band-aid" crisis management counseling program but as a fully integrated part of the school curriculum in that "pastoral care" is often timetabled as an "education for living" course. US and Irish students held the highest index for caring in teaching and learning of all groups.

The religious ideology

The religious factor is an independent variable that cannot be ignored in the value research enterprise. In previous field work I found significant differences between the values of Catholic and Protestant high school students in Northern Ireland and the relationship between races in Ulster and North America. Values may be "pre-cursive" rather than acquired as the result of the socialization process. Children grow up to vote and practice religion as their parents did. That is, values may be ascribed at birth by virtue of being born into a Protestant or Catholic or Muslim household. The chief influence upon what is learned about morals, ethics and behavior may be decided by birth into a particular religious group. It is noteworthy that the American students – almost entirely Protestants and church members – ranked the religious values *Forgiving* and *Salvation* higher than all other respondents, who were Catholics, in the main (see Table 11.5). In fact the value *Salvation* shows the greatest differences of all thirty-six values between respondents, being ranked first by the American undergraduates and third by the graduate students compared with rankings of twelfth, fourteenth and seventeenth by Costa Ricans, Palestinians and Irish teachers and graduate students in that order. *Salvation* is a value not as much emphasized in Catholic doctrine, where reading the Bible for "salvation" does not enjoy the primacy of position it does in Protestant religious groups.

In our religious model the value *Forgiving* also demonstrates large differences between Americans and other sub-groups, with fourth place for East

Table 11.5 The cumulative religious index

	USA (ug) N = 140	USA (g) 54	C.R. 27	PAL. 147	IRE. 302
Salvation	(1)	(3)	(12)	(14)	(17)
Forgiving	(4)	(4)	(9)	(12)	(6)
Cumulative index	5	7	21	26	23

Note: Numbers in parentheses represent the median ranking for each group.

Carolina University students and twelfth place for Palestinians. These religious model results might further suggest that the effects of Protestantism and its religious values are effective in the socialization of those choosing education as a career in eastern North Carolina. Sociologists and anthropologists often underestimate the effects of religion in the socialization process. Salvation is to be counted as a fundamental part of the Protestant ethic, which may, in certain circles, be alive and well in rural America and in education. This partial picture of a Christian teacher holds up when church membership and attendance are identified. In a national sample *Salvation* ranked third on average for those who attended church each week and dropped linearly to eighteenth for those who never attend church. Similarly, *Forgiving* ranked second for those attending church weekly and decreased to eleventh for non-attendees at church. As a correlative, the composite median ranking of *Salvation* came first for those who said "religion is very important" and last for those stating "religion is not at all important." The comparable result for *Forgiving* is sixth for those regarding religion as important and thirteenth for those regarding it as unimportant – these findings are consistent across socio-economic status positions. There seems to be a quite strong correlation between the "caring model" values of *Loving* and *Helpful* as these were ranked second and fifth by our American teachers. While not perhaps universal Christian educator values, these do appear to be American educator values, suggesting the import of religion on educators' values. It was expected that the religious value orientation would be a powerful priority in nations like the USA where havens were founded to escape religious persecution. The results turned out to be in conformity with this hypothesis – yet interestingly the USA does not allow religion to be a formal part of public schooling today. These data show American undergraduates and graduate students to hold the highest priority of all six value perspectives for the religious ideology.

The political ideology

Rokeach (1973) has noted that the values *Freedom* and *Equality* are the two "political" values in the survey (see Table 11.6). The Value Survey may be sensitive to differences across cultures. *A World at Peace* was ranked highest (fifth) by Palestinians. This may be self-evident from a culture where political violence and terrorism are day-to-day commonplaces. The political value *Freedom* was also ranked very high by Palestinians (second), Costa Ricans (third) and by Irish teacher education students (fifth). The other political value, *Equality*, shows little difference across groups, being ranked between ninth and twelfth for all of them. In the earlier Irish study of value differences between Catholics and Protestants in Northern Ireland, *Equality* differed significantly (P > 0.001) with Catholics ranking it sixth and Protestants eleventh. Thus, it may be the case that different social institutions

Table 11.6 The cumulative political index

	USA (ug)	USA (g)	C.R.	PAL.	IRE.
N =	140	54	27	47	302
Freedom	(6)	(7)	(3)	(2)	(5)
Equality	(9)	(12)	(11)	(10)	(11)
Peace	(7)	(9)	(10)	(5)	(7)
Cumulative index	22	28	24	17	23

Note: Numbers in parentheses represent the median ranking for each group.

(churches, schools) and cultures have a deterministic and ascriptive effect on value formation.

The effects of Christian institutions are reflected mainly in the "religious" values *Salvation* and *Forgiving*. Further, the effects of political institutions and the conditions of minority populations may be reflected in the ranking of the two distinctly "political" values of *Equality* and *Freedom*. Even though a systematic cross-cultural approach to value inquiry may be still in the future some data have emerged which illuminate the discussion. The relatively low ranking given by respondents in all samples might suggest that multicultural education and other programs emphasizing equality are not matched with the value preferences of teachers.

The social ideology

Teachers are caring agents and charged with a deep concern and responsibility for acting in the place of parents. Few would deny the social and humanistic nature of teaching. Do cross-cultural groups of teachers rank social values highly? The data illustrate some quite remarkable differences in the ranking of the three values *Cheerful*, *Happiness* and *Friendship* which collectively define the model I have called "social-humanistic" (see Table 11.7). There are quite significant differences in ranking these values between the Irish respondents and the other groups. The Irish, noted for their hospitality and sociability, came highest in ranking these values. In fact, of all thirty-six values, the ranking of *Cheerful* shows the second greatest difference between groups (after *Salvation*). *Cheerful* was ranked fifth by the Irish and thirteenth by the Palestinians. Perhaps as well as aiming at enabling children to be literate and numerate we ought to include being *sociate*. The old tune informs us that "When Irish eyes are happy all the world is bright and gay": the Irish respondents ranked *Happiness* first, while the American graduates ranked it eighth, undergraduates third; the Costa Ricans placed it fifth and the Palestinians ninth as a terminal value preference. The concept of Irish sociability or "mateship" is further supported by the Irish ranking

Table 11.7 The cumulative social-humanistic cumulative index

	N =	USA (ug) 140	USA (g) 54	C.R. 27	PAL. 147	IRE. 302
Cheerful		(12)	(11)	(7)	(13)	(5)
Friendship		(5)	(10)	(8)	(8)	(3)
Happiness		(3)	(8)	(5)	(9)	(1)
Cumulative index		20	29	20	30	9

Note: Numbers in parentheses represent the median ranking for each group.

Friendship third while the Americans ranked it fifth (undergraduates) and tenth (graduates); the Costa Ricans and Palestinians put it eighth. Finally, the Irish ranked *Cheerful* fifth while the American undergraduates placed it twelfth and graduates eleventh; the Costa Ricans ranked *Cheerful* seventh and the Palestinians ranked it thirteenth. This social factor is viewed by many in Irish life and culture as contradictory to the value placed on success and achievement – interestingly the Irish rank the value *Ambitious* lowest of all groups. The author would wholeheartedly support this finding after twenty-two years of living in Ireland both north and south of the border.

The personal ideology

All groups demonstrate the highest preference for the "personal" values (see Table 11.8). Perhaps the most striking finding of the study is that the American, Costa Rican and Irish teachers ranked *Honest* first, with the Palestinians placing it fourth on the list of instrumental values. *Responsible* was rated second by the US graduates and Costa Rican teachers and third by US undergraduates and Irish teachers. The terminal value *Self-Respect* was

Table 11.8 The cumulative personal index

	N =	USA (ug) 140	USA (g) 54	C.R. 27	PAL. 147	IRE. 302
Honest		(1)	(1)	(1)	(4)	(1)
Inner Harmony		(8)	(4)	(4)	(6)	(2)
Responsible		(3)	(2)	(2)	(7)	(3)
Self-Respect		(2)	(2)	(1)	(1)	(4)
Cumulative index		14	9	8	18	10

Note: Numbers in parentheses represent the median ranking for each group.

ranked first by the Costa Rican and Palestinian respondents; second by the Americans; and fourth by the Irish. All four groups gave a reasonably high rank (second through eighth) for the terminal value *Inner Harmony*. A picture emerges of teachers who think of themselves as sincere, spiritually grounded and responsible adults striving towards self-actualization and realization. A compelling personal development model.

Overall results

Tables 11.1 and 11.2 show the terminal and instrumental value medians and composite rankings of values for the five sub-groups. It is fascinating to note the extraordinary number of similarities in the ranking of both terminal and instrumental values across different cultures on three continents. Tables 11.3 through 11.8 show the Cumulative Value Indexes for the six value factors identified as important curriculum and personal value orientations. It is instructive to note that these six value factors closely resemble the six value ideologies discussed in Chapter 1 and identified by others as guiding curriculum beliefs.

Group 1: USA undergraduates (N = 140)

The results show that USA undergraduate *ED3200* students rank *Salvation*, *Self-Respect* and *Happiness* at the top of their end-states of existence. At the bottom, in rank order are: *An Exciting Life*, *Social Recognition* and *A World of Beauty*. These choices suggest that the Protestant ethic is alive and well. The students ranked *A World at Peace* seventh on their list, which may suggest that while important it is a value already realized in Eastern North Carolina. Among instrumental value choices the top rankings were given to *Honest*, *Loving* and *Responsible*.

Group 2: USA graduate students (N = 54)

USA postgraduate students consisted of 34 MA (education) and 20 EdD students. At the top of their terminal value list were: *Family Security*, *Self-Respect* and *Salvation*. Ranked at the bottom were: *Pleasure*, *A World of Beauty* and *Social Recognition*. *A World at Peace* was ranked ninth. Among instrumental values the highest rankings were ascribed to being *Honest*, *Responsible* and *Loving*, which was identical with USA undergraduates. These similarities bear out some continuity across time and career orientation of education students in Eastern North Carolina. One may well ask how these data compare with teacher education students overseas.

Group 3: Costa Rican educators (N = 27)

This sub-group ranked the terminal values *Self-Respect*, *Family Security* and *Freedom* highest and *Social Recognition*, *Pleasure* and *National Security* lowest. *A World at Peace* was ranked tenth. Instrumental values ranked highest were *Honest*, *Responsible* and *Loving*. The least desirable were: *Imaginative*, *Ambitious* and *Obedient*.

Group 4: Palestinians (N = 147)

Education undergraduates at Bethlehem University ranked *Self-Respect*, *Freedom* and *Family Security* highest and *Pleasure*, *An Exciting Life* and *A World of Beauty* at the bottom. *A World at Peace* was ranked fifth, indicating the priority for these students of a peaceful culture. When instrumental value system rankings are analyzed the values *Intellectual*, *Ambitious* and *Logical* come first through third, and lowest ranked values are *Helpful*, *Obedient* and *Imaginative*.

Group 5: Republic of Ireland pre-service teacher education students (N = 302)

The Irish respondents were graduates embarked upon the one-year postgraduate Higher Diploma in Education course and represented a quite different value picture. At the top of the terminal value system came: *Happiness*, *Inner Harmony*, *True Friendship* and *Self-Respect*. At the bottom were: *Social Recognition*, *Salvation* and *National Security*. The value *A World at Peace* comes seventh on their list. When instrumental rankings are examined we find that being *Honest*, *Loving* and *Responsible* were ranked highest and being *Logical*, *Clean* and *Obedient* were the least desirable choices. Some comments are in order about the sociability of Irish culture. Irish life and culture focus around the concept of the primacy of the family, love, community and friendship. It is not surprising to find the Irish ranking *Happiness* and *True Friendship* at the top of their terminal value structure.

Taking the findings as a whole, education students and teachers show remarkable similarity in the structure of their terminal value systems: Overall, the value *Self-Respect* appears in the top three choices across all five groups of educators. *Salvation* is ranked by both American groups highly and *Family Security* is ranked at the top by three groups: USA graduates, Palestinians and Costa Ricans. It may well be that teaching attracts individuals with a deep sense of self-respect and concern for family life. For the purposes of this analysis, it was believed that a cross-cultural value inventory would provide social indicators of the quality of life and value preferences that would ultimately be of value in curriculum development for intergroup harmony. Table 11.1 shows the terminal value medians and composite rankings for the student survey. For all students, at the top come *A World at Peace*, *Freedom* and *Happiness*. At the bottom of the terminal list come *National Security*, *Social Recognition* and *Salvation*. This suggests that peace in the world is a leading value in the provision of freedom and happiness.

These value analyses provide interesting "mirrors for behavior" but they may be more like funhouse mirrors which distort useful data for curriculum development work. The remainder of this chapter is devoted to exploring the values of students and teachers, and the implications for educational programs.

Values and teaching

What values ought the teacher and curriculum foster? It is reasonable to think that as a result of our teaching undergraduates would be more rational, reflective, autonomous, open-minded and sharing a critical responsibility. Our efforts at multicultural education aim undoubtedly at cultivating modes of sensitivity, tolerance and mutual understanding. Yet their effects are unknown to us yet. I have argued elsewhere (McKernan, 1996) against a "division of labor" in teaching and research and it follows that if we are after reflective students and practitioners then the values inherent in the research process ought to be prioritized. I think here of the concern for evidence; the passion for inquiry, curiosity and truth. The philosopher John Dewey spent the great part of his life promoting a reflective process of inquiry which could be applied to both fact and value problems. Such a process constitutes elements of problem posing, hypothesis formulation, action and experimentation, consideration of effects and conclusions; in effect the adoption of the inductive process (Dewey, 1938).

I wish to suggest that educators' values may function, then, as quality indicators revealing ideological models, be they "religious," "political," "educational," "caring" and so on. I wish to further argue that what we ought to aim at is a model that constitutes *educational values* – that seek our educational aims. These would not be instrumental values like "efficiency" or "effectiveness" but conceptualizations of qualities or values that the educational process seeks to foster, for example reflectiveness, critical capabilities, tolerance, understanding, multicultural sensitivity and, above all, imagination for realizing potential. These educative values thus become our principles of procedure – they are not outcomes or products in the sense of objectives because they are realized in and through the process and practice of education. They are thus *enabling conditions*. Construed in this manner we cannot predict the outcomes of these educational values. What teachers have within their power, and I count myself in these ranks, is the extent to which they can establish these conditions and processes in classrooms and the extent to which they are educational – not the outcomes of these processes.

R.S. Peters (1966) claimed that when we talk about aims we are talking about "qualities of mind," and he argued that these are analyzed not into outcomes which are extrinsic to processes but as *principles of procedure* providing criteria for what is to count as *an educational process*. Stenhouse (1975) translated Peters' philosophy into curriculum and it was from within these experiments that the "teacher-researcher" movement was reborn in Britain in the 1970s. These are very different values than those governing the "production-consumption" model of education and the diet of the technical rationalists and neo-essentialists. One area of value concern for the present author lies in the encroachment of technical rationality and curriculum design through outcomes and behavioral objectives. This engineering model of education is akin to testing a curriculum as a product against some specification or blueprint it is designed to meet. Beware of publishers and curriculum developers who come bearing "solutions" rather than as persons who wish to "explore problems."

An understanding of the concept of *education* may not solve our problem but it may provide analytical lenses for critical reflection and action. Education has a great deal to do with the concepts of personal inquiry and the relationship between tutor and student is characterized by the twin concepts of "care" and "love"; concepts which are little written about by educationists. Thus, it is argued that education is philosophically about developments of the student which are achieved through learning and through the cultivation of the rational mind. This is not to say that education has only to do with intellectual development; it also has to do with aesthetic, physical, social, emotional, moral and vocational development. What is indicated is that all of these involve elements of knowledge and cognitive development, rational understanding and powers of reason. It is assumed nowadays by many students, parents and others that the primary purpose of education is to contribute to one's vocational and economic life. While this essentially narrow and *instrumental* or *utilitarian* purpose is indeed an argument made by some, it is not the only reason, nor in any view the major reason, for education; yet the *social market* advocates go further and stipulate that accountability is required because public funds are being expended on "investment spending."

There is a more fundamental purpose of education – that of developing the individual as a person. This is correlative with the teachers' preferences in these surveys. The personal is highly prized. This leads to the conviction that education must not be seen as merely an investment in the economy but also as a service to be judged by the contribution it makes to the well-being of the individual. This means simply that education is, in itself, a good thing. Education is intrinsically worthwhile and justifiable. Proponents of the *social market perspective* would argue that education is justifiable for its extrinsic utility – because it leads to jobs and economic wealth – the instrumentalist position. However, part of our problem is that there are alternative conceptions of education as well as wrong ones.

To set the curriculum by objectives to be achieved conforms to some instrumentalist justification – because it leads to something – it is akin to taking a means to an end. In a sense, to have objectives is to set limits to human speculation and development. But an experience may be educational because of its intrinsic value – it can be justified simply because it is desirable and enjoyable for its own sake, as in the case of reading poetry or painting landscapes.

In my view, several conditions, or criteria, are necessary for something to count as education. Something counts as *education* because it involves knowledge and understanding and has its own in-built standards of excellence immanent in it; rather than because it leads to an objective. Something can be picked out as educational also because it is desirable and permeates one's way of looking at things. A skilled and trained ballet dancer or mechanic is not necessarily educated because of their skill and performance abilities alone. Yet certain forms of knowledge, for example philosophy, mathematics and history, are educational because they are justifiable in terms of their own standards and worth. They have an organized structure and body of knowledge; they have key principles and concepts that give the particular discipline structure; they have respected methods of adding new knowledge to the subject; and finally, some have tests of proof, such as mathematics.

The content for curriculum ought to be selected not because it leads to some operationalized objective but rather because this content and its implementation serve as principles of procedure for realizing our values. Our everyday talk about the goals of education does not assume that we are speaking of the extrinsic outcomes of an educational process. But rather, and here is my main assertion in this book, we are speaking about values which constitute a process which is educational. Our values are realized *in* rather than as a result *of* education. I have witnessed this practical rationality in the work of many innovatory teachers. We need to articulate the specification of an educational process. How can we predict in advance of teaching what the outcomes of a truly educative encounter will be? In our procedural model education will be successful to the extent that the outcomes of curriculum for a student are unpredictable.

Curriculum and teaching ought to promote inquiry as the mode of improvement. Such a stance is opposed to an outcomes-based education style of design. I am concerned with education as a process – not as product. This means that we design our aims so that they will be realized through the implementation of certain "principles of procedure." It is today quite radical to adopt an anti-objectives approach. But I believe I am right to do so.

The issue for me and my colleagues was: could we design a curriculum and pedagogy satisfactorily other than through a strict objectives model cast in an ends-means scenario? We believed we could, and we did. This is what I have called a "process-inquiry model" as opposed to the "objectives model" of curriculum design. We were essentially aiming at getting students to understand controversial value issues through a broadly based set of teaching strategies and inquiry-based learning through group discussion. Thus, central to the heart of this thesis is to design a method of handling value issues which would protect students from teacher bias and moralizing, while advancing the student's understanding. This entailed the development of two roles for project teachers: values clarification and "procedural neutrality." Both, it must be pointed out, are value-laden and committed stances.

Results in perspective

In conclusion, the human values and ideologies study shows teachers to be *Honest*, *Loving* and *Responsible* people who seek *Family Security* and *Self-Respect* as means and ends respectively. These denote a new *Personal*, *Care-giving* and *Social-Humanistic* model of teaching based upon the realization of personal qualities such as sincerity and truthfulness in teachers who are at once reliable and dependable in the discharge of their duties. The "Religious factor" in the Protestant work ethic is highly valued by the American respondents, suggesting that the religious motive in capitalism may not have diminished but rather has flourished in this region of the nation, with religious beliefs and orthodoxy having a significant effect on behavior in schools.

The implications for teaching are profound. On my view, teachers should beware of moralizing on value issues and the controversial issues exhumed in the classroom. Helping students clarify their own values would be more beneficial for aiding self-realization. I have attempted to begin to outline a stance which would have *an educational process* as a priority and not educational objectives – and teachers working within this stance would seek to employ values as *principles for procedure* within their subject field. Thus, procedural values become the aim in a curious twist of rational planning. Teachers are invited to develop their classroom stance in light of valued educational procedures and to collect evidence about their performance, indicating a distinct teacher-researcher mandate leading to and extending the professional role. In short, along with Richard Peters we are committed to helping our students adopt rational procedures for arriving at substantive values.

Some research questions remain. Do the various values in the survey have the same meaning for respondents in different cultures? For example, communal groups may interpret the values in very different ways. Finally, some omissions may be evident. It seems to me that values like *Inquiry*, *Tolerance*, *Empathy* and *Rationality*, to name but a few, are questionably absent from the survey instrument. Nevertheless, it seems to me that many universal values are contained in the instrument and these data provide a start for cross-cultural teacher value research.

Part IV

Curriculum and evaluation

The critical domain

Chapter 12

The countenance of evaluation and the special place of action research

> Curriculum research must be concerned with the painstaking examination of possibilities and problems. Evaluation should, as it were, lead development and be integrated with it. Then the conceptual distinction between development and evaluation is destroyed and the two merge as research. Curriculum research must itself be illuminative rather than recommendatory as in the earlier tradition of curriculum development.
>
> Lawrence Stenhouse (1975: 122)

This final chapter is of singular significance. In it I shall endeavor to outline the face and purposes of evaluative judgment in curriculum and the unique professional role educational action research can contribute with the teacher, or professor, acting as a researcher. Thus, the chapter shall attempt to show how various strands of evaluation practice together with action research may help with the improvement of practice and to judge the effects of educational interventions. The onus is upon evaluation of the curriculum as a "proposal," or hypothetical idea, being implemented. This is the research inquiry aspect that accompanies the process model described in Part 2. We must try to detach ourselves from the constrictions of the product-outcomes model of curriculum. Underpinning this remit of the teacher as action researcher is a belief that practice is best improved by educators working on problems they have identified themselves. Action research is a type of self-evaluation done by practitioners on the problems they experience. Actions are taken to solve problems and inquiry is mounted to monitor the process of change.

Most of what has developed as evaluation theory has come from attempts to judge experimental and innovative practices in courses of study – for example curriculum materials production, student knowledge and behavior or teaching styles – in the field. These are mainly attempts to understand if the development was implementable and worthwhile. Assessment of students is only one narrow strand of this enterprise, which has branched out to include qualitative evaluations, teacher self-evaluation, school and curriculum review, curriculum research, action inquiry and, more recently, attempts to develop appraisal of teacher work. This has come about in the attempt to shift the focus of accountability from that of curriculum reform to teacher reform.

In North America, Europe and many other parts of the world, education systems are most definitely at risk from the lock-step linear ends-means model of curriculum and assessment. It is at risk from an enemy within its own ranks; that enemy is a dogmatic aspiration to enshrine program-building and evaluation around a limited objectives model and its concomitant assessment technology. The value and quality of an educational system can be judged by an examination of three critical features: first its system of teaching and teacher education; second its system of assessment and evaluation; and finally with regard to its curriculum. Most teachers revere the "marking (objectives) model" instead of the "critical judgment (educational process) model." The main problem with the objectives model is that it measures and makes assessment without going deeply into explanation or that discourse which will enhance our understanding of the curriculum in operation. This is what I mean by calling it a "marking model." Outside of assigning a number value to each student's performance we cannot learn very much from this style of evaluation. We might not want to throw it out altogether but simply engage other styles of evaluation that will give us thick description, practical reasoning and situational understanding. For this task, we require special criteria by which to evaluate the curriculum. I believe we can only advance knowledge *of* curriculum and evaluation by looking at the issues and problems thrown up *by* the curriculum – instead, evaluators seem to go for "solutions," and by doing so they avoid these perennial problems and issues.

It is the task of all with an educational responsibility – whether in schools or in the university, and of teacher education programs – to commit to the aim that education is not about passive acceptance of instruction as a "rhetoric of conclusions," as Stenhouse (1983) so aptly put it. We must avoid such a goal. Knowledge has been won through research and inquiry and it cannot be divorced from the process which gave it warrant. Thus research is part and parcel of the stance any educator must take.

Training and education of teachers is always an uncertain "growth point" simply because our aim is more growth, not contentment with some minimal mastery or finality. These growth points are thus provisional ground and it is the task of a College of Education to keep this potential always open. Construed this way, education is an art, a social practice, that requires reflective engagement of the curriculum, its purposes and effects; in short, the exercise of the reflective art of judgment, in pursuit of improvement. Evaluation is the art of judging the worth, or value, of educational activities, including pupils, personnel, materials, programs, teachers and even entire systems using quantitative and/or qualitative data. Its methodology is varied to suit the purposes of the judgment exercise. It is not something of a mastered task. This seems to me to suggest that "evaluation" has at least six purposes:

1   curriculum program evaluation;
2   curriculum research;
3   teacher appraisal;
4   teacher self-evaluation;
5   student assessment;
6   action research as evaluation.

The nature of evaluation as professional judgment

The concept of evaluation is often narrowly construed and widely misunderstood. Most think of it as a "marker mentality" when in fact it is more akin to "judgment." Most traditional accounts of evaluation have tried to ape the fourth stage of the Tyler Model (1949) of the evaluation of ends, usually meaning "Have the students reached the desired specified behavioral (performance) objectives?" This often rests upon an assumption that tests of student achievement are the best tool for evaluation. I will refer to student outcomes under "assessment," which I believe to be quite a different type of judgment act than what policy-makers or the public see as education being publicly accountable, or rather "accountability" and value for money and for resources. Issues in curriculum development are not merely theoretical and practical but also highly social and political.

Who will have power to authorize change? How are faculty, students, administrators and others to be involved in curriculum change? Evaluation is the making of judgments based upon evidence gathered so as to assign "value" or lack of it to a person, program, curriculum or system. Evaluation may be quantitative or qualitative.

Another type of judgment is concerned with whether educational programs and curricula are worthwhile as innovatory practices – here the goal is to judge curriculum in action as a programmatic concern. Does the new IT keyboarding module justify its startup costs? This is the purpose of curriculum program evaluation, or course improvement – does it "pan out"? Does the IT module do what it is intended to accomplish? Are the unit materials relevant, appropriate to the key concepts? Much of the best work in improving education lies in this domain. There is also teacher self-evaluation, a highly valuable searching of one's own performance. Finally, there are the judgments made by others of teacher performance, for example peer review, or what is referred to as "appraisal." For instance, those checklists that are used with pre- and in-service educators to appraise their performance.

Then there is the educational and curriculum research that is done in the main by external researchers focused upon the curriculum, to understand the effects of teaching, learning and curriculum development. Imagine, for example, a feminist sociologist who might examine the curriculum choices of girls and boys in an analysis of hypotheses conceived in terms of career or college choices based on her theory of gender-socialization bias. Or, a reading specialist's examination and research of a curriculum in terms of its efficiency level in matching the correct reading level with chronological age and place in class. Internal teacher action research may focus on ways in which gender equality can be improved within the classroom structure – say by monitoring closely to ensure that the questions put to boys and girls have an equal proportionality.

It seems that evaluation, assessment, appraisal, research and accountability have all become seriously blurred, misunderstood and, sadly, misused by students and practitioners of education. Initial and in-service educators and policy-makers need to sort these various reflectic arts of judgment and make determinations about which serve different audiences correctly. It is no simple matter – but many of the curriculum problems today exist because such a work ethic has not existed.

During the 1960s there was a concern for evaluation of new innovatory programs: course development in mathematics, biological science, humanities and so on. This idea of program evaluation in curriculum development moved quite quickly to accountability and student assessment. Indeed, high stakes tests and measurement seem to be the sole concern under recent state and federal education initiatives. Funding is politically linked to progress – in say mathematics and reading improvement – as evidenced in student test scores. This narrow view of assessment as evaluation needs re-addressing by responsible educators and policy-makers.

After the mid-twentieth century, evaluation theory developed rapidly, mainly in response to the many curriculum development projects. Evaluation theory in curriculum needs to take account, separately, of each of these functions. Too often the results of student achievement tests are used to decide entirely the fate of curriculum and teacher performance, and the data are used to make decisions inappropriately. Stenhouse argued (1975: 122) that "Evaluation should lead development and be integrated with it. Then the distinction between development and evaluation is destroyed and the two merge as 'research'."

The political nature of evaluation

Too often decisions are political, rather than in the best interest of what is valuable in educational terms. It is crucial that appropriate persons are charged with doing evaluation. Barry MacDonald, the UK-based Humanities Curriculum Project evaluator, devised a model of evaluation that is described as being "democratic" (Hamilton, 1976). It is somewhat surprising to read of "empowerment evaluation" (Fetterman, 2001) today as a "new" form when in fact it resembles closely MacDonald's "democratic evaluation" model by allowing all the users of a program a "voice" in the evaluation. Essentially, MacDonald saw evaluation as an extremely political act and argued that there are three types of evaluation: Bureaucratic, Autocratic and Democratic.

Bureaucratic Evaluation is provided as a service to central government agents. It is not independent – control rests with the values of the bureaucrats who control resources. The evaluators start out by accepting the values of the bureaucrats and try to help them with their mission. It is understood that evaluation will offer data that will help bureaucrats forward their mission or policy.

Autocratic Evaluation is a conditioned, quasi-independent in nature, form of evaluation service to government agents or central authority which offers "external validation" of central policy or policies in exchange for compliance with its recommendations. The evaluator retains ownership of the data – thus not allowing clients to change or influence the evaluation recommendations once made by the evaluator. The evaluator is often one who seeks refuge in the principles of research, and the research community, objectivity and the positivist traditions of science. The evaluator is sole expert and "judge."

In MacDonald's model of Democratic Evaluation, ownership is held by all the stakeholders in the program being evaluated. Thus, it would seem that all the criticism today about the Empowerment Evaluation Model (Fetterman, 2001) may well be deserved. On the democratic model evaluation is a service to the educational community and stakeholders. It understands that a variety of issues and values are embedded and seeks to appraise these democratically by allowing all participants ownership and right of appeal. The evaluator is an honest broker who allows access to data to all. Moreover, there is an attempt to make the evaluation readable and accessible by all – not just an educated elite. MacDonald argued that the chief characteristics are: confidentiality, negotiation and access.

Fetterman and his colleagues (Fetterman, 2001; Fetterman *et al.*, 1996) have promoted "empowerment evaluation," arguing that it is democratic and that it comprises three parts: first, a description of the program's "mission" statement; second, a "taking stock" in which the values and ideology of what is being aimed at are explored by all those with a stake in the project; third, "planning for the future," in which strategies are worked out to allow the innovatory program to move forward. Fetterman also uses evaluation as a problem-informing and -solving exercise akin to the character of action research:

> Perhaps what distinguishes the discourse on empowerment most clearly is its acknowledgement and deep respect for people's capacity to create knowledge about, and solutions to, their own experiences.
>
> (2001: 147)

I would argue that a climate of distrust and loss of confidence in schools and teachers has been deliberately created over the past few decades; mainly by legislators and policy-makers, who want teachers and schools to prove they are competent. The irony is that the accountability movement pushes educators for results but does little to allow them to take responsibility for the creation of their curricula. Often the only data collected are test scores and that, at times, records trivial learning because the technology of the testing industry is available. Quite often these data are used wrongly to lay blame at the feet of programs, teachers and of late, the work of teacher education institutions.

1. Curriculum program evaluation

Evaluation is the assignation of "worth" or value to a program, activity, course, and set of experimental materials, students, teachers or school systems. It is the rendering of a judgment as its outcome which is the best evidence for future action, or possibly non-action, about the subject of inquiry. Evaluation is a value judgment and has several purposes: making decisions about individual students (what I would refer to as assessment) and teachers; making decisions about educational programs; and finally, making decisions about systems, administrators and regulations. Using evaluation for student assessment and course improvement is a more useful type in improving education than the remaining two types above. Stufflebeam (1971) posited that evaluation counted as the gathering of information upon which to make decisions of the worth of educational programs, persons and systems.

Evaluation then is open to a wide variety of empirical tests, where appropriate, as well as qualitative styles of judgment. It is clearly concerned with the making of value judgments about some aspect of educational activity, be it students, teachers or school/curriculum projects. MacDonald argued for "democratic evaluation" this way:

> Evaluation is the process of conceiving, obtaining and communicating information for the guidance of educational decision making with regard to a specified program.
>
> (1973: 1–2, cited in Stenhouse, 1975: 112)

The activities of evaluation traditionally enjoined scientific and psychometric approaches to measurement of change that was dominant in educational research. Yet the shifts and complexities of curriculum projects were not easily measured using such instrumentation. This traditional type of evaluation was hopelessly inadequate in capturing any essence of these project complexities. At base, evaluation is ultimately about the art of making judgments based on data. These judgments may not necessarily be based on quantitative or empirically derived data such as numbers. Indeed, there was for a time a flourishing development in the 1970s through 80s of curriculum program evaluation characterized by models such as "Democratic Evaluation" (MacDonald, 1975), "Illuminative Evaluation" (Parlett and Hamilton, 1972), "Goal Free Evaluation" (Scriven, 1967), "Connoisseurship" (Eisner, 2002), "Responsive Evaluation" (Stake, 1967) and "Empowerment Evaluation" (Fetterman, 2001). Much of this innovatory design was qualitative rather than quantitative/scientific in style. Evaluation became more readable and humanistic. Ethnographic accounts describing the culture of institutions allowed teachers and others to "see" and understand more fully the educational values being implemented. It was living proof that improvement was possible through alternative ways of studying innovations in education.

Before the current period of retrenchment there was a halcyon era of curricular experimentation across Western nations that yielded great developments in evaluation theory, curriculum research, organization, theory and teacher development. Sadly, experimental curriculum development and evaluation styles have given way to greater federal and state controls in determining what the aims, content and assessment of curriculum shall be. Teachers have been cast in the role of functionaries in large bureaucracies. Local schools are dis-empowered from innovation. This fact does not mean that educators have to give up their aspirations for true education. The task now is to convince legislators and policy-makers that the false industrial values mandated in the name of quality are as empty now as they were during the period of "Efficiency in Education" of Franklin Bobbitt, Frederick Taylor and the scientific managerialism they advocated. Americans have always had a love affair with the possibility of science. Thorndike and others revered a science of education that would make teaching and learning a "technology of practice" in the words of Elliot Eisner (2002).

The now largely discredited theory of Behaviorism also played a large part in gaining steerage of curriculum and assessment; breaking down learning into micro-tasks in a system of inputs and outputs where learning was seen as "behavior change" and prescribed in the form of "intended learning outcomes" (ILO) which in curriculum took the shape of behavioral objectives. The test was the thing that would prove progress. This belief still holds a premium bunting in every state education policy in the USA.

The history of American and British curriculum shows how the Behaviorists, since the turn of the twentieth century, have shaped curriculum and evaluation. Franklin Bobbitt, an engineer and a professor of administration at the University of Chicago, described his theory as:

> The central theory (of curriculum) is simple. Human life, however varied, consists in the performance of specific activities. Education that prepares for life is one that prepares definitely and adequately for those specific activities. However numerous and diverse they may be for any

social class they can be discovered. This requires only that one go out into the world of affairs and discover the particulars of which these affairs consist. These will show the abilities, attitudes, habits, appreciations and forms of knowledge that men need. These will be the objectives of the curriculum. They will be numerous, definite and particularized. The curriculum will then be that set of experiences which children and youth must have by way of attaining these objectives.

(Bobbit, 1918: 14)

One must also bear in mind that research and evaluation differ between nation states. In the USA teachers and schools are not the agents who make evaluation decisions. These decisions are made by supervisors in State Departments of Education, who have the administrative leadership power to control schooling. In centralized systems such as Ireland, France and Sweden, decisions are made by government officials for the entire school system.

Since the objectives model originated in the USA, and has a long and dominant history there, the emphasis has always been on using objectives in curriculum because they are the targets of all evaluation work. This is, I further believe, part of the curious romance educationalists have had with science and technology. To wit, we shall only know if a curriculum works if the objectives are met. I have argued in this book that there are alternatives to the ends-means model of justifying curriculum through the meeting of objectives. We must ask "Who is the most important audience for evaluation?" I argue it is teachers. Teachers will ask "Will I, or my students, gain benefit from this curriculum?" In the USA curricula are advanced as "directives" for teachers to implement, with the key question being "Will it work?" This is quite different to the concerns posed by teachers, who are more concerned that an innovative curriculum offer something worthwhile for students. Further, what is regarded as worthwhile will vary among schools and students. Therefore, a model based on objectives asks for a Fail/ Pass result when what is required is a full and thick description of understanding the complexities of a curriculum in practice across different schools. Stenhouse suggested:

It can be argued that conventional objectives-type evaluations do not address themselves to understanding the educational process. They deal in terms of success or failure. But a programme is always a mixture of both and a mixture which varies from setting to setting.

(Stenhouse, 1975: 109)

The problem, it seems to me, is that instead of asking teachers to be investigators of the problems thrown up by curriculum, the state has conceived curriculum development to be seen as the offering of solutions from outside the school. Evaluation is set up politically as an external activity, not an internal professional mandate. In fact, of all the audiences most directly affected by curriculum, pupils, parents, community and teachers often have the least power to make decisions. This is so because the state does not see the school or its workers as being able to make decisions about the curriculum. If the state did see teachers as researchers and developers they would allow schools to engage in curriculum research and development work and a whole school review and plan for growth would be possible. In a nutshell, the strategy adopted in the USA works against teachers as researchers and professional development agents.

2. Curriculum research

Research is systematic inquiry made public. Good evaluations require evidence to help judgment and research provides excellent evidence that can feed evaluation. When used with the curriculum it is normally carried on by external professional researchers in institutes and universities as well as by teachers in schools. This book advances the idea that the current "division of labor" between researchers and teachers is unhealthy and counterproductive. It supports the idea that research belongs to the teacher and that the teacher should work as an action researcher to solve problems where she or he can. Thus teachers making appraisals of their own work becomes the basis for professional development. Indeed, John Dewey held this view (1929), writing a chapter titled "The Teacher as Investigator" in his classic *The Sources of a Science of Education*. Dewey remarked that the results that would come from this "un-worked mine" of teachers as investigators would be truly worthwhile. This is a view of research as a "reflectic art." The teacher's work is in the transaction of knowledge, skills and values. The social practice of education engages the teacher in a scene in which these transactions are negotiated and improved. It provides a framework that makes possible the development of the art of teaching. Stenhouse argued that the "really important thing about curriculum research is that, in contrast to books about education, it invites the teacher to improve his art by the exercise of his art" (1983: 157). One learns through critical practice. Art is improved by doing sketches – there cannot be complete mastery, only higher aspirations. This will mean that the development of curriculum, teaching or whatever is a dialectic between ideas, and testing ideas in action in classrooms.

Stenhouse (1981) defined research as "systematic self-critical enquiry made public" and he goes on to suggest that research is not confined to empirical tests alone – their use is encouraged where appropriate. Stenhouse was of the belief that research should be conducted by teachers. I call this teacher-as-researcher style of inquiry and curriculum development action inquiry or research. Research-based teaching is casting the educator in the role of speculator – or inquiry agent – rather than the role of purveyor of instruction and facts or teacher as authority, which I believe is the role that teacher education programs hold in mind today. This is a very grave error. The idea of research-based teaching is not even widely practiced in universities, let alone schools. But excellent research-based teaching is not like mastery of, say, driving a steam shovel; it is always an uncertainty, a high ambition. It is more an art that must be constantly developed. To teach a rhetoric of conclusions as research results would be to lower our sights – yet that seems to be the practice that is sought.

In earlier work on how to conduct action research (McKernan, 1991, 1996), I attempted to set out methods and techniques for conducting curriculum action research as there was not a comprehensive manual on the methodology of action inquiry at that time. We must remember that the curriculum and research into curriculum is the medium by which teachers will improve their art, and the curriculum is also the medium by which the student learns. In doing this research the educator relies upon his or her research-based knowledge and not the authority of others. "Research" is a word that has connotations of the "expert" for teachers, and therefore, perhaps, a more user-friendly concept is "inquiry." That is, more teachers will understand and warm to inquiry in action, or "action inquiry," as a function of their work, as opposed to "action research." We should also respect that there is another side to this: that of "action learning" (Revans, 1982), where the knowledge that improves practice is learned and stored as practical wisdom.

3. Teacher appraisal

Teacher appraisal and peer review of professors is *a la mode* in schools and colleges nowadays. It would seem to contain two aspects: "evaluative" (to make decisions on merit pay, promotion and even termination); and "developmental" (to aid in career growth, teaching competence, in-service planning and learning and so on). It is also an international phenomenon, being established as a Statutory Regulation in England in 2000 to be administered by the Board of Governors for each school in England.

In Canada, the provinces are making teacher appraisal the law. The *Quality in the Classroom Act, 2001* and the Ontario Teacher Testing Program were two of the government's commitments in the blueprint. The comprehensive program was first announced in May, 2000. The Ontario Teacher Testing Program will ensure that both new and experienced teachers have the up-to-date training, knowledge and skills to help students succeed and achieve. The *Quality in the Classroom Act, 2001* put in place two more components of the government's teacher testing program.

The highlights in the Ontario Teacher Testing Program include:

- a qualifying test for new teachers in Ontario;
- a comprehensive performance appraisal system;
- a mandatory professional development requirement;

- a language proficiency test for teachers coming to Ontario who received their training in a language other than English or French;
- an induction program for new teachers; and
- a teacher excellence recognition system.

This system does allow for students and parents to provide feedback to teachers. Teachers are evaluated twice in their first two years and then twice a year in three year cycles by the school vice-principal or principal. Inputs from parents and students are just one component of these performance appraisals, which will also include:

- the teacher's level of commitment to the pupils;
- the teacher's knowledge of the curriculum, and other factors.

The appraisals are planned every three years for experienced teachers and twice in each of the first two years for new teachers or those moving to another school board. The Ontario Teacher Testing Program is based on programs in other jurisdictions. The government argues that it is similar to the requirements for other professions, such as doctors, lawyers, nurses, architects and occupational therapists. It follows on from recommendations from Ontario's education partners and recommendations from the 1995 Royal Commission on Learning.

Some, of course, are rooted in notions of teacher professional development, but more often than not appraisal schemes are implemented through "performance indicators" as a form of accountability, data on which to base, say, merit pay decisions, tenure appointments, indeed even for getting rid of professors who do not seem to be working effectively in terms of the schemes and rubrics drawn up. Tenure has for all intents and purposes been abolished under peer review, which can have political effects when carried out by administrators and colleagues with personality and professional differences. Indeed, even the standard form for measuring "teacher effectiveness" used in North Carolina public schools has not been developed by master teachers, but rather by academic psychologists. It says nothing about the subject content *per se*, only what type of activity was being engaged, for example questioning or lecturing, and thus is not penetrable. These schemes of appraisal have been implemented under the guise of "Teacher Quality" in an instrumental system hell-bent on playing a numbers game.

These "performance indicators" did not come from the teaching profession, but rather from external agents with an agenda. The justification is that these are reliable data on the quality of teaching. Perceptions of teacher effectiveness held by teachers differ markedly from those of state and LEA officers implementing teacher performance indicators. What the politicians and policy-makers have in mind is a social market ideology in which education is seen as a product that must be controlled. Elliott has written coherently about the assault of this social market mentality as a device implemented by Conservative market forces (1993: 51–64).

4. Teacher self-evaluation

Perhaps the most significant characteristic of the professional educator is the willingness to subject oneself to a searching self-evaluation for the sake of self-improvement. One could not be a reflective practitioner without study of one's practice. One criticism of self-evaluation is that it may indeed lack objectivity (Kelly, 1989: 204). Yet these difficulties may be helped through the use of peer-review where colleagues, familiar with the teacher's agenda and work, can conduct an evaluative study of him or her.

In the public universities of North Carolina all faculty (even those with tenure) must undergo a peer review at least every five years to continue to hold their position. Normally this means taking stock of the annual report for each faculty member's ratings on teaching, service and research work based on a five-point scale with minimal effectiveness being set at 2.0.

Action research is useful for the purpose of self-evaluation of faculty, or schools, and is increasing in school districts where professional development is valued.

5. Student assessment

To assess is to measure and quantify. For example, if I request an assessment of my house I am given a quantitative figure, of say $200,000 in value. I prefer to think of assessment as a measurement or judgment based upon numbers. This helps me understand that this type of judgment is quite distinct from statements of value such as "That is a good history module." Assessment data on their own are not enough to render a true judgment of a curriculum. This is why multiple forms of evaluation can add validity and reliability to evaluation work.

A great deal of what is understood to count as evaluation is set within the parameters of the "objectives model" of curriculum evaluation. That is, has the student performed a behavior which is evidence for understanding that the stated intended learning outcome has been achieved? Testing of knowledge dominates on this view of judgment as assessing the attainments of students. A great many of the outcomes here have to do with modification of learning so that the desired behavior is performed by students. This leads oftentimes to teachers' complaints that state tests determine the type of curriculum experiences students have – teachers will "teach to the test" to get results. This is just the sort of thing that is happening in the USA due to the political pressures of the No Child Left Behind (NCLB) Act of 2001. Also, those objectives which can easily be mastered and taught will tend to monopolize the curriculum. Assessment, like other forms of judgment, is no easy task. Stenhouse made the telling remark that the simple assessment of the attainment of objectives is concerned only with the success or failure of the programme; it is not concerned with an *understanding* of it. It assesses without explaining (Stenhouse, 1975: 95). Indeed, Chapter 4 has argued for the limitations of objectives, not least in distorting the proper structure and epistemology of the subject being studied. My position on assessment is that with training this is satisfactory, but when it comes to induction into the forms of knowledge as an education, then pre-specification of ends is a profound distortion. Most professors and teachers follow some form of "summative evaluation" where students are tested for grades at the end of a course. Professor Denis Lawton, of the University of London, once remarked that this was like "doing military intelligence when the war is over." His point was obvious; leaving evaluation as summative will not help the student, who has now terminated his or her studies. Evaluation should improve a student, not set out to "prove" what she or he has learned.

6. Action research and evaluation

Action research is inquiry conducted by a practitioner to improve the quality of that practice in a social setting through the researching of action, by the practitioner, in a reflective manner. One technique for reflecting upon the action is a modification of the concept of triangulation (Denzin, 1970), which the author calls quadrangulation. It seeks to use various actors, data, research methods and theories to gain insight into the problem at hand (McKernan, 1996).

The Ford Teaching Project in the United Kingdom asked teachers to gain a more comprehensive perspective over theory, actors and research methods by correlational and collaborative "triangulation" of the data actors and methods. The author has demonstrated the use of triangulation in attempts to teach the methodology of action research (McKernan, 1996). However, this method of triangulation can be further strengthened by adding another full dimension to the research technique: Quadrangulation is not only a powerful research method but it is a compelling evaluation strategy for curriculum hypotheses being tested in action.

Trow (1957) suggested that social researchers ought to abandon the arguments of favoring one method over another. The sides, or planes, of quadrangulation are:

1   theory/concepts: seeing a curriculum conceptually;
2   actors and participants: often there will be multiple actors, students, teachers, researchers and so on – their perspectives can be viewed individually and contrasted against other actors;
3   data and evidence: qualitative and quantitative data can be compared;
4   methodological: triangulating various methods such as field notes with

video footage or combining questionnaire data with structured interview accounts.

The more rigorous the data and perspectives the more powerful the validity
of results. Consider the case of the teacher using classroom discussion when
she or he adopts a "neutral chair" role. The teacher allows an external
researcher to film the classroom action. This collaboration of teacher and
researcher represents the first plane or side of the quadrangle. The second
side involves students looking at a video clip of the discussion along with
their teacher. This account is then, third, discussed by the teacher and
researcher alone, and finally the video is seen by other teachers in the school
involved in the curriculum project. Various theories of practical action and
methods such as interviews may be used with the students and teachers to
throw up new perspectives and hypotheses about how to improve discussion
as a strategy for understanding. It needs to be pointed out that "quadrangulation" is not just using four sets of actors – but rather multiple methods,
actors, data and concepts/theories all brought to bear upon the study of the
research problem. In this way one can exhume a better "grounded theory" to
explain what is going on in the setting being researched.

Action research seeks to change and improve a problematic situation
through the testing of alternative forms of human action on a problem and
the monitoring of the effects through research. Once data have been gathered the critical result of action research is making a judgment of choice on
what to do next. Thus action inquiry provides for judging value choices and
making evaluations of action.

The research techniques fall into several types:

1   *Narrative and Observation Techniques* such as participant and non-partici-
    pant observation, anecdotal records, case study, diary/journals, video and
    photographic records, checklists, rating scales and field notes;
2   *Survey and Self Report Techniques* including attitude scales, questionnaires,
    interviews and life histories;
3   *Pedagogical Techniques* such as brainstorming, neutral chairperson in
    discussion, action inquiry seminars and so on;
4   *Critical Techniques* such as quadrangulation, student and teacher evalua-
    tions, peer review, triangulation, literary criticism and connoisseurship.
    The intent here is to not merely describe and interpret but to criticize
    an intervention (McKernan, 1996).

Accountability

As public servants, we are held accountable for the results of our professional
performance. Students, administrators and indeed parents, along with
teachers, are being held accountable nowadays. The real question becomes

"What sort of accountability is appropriate?" For example, quality indicators, developed by teachers (Elliott, 1993), would provide data that would make teacher quality indicators available. Hamilton (1976) reminds us that accountability has been around at least since the time of Socrates. For example, the most important aspect of Greek society was not the democratic process of elections but rather the calling to account of those who held high office in the state so as to judge their performance. One such notorious event was the trial of Socrates himself. We have often overlooked this in our contemporary democratic process. A recent *New York Times* piece commenting on the Report of the Commission investigating the intelligence failures surrounding 9/11 quipped that, while honorable, the report was "toothless" in the sense that it blamed no one person or agency. The purpose of an evaluation is to judge.

Accountability takes place after the fact. That is, it only comes into play after professional actions have been taken. The real question is not whether professors, teachers and administrators are accountable but how that accountability operation is to be conducted.

Two major models of accountability have been operating. First is the instrumental, pre-specified standard or criterion type implemented as intended outcomes. This counts as an extrinsic type of accountability, like the Tyler objectives model. Second is a professional development model, which views quality as intrinsically tied to the professional work (Sockett, 1976) which admits adherence to principles of practice rather than results embodied in student performances. Such a model supports the thesis of this book – that improvement does not come from pre-specification and testing of behavior; but rather, that the standards and educational values, what Elliott calls "educational ethic," resides in adhering to principles embedded in the process of education itself and not its results or exit outcomes. This is a complex task but one which should not discourage educators because its conduct will result in better opportunities to improve.

Another point should be made here – teachers need to be involved in this type of accountability exercise themselves, just as they need to be involved in research, course evaluation, appraisal and assessment. To date in our democracy teachers are generally excluded from involvement in all of these activities that ultimately rest on their professionalism and development. It is a very odd scenario. What is required is a Teacher and Schools Council for Curriculum and Research, as I have argued in Chapter 2.

Schools as critical democratic communities of learning

The school is the best place for teachers to develop curriculum and teaching because it allows practitioners to exercise judgment in relation to the development of their reflective arts. To do this I believe teachers require significant support; not always monetary in nature. Teachers require curriculum development and research *time*. Teachers need to be able to meet as curriculum development teams and as researchers. Why are teachers not evaluated in terms of their research and service as well as teaching activities, as college professors are? An end to this division of labor will be most helpful in making teachers, just as professors, better artists.

Teachers need access to collaborative networks. Some have already been established, for example the Classroom Action Research Network (CARN) based in the School of Education at the University of Norwich, East Anglia. The organization produces *Educational Action Research*, a world-class journal of which many authors are classroom teachers from around the world.

Concluding comments

In conclusion, the proposition is that the curriculum can be substantially reformed and improved through the practice of "the reflective arts" of teacher research and school-based curriculum development, involving members of the school community as critical researchers and reflective practitioners. Curriculum development and the act of research and critical reflection belong to the members of the school community – not to external agents and agencies. There is little doubt that local administrators, teachers, pupils and parents are the key operators in this movement for democracy in educational reform.

Stenhouse (1975: 143) stated: "It is not enough that teachers' work should be studied: they need to study it themselves." Action research is perhaps the most suitable research methodology for investigating and solving curriculum and practical classroom problems. I take as a definition that of Elliott (1993: 69): "Action research may be defined as the study of a social situation with a view to improving the quality of action within it." At base action research seeks to inform the practical judgment of actors in real situations that are problematic. It is not so much concerned with the production of theory and conceptual frameworks as it is in obtaining useful results that improve practice for individuals in difficult situations.

I further argue that the field of curriculum, both in theory and practice, depends to a large extent upon evolving a critical process of research and development by teachers using other professionals to support their work. Action, and reflection on those actions, is the responsibility of teachers. Teachers need a research tradition based on classrooms rather than laboratory experiments. Such a research tradition will feed teachers ideas and be eminently accessible to them. It is difficult to believe that classrooms and curriculum can ever be improved without the participation of teachers in that improvement.

Yet obstacles abound in requesting teachers to not only become researchers but to simply become more reflective about their work. One problem is that university academics, more often than not, are inexperienced school teachers themselves – they go on to advocate a rhetoric of teacher development which includes school improvement and research briefs and they are seen largely to have huge credibility problems by the population of practicing classroom teachers. Personally, the folk who enjoy successful reputations do not suffer this credibility problem.

Bennett (1993) argues that if teachers are to contribute to the betterment of schools and curriculum then they need to have proper support from both members of the school community and district office. Teachers cited that they needed greater skill and understanding of research methods to take on this task, something which Stephen Corey (1953), of Teachers College, commented upon with the birth of action research in education.

- Teachers needed school and administrative support for research.
- The definition and role of the teacher would have to be reconceptualized and refined to include a research brief.
- Teachers required staff development training for research, conference attendance and more research resources.
- Teachers needed to test research findings in their own classrooms and settings.

Action inquiry such as Dewey's reflective stages of thought is an inductive process that allows educators to grow through research. For Dewey, reflective thinking has five stages: suggestion, intellectualization, hypothesizing, reasoning and testing the hypothesis by overt action. Dewey argued that the sequence of these stages was not necessarily fixed. The "aim of living," he wrote, "is not perfection as a final goal, but the ever enduring process of perfecting, maturing refining." The goal of education is not reaching some target but simply growing and reaching for more and more growth.

In *Education, Authority and Emancipation*, Stenhouse (1983: 185) argued that research counts as "systematic self-critical inquiry made public." His idea was to shift the balance of power from the teacher as *an authority* to the students. The teacher could be *in authority* but in reflective and research-based teaching the teacher had to depreciate his or her claim to being *an authority* on a subject. This type of systematic inquiry, which Stenhouse wished for students and teachers, was in essence a pattern of action learning through the thoughtful study of problems and issues. This form of study becomes research when it is publicly disclosed, say through publication – the act of disclosure evokes a critical response counting as new knowledge established through soundly based methods and being in some sense new. Teachers require prerequisites for this work. First, they need *imagination* to initiate projects and inquiries suitable for student involvement. Second, they require sound judgment so as to discipline the inquiry.

These attributes very much operate as principles of procedure, or values embodied in the process of education. We must commit to the view that the teacher, as a critic and scholar, can criticize the work of her or his pupils, so that they may learn together just as scholars who are critical of work in their field engage in discussion and dialogue with fellow scholars. Should not our students be treated with the same respect? Our curriculum needs to be knowledge based and we need to understand that a knowledge-based education is for everyone – not only scholars – and obligates the teaching profession to the great struggle with the immediate consequences of pursuing such an aspiration and ideal. We must also accept that we can never be content with mastery of curriculum. Knowledge is provisional and static. We require the principle or belief that we need to develop and grow further in our understanding and knowledge and skill. Our schools need to adopt the mission of the university, which is to extend our knowledge, not merely to transmit that which we hold in stewardship, and which was developed by previous generations of scholars. A number of scholars and curriculum workers are beginning to craft their own notions of "reflective practice." Reflection is in reality a form of specialized thinking arising from a troublesome or difficult concrete situation. It begins with a perceived problem.

Donald Schon has been perhaps the key influence on the promotion of "reflective practice" since the time of Dewey. Through his work (1983, 1987) he has developed a conception of reflection-in-action that empowers the professional to take action and to redeem knowledge from these actions through personal inquiry. This conception refutes directly what he calls "technical rationality" (1983: 21), that is, the notion that a well-built, science-like corpus of knowledge exists that can prescribe correct action and lead to precise predictions and control. For Schon, the practical world requires one with an "epistemology of practice implicit in the artistic, intuitive processes which some practitioners do bring to situations of uncertainty, instability, uniqueness, and value conflict" (1983: 49). Practitioners' messy problems do not fit into the precise domains of the technical-rational model of science. Schon conjures up the situation as one in which the inquirer holds a "conversation" with the problem situation. There is then a reflective exchange between the agent and the problem in which:

> the situation talks back, the practitioner listens and as he appreciates what he hears, he re-frames the situation once again.
>
> (1983: 131–32)

This conversation is one in which the reflective agent leans towards "appreciation, action and re-appreciation" (1983: 132). Schon, wishing to extend his model to reflective teaching, commented that:

> By reflective teaching I mean what some teachers have called "giving the kids reason": listening to kids and responding to them, inventing

and testing responses likely to help them get over their particular diffi-culties in understanding something, helping them build on what they already know but cannot say, helping them coordinate their own sponta-neous knowing-in-action with the privileged knowledge of the school.

(1987: 19)

Reflective teaching, says Schon, is a kind of research. He argues that it is not research *about* or *for* practice but it counts as research *in* practice. This is a point made by Elliott (1981) and McKernan (1996), that there is no division of labor in teaching and educational research; the teachers need to be researchers of their practice, not the recipients of meaning handed to them by external researchers. There are some guidelines for *reflective teaching*. The practitioner needs to:

1   become *curious* about the things students say and do;
2   make sense of, and respond to, the issue that holds one's curiosity;
3   enter into our thoughts and ways of thinking about the problem, *partic-ularizing* his or her description with other observers' (agents in the action inquiry) descriptions so as to arrive at a more complete under-standing.

Elliot Eisner sums things up nicely:

To create schools that genuinely educate, policymakers must pay atten-tion to the deep aims of the enterprise, to the structure that schools possess, to the curriculum that they offer, to the quality of teaching that occurs, and to the forms of evaluation and assessment that are employed to understand its consequences. In short an array of interacting factors must be taken into account in both planning and assessing the conse-quences of schooling.

(2002: 383)

My simple conclusion is that we shall only learn from recognizing and under-standing our failures. It was Stenhouse who bravely stated that it is teachers and other practitioners who, in the end, will be the ones who significantly improve curriculum and learning through research, by understanding their practice.

What is required is a practical and critical science of situational under-standing through the generation of research data and grounded theories for action and reflection on action. Data and theories generated by practitioners. Nothing less will qualify. The development of this practical wisdom and critical disposition, garnered through classroom inquiry, is a responsibility and a task for each educator.

References

Preface

Apple, M. (1979) *Ideology and Curriculum*, London: Routledge and Kegan Paul.

Bentley, J. (1963) *An Outline of American Philosophy*, Paterson, NJ: Littlefield, Adams and Co.

Bobbitt, F. (1918) *The Curriculum*, Boston, MA: Houghton Mifflin.

Carr, W. and Kemmis, S. (1986) *Becoming Critical: Education, Knowledge and Action Research*, Lewes, Sussex: Falmer Press.

Corey, S. (1953) *Action Research to Improve School Practices*, New York: Teachers College Press.

Eisner, E.W. (1983) "Teaching as art and craft," *Educational Leadership*, 40 (4): 4–13.

Elliott, J. (1991) *Action Research for Educational Change*, Philadelphia, PA: Open University Press.

—— (ed.) (1993) *Reconstructing Teacher Education*, London: Falmer.

Freire, P. (1972) *Cultural Action for Freedom*, London: Penguin.

Gadamer 1980.

Habermas, J. (1972) *Knowledge and Human Interests*, London: Heinemann.

McKernan, J. (1996) *Curriculum Action Research: A Handbook of Methods and Resources for the Reflective Practitioner*, 2nd edn, London: Kogan Page.

Pinar, W.F. and Grumet, M. (1981) "Theory and practice and the reconceptualization of curriculum studies," in Lawn, M. and Barton, L. (eds) *Rethinking Curriculum Studies: A Radical Approach*, New York: John Wiley, and London: Croom Helm, pp. 20–42.

Pinar, W.F., Reynolds, W.M., Slattery, P. and Taubman, P.M. (1995) *Understanding Curriculum: An Introduction to the Study of Historical and Contemporary Discourses*, New York: Peter Lang.

Reid, W.A. (1978) *Thinking about Curriculum*, London: Routledge and Kegan Paul.

Schubert, W.H. (1980) *Curriculum Books: The First Eighty Years*, Lanham, MD: University Press of America.

Schubert, W.H., Lopez-Schubert, A.L., Thomas, T.P. and Carroll, W.M. (eds) (2002) *Curriculum Books: The First Hundred Years*, New York: Peter Lang.

Schwab, J.J. (1969) "The practical: a language for curriculum," *School Review* 78, 1–23.

Shumsky, A. (1958) *The Action Research Way of Learning: An Approach to In-service*

Education, New York: Bureau of Publications, Columbia University, Teachers College.

Skilbeck, M. (1976) "School-based curriculum development," in Walton, J. and Welton, J. (eds) *Rational Curriculum Planning: Four Case Studies*, London: Ward Lock.

Smith, B.O., Stanley, W.O. and Shores, J.H. (1957) *Fundamentals of Curriculum Development*, New York: Harcourt, Brace and World.

Stenhouse, L. (1968) "The Humanities Curriculum Project," *Journal of Curriculum Studies*, 1 (1): 26–33.

—— (1975) *An Introduction to Curriculum Research and Development*, London: Heinemann.

—— (1983) *Authority, Education and Emancipation*, London: Heinemann.

Tanner, D. and Tanner, L. (2007) *Curriculum Development: Theory into Practice*, 4th edn, Upper Saddle River, NJ: Pearson Education.

1 The curriculum and its ideological conceptions

Apple, M. (1995) "Is there a curriculum voice to reclaim?," in Ornstein, A.C. and Behar, L.S. (eds) *Contemporary Issues in Curriculum*, Boston, MA: Allyn and Bacon, pp. 34–40.

Bloom, B. (1995) "The search for methods of instruction," in Ornstein, A.C. and Behar, L.S. (eds) *Contemporary Issues in Curriculum*, Boston, MA: Allyn and Bacon, pp. 208–25.

Bobbitt, F. (1918) *The Curriculum*, Boston, MA: Houghton Mifflin.

—— (1924) *How To Make a Curriculum*, Boston, MA: Houghton Mifflin.

Carr, W. and Kemmis, S. (1986) *Becoming Critical: Education, Knowledge and Action Research*, Lewes, Sussex: Falmer Press.

Connelly, M. and Clandinin, J. (1988) *Teachers as Curriculum Planners: Narratives of Experience*, New York: Teachers College Press.

Corey, S. (1953) *Action Research to Improve School Practices*, New York: Teachers College Press.

Cremin, L. (1974) *The Transformation of the School*, New York: Knopf.

Cubberley, E.P. (1934) *Public Education in the United States*, Boston, MA: Houghton Mifflin.

Dewey, J. (1910) *How We Think*, New York: D.C. Heath.

—— (1916) *Democracy and Education*, New York: Macmillan.

—— (1938) *Logic: The Theory of Inquiry*, New York: Henry Holt.

Dunne, J. (1997) *Back to the Rough Ground: Phronesis and Techne in Modern Philosophy and in Aristotle*, London: Notre Dame University Press.

Egan, K. (1990) *Romantic Understanding: The Development of Rationality and Imagination, Age 8–15*, New York: Routledge.

—— (1992) *Imagination in Teaching and Learning*, London: Routledge.

—— (2005) *An Imaginative Approach to Teaching*, San Francisco, CA: Jossey Bass.

Eisner, E.W. (1981) "On the differences between scientific and artistic approaches to qualitative research," *Educational Researcher*, 10 (4): 5–9.

—— (1983) "Teaching as art and craft," *Educational Leadership*, 40 (4): 4–13.

—— (2002) *The Educational Imagination: On the Design and Evaluation of School Programs*, 3rd edn, Upper Saddle River, NJ: Merrill Prentice Hall.

Eisner, E. and Vallance, E. (eds) (1974) *Conflicting Conceptions of Curriculum*, Berkeley, CA: McCutchan.

Elbaz, F. (1983) *Teacher Thinking: A Study of Practical Knowledge*, London: Croom Helm.

Elliott, J. (1976) "Developing hypotheses about classrooms from teachers' practical constructs," *Interchange*, 7 (1): 2–22.

—— (1991) *Action Research for Educational Change*, Philadelphia, PA: Open University Press.

—— (ed.) (1993) *Reconstructing Teacher Education*, London: Falmer.

Freire, P. (1970) *Pedagogy of the Oppressed*, London: Penguin.

—— (1972) *Cultural Action for Freedom*, London: Penguin.

Giroux, H.A. (1994) "Teachers, public life and curriculum reform," in Ornstein, A.C. and Behar, L.S. (eds) *Contemporary Issues in Curriculum*, Boston, MA: Allyn and Bacon, pp. 41–49.

Giroux, H. and McLaren, P. (1986) *Critical Pedagogy, the State, and Cultural Struggle: Teacher Empowerment and School Reform*, Albany, NY: State University of New York Press.

Gramsci, A. (1971) *Selections from the Prison Notebooks of Antonio Gramsci*, ed. and trans. Quintan Hoare and Geoffrey Nowell Smith, London: Lawrence and Wishart.

Greene, M. (1986) "Philosophy and teaching," in Wittrock, Merlin (ed.) *Handbook of Research on Teaching*, 3rd edn, New York: Macmillan.

—— (1995) *Releasing the Imagination: Essays on Education, the Arts, and Social Change*, San Francisco, CA: Jossey-Bass.

Gutek, G.L. (1995) *A History of the Western Educational Experience*, 2nd edn, Prospect Heights, IL: Waveland Press.

Habermas, J. (1976) *Communication and the Evolution of Society*, Boston, MA: Beacon Press.

Hamblin, D. (1984) *Pastoral Care: A Training Manual*, Oxford: Basil Blackwell.

Harris, W.T. (1898a) *Psychologic Foundations of Education*, New York: D. Appleton.

—— (1898b) "My pedagogical creed," in Lang, O.H. (ed.) *Educational Creeds of the Century*, New York: Kellogg, pp. 36–46.

Hirst, P. H. (1976) "The logic of the curriculum," in Golby, M., Greenwald, J. and West, R. (eds) *Curriculum Design*, London: Croom Helm, pp. 181–93.

Hodgkinson, H.L. (1957) "Action research – a critique," *Journal of Educational Sociology*, 31 (4): 137–53.

James, W. (1992) "The sentiment of rationality," in *William James: The Writings 1878–1899*, New York: Library of America.

Johnson, M. (1967) "Definitions and models in curriculum theory," *Educational Theory*, 17: 127–40.

Kelly, V. (1989) *Curriculum: Theory and Practice*, 3rd edn, London: Paul Chapman.

Kerr, J.F. (ed.) (1968) *Changing the Curriculum*, London: University of London Press.

Klafki, W. (1975) "Decentralised curriculum development in the form of action research," in *Council of Europe Information Bulletin*, Number 1, S. 13–22.

Kliebard, H.M. (1970) "The Tyler rationale," *School Review*, 78 (2): 259–72.

—— (1975) "Reappraisal: The Tyler rationale," in Pinar, W.F. (ed.) *Curriculum Theorizing: The Reconceptualists*, Berkeley, CA: McCutchan, pp. 70–83.

—— (1995) "The Tyler rationale revisited," *Journal of Curriculum Studies*, 27 (1): 81–88.

Lewin, K. (1948) *Resolving Social Conflicts*, New York: Harper and Row.

McCutcheon, G. (1995a) *Developing a Curriculum: Solo and Group Deliberation*, White Plains, NY: Longmans.

—— (1995b) "Curriculum theory and practice for the 1990's," in Ornstein, A.C. and Behar, L.S. (eds) *Contemporary Issues in Curriculum*, Boston, MA: Allyn and Bacon, pp. 3–9.

MacDonald, B. (1971) "The evaluation of the Humanities Project: a holistic approach," *Theory Into Practice*, 10: 163–67.

Macdonald, J.B. (1982) "How literal is curriculum theory?," *Theory Into Practice*, 21 (1): 55–61.

McKernan, J. *et. al.* (1985) *Learning for Life: Tutor's Guide*, Dublin: Gill and Macmillan.

—— (2006) "Validity and choice in action research: a response to Peter Reason," *Journal of Management Inquiry*, 15 (2): 204–06.

Marsh, C. and Willis, G. (2007) *Curriculum: Alternative Approaches, Ongoing Issues*, 2nd edn, Upper Saddle River, NJ: Merrill.

Oakeshott, M. (1966) *Experience and its Modes*, Cambridge: Cambridge University Press.

—— (1981) *Rationalism in Politics and Other Essays*, London: Methuen.

Ornstein, A.C. and Levine, D.U. (2006) *Foundations of Education*, 9th edn, Boston, MA: Houghton Mifflin.

Parlett, M. and Hamilton, D. (1972) "Evaluation as illumination: a new approach to the study of innovatory programmes," occasional paper of the Centre for Research in the Educational Sciences, Edinburgh: University of Edinburgh.

Peters, R.S. (1966) *Ethics and Education*, London: Allen and Unwin.

Phenix, P. (1974) *Realms of Meaning*, New York: McGraw-Hill.

Pinar, W.F. (ed.) (1975) *Curriculum Theorizing: The Reconceptualists*, Berkeley, CA: McCutchan.

Pinar, W.F., Reynolds, W.M., Slattery, P. and Taubman, P.M. (1995) *Understanding Curriculum: An Introduction to the Historical and Contemporary Curriculum Discourses*, New York: Peter Lang.

Raths, L., Harmin, M. and Simon, S. (1966) *Values and Teaching*, Columbus, OH: Merrill.

Reason, P. (2006) "Validity and choice in action research," *Journal of Management Inquiry*, 15 (2): 193–201.

Reid, L.A. (1978) *Thinking about the Curriculum: The Nature and Treatment of Curriculum Problems*, London: Routledge and Kegan Paul.

Rudduck, J. (1989) "Practitioner research and programmes of initial teacher education," *Westminster Studies in Education*, 12: 61–72.

Russell, B. (1950) *Unpopular Essays*, London: Allen and Unwin.

Sanders, D. and McCutcheon, G. (1986) "The development of practical theories of teaching," *Journal of Curriculum and Supervision*, 2 (1), Fall: 50–67.

Sartre, J.P. (1949) *Literature and Existentialism*, New York: Citadel Press.

Schools Council for Curriculum and Examinations (1975) *The Whole Curriculum 13–16*, London: Evans Methuen Educational.

Schubert, W.H. (1986) *Curriculum: Perspective, Paradigm and Possibility*, New York: Macmillan.

Schwab, J.J. (1969) "The practical: a language for curriculum," *School Review*, 1–23.

Scriven, M. (1973) "Goal-free evaluation," in House, E. (ed.) *School Evaluation: The Politics and Process*, Berkeley, CA: McCutchan.

Skilbeck, M. (1984) *School-Based Curriculum Development*, London: Harper.

Smith, B.O., Stanley, W.O. and Shores, J.H. (1957) *Fundamentals of Curriculum Development*, New York: Harcourt, Brace and World.

Sockett, H.T. (1976) *Designing the Curriculum*, London: Open Books.

Stake, R. (1967) "The countenance of educational evaluation," *Teachers College Record*, 68: 523–40.

Stenhouse, L. (1975) *An Introduction to Curriculum Research and Development*, London: Heinemann.

Tyler, R. (1949) *Basic Principles of Curriculum and Instruction*, Chicago, IL: University of Chicago Press.

Warnock, M. (1973) "Towards a definition of quality in education," in Peters, R.S. (ed.) *The Philosophy of Education*, London: Oxford University Press.

Webb, L.D., Metha, A. and Jordan, K.F. (2003) *Foundations of American Education*, 4th edn, Upper Saddle River, NJ: Merrill Prentice Hall.

Whitehead, A.N. (1929) *The Aims of Education and Other Essays*, New York: Macmillan.

Wiles, J. and Bondi, J. (2007) *Curriculum Development: A Guide to Practice*, 7th edn, Upper Saddle River, NJ: Pearson Education.

2 Curriculum, quality and freedom

American Association of University Professors (AAUP) (1940) *Statement on Academic Freedom*, Washington, D.C.: AAUP.

Apple, M. (1995) "Is there a curriculum voice to reclaim?," in Ornstein, A.C. and Behar, L.S. (eds) *Contemporary Issues in Curriculum*, Needham Heights, MA: Allyn and Bacon, pp. 34–40.

Dewey, J. (1966) *Democracy and Education*, New York: Free Press.

Donohue, J.W. (1968) *St. Thomas Aquinas and Education*, New York: Random House.

McKernan, J. (1996) *Curriculum Action Research: A Handbook of Methods and Resources for the Reflective Practitioner*, 2nd edn, London: Kogan Page.

—— (2004) "The social market ideology and higher education," *College Quarterly*, 8 (1), Winter: 1–8, www.collegequarterly.ca.

Mulcahy, D.G. (2002) *Knowledge, Gender and Schooling: The Feminist Thought of Jane Roland Martin*, Boston, MA: Bergin and Garvey.

Warnock, M. (1973) "Towards a definition of quality in education," in Peters, R.S. (ed.) *The Philosophy of Education*, London: Oxford University Press, pp. 112–22.

Whitehead, A.N. (1929) *The Aims of Education and Other Essays*, New York: Macmillan.

3 Curriculum design and theorizing

Anyon, J. (1980) "Social class and the hidden curriculum of work," *Journal of Education*, 162 (1): 67–92.

Apple, M. (1979) *Ideology and Curriculum*, London: Routledge and Kegan Paul.

Beauchamp, G.A. (1975) *Curriculum Theory*, 3rd edn, Wilmette, IL: Kagg.

Block, J. (ed.) (1971) *Mastery Learning*. New York: Holt, Rinehart and Winston.

Bloom, B.S. (ed.) (1956) *Taxonomy of Educational Objectives: Cognitive Domain*, New York: David McKay.

—— (1981) *All Our Children Learning: A Primer for Parents, Teachers and Other Educators*, New York: McGraw-Hill.

Bobbitt, F. (1918) *The Curriculum*, Boston, MA: Houghton Mifflin.

—— (1924) *How to Make a Curriculum*, Boston, MA: Houghton Mifflin.

Bode, B.H. (1927) *Modern Educational Theories*, New York: Macmillan.

Bourdieu, P. and Passeron, J. (1977) *Reproduction in Education, Society and Culture*, London: Sage.

Charters, W.W. (1923) *Curriculum Construction*, New York: Macmillan.

Davies, I.K. (1976) *Objectives in Curriculum Design*, Maidenhead: McGraw-Hill.

Dewey, John (1900) *The School and Society*, Chicago, IL: University of Chicago Press.

—— (1902) *The Child and the Curriculum*, Chicago, IL: University of Chicago Press.

—— (1916) *Democracy and Education*, New York: Macmillan.

—— (1929) *The Sources of a Science of Education*, New York: H. Liveright.

Eisner, E.W. (1974) "Instructional and expressive objectives: their formulation and use in curriculum," AERA Monograph Series on Curriculum Evaluation No. 3, in Golby, M. (ed.) *Curriculum Design*, London: Open University Press.

—— (1979) *The Educational Imagination*. New York: Macmillan.

—— (1991) *The Enlightened Eye*. New York: Macmillan.

Eisner, E.W. and Vallance, E. (1974) *Conflicting Conceptions of Curriculum*, Berkeley, CA: McCutchan.

Elliott, J. (1991) *Action Research for Educational Change*, Milton Keynes: Open University Press.

Freire, P. (1970) *Pedagogy of the Oppressed*, trans. M.B. Ramos, New York: Seabury Co.

—— (1973) *Education for Critical Consciousness*, New York: Seabury Co.

Froebel, F. (1896) *The Education of Man*, trans. W.M. Hailman, New York: Appleton.

—— (1899) *Education by Development*, New York: Appleton.

Giroux, H.A. (1982) "Power and resistance in the new sociology of education: beyond theories of social and cultural reproduction," *Curriculum Perspectives*, 2 (3): 1–14.

Greene, M. (1975) "Curriculum and consciousness," in Pinar, W. (ed.) *Curriculum Theorizing: The Reconceptualist*, Berkeley, CA: McCutchan, pp. 299–317.

Grumet, M, (1981) "Restitution and reconstruction of educational experience, an autobiographical method for curriculum theory," *Journal of Curriculum Theorizing*, 1 (1): 191–257.

Gwynn, J.M. (1945) *Curriculum Principles and Social Trends*, New York: Macmillan.

Herrick, V.E. and Tyler R.W. (eds) (1950) *Towards Improved Curriculum Theory*, Chicago, IL: University of Chicago Press.

Hirst, P. (1965) "Liberal education and the nature of knowledge," in Archambault,

Reginald D. (ed.) *Philosophical Analysis and Education*, London: Routledge and Kegan Paul, pp. 113–38.

Hirst, P. and Peters, R.S. (1970) *The Logic of Education*, London: Routledge and Kegan Paul.

Huebner, D. (1975) "Curricular language and classroom meanings," in Pinar, W. (ed.) *Curriculum Theorizing: The Reconceptualists*. Berkeley, CA: McCutchan, pp. 217–37.

Hutchins, P.M. (1968) *The Learning Society*, New York: Praeger.

Kelly, V. (1989) *Curriculum: Theory and Practice*, 4th edn, London: Paul Chapman.

Kemmis, S. (1986) *Curriculum Theorizing: Beyond Reproduction Theory*, Geelong, Victoria: Deakin University Press.

Kilpatrick, W. (1918) "The project method," *Teachers College Record*, 19 (4): 1–26.

Lawn, M. and Barton, L. (1980) "Curriculum studies: reconceptualism or reconstruction?," *Journal of Curriculum Theorizing*, 2 (1): 47–56.

McCutcheon, G. (1995) *Developing the Curriculum: Solo and Group Deliberation*, White Plains, NY: Longman.

Macdonald, J.B. (ed.) (1971) *Curriculum Development in Relation to Social and Intellectual Systems*, Seventieth Yearbook of the National Society for the Study of Education. Chicago, IL: University of Chicago Press.

—— (1975) "Curriculum and human interests," in Pinar, W. (ed.) *Curriculum Theorizing: The Reconceptualists*, Berkeley, CA: McCutchan.

Mager, R.F. (1962) *Preparing Instructional Objectives*, Palo Alto, CA: Fearon.

Marsh, C. and Willis, G. (2007) *Curriculum: Alternative Approaches, Ongoing Issues*, 4th edn, Upper Saddle River, NJ: Pearson.

Martin, J.R. (1984) "Bringing women into educational thought," *Educational Theory*, 34 (4): 341–53.

Montessori, M. (1949) *Childhood Education*, trans. A. M. Joosten, Chicago, IL: Henry Regnery Press.

—— (1967) *The Absorbent Mind*, New York: Holt, Rinehart and Winston.

Morrison, H.C. (1926) *The Practice of Teaching in the Secondary School*, Chicago, IL: University of Chicago Press.

Mulcahy, D.G. (1981) *Curriculum and Policy in Irish Post Primary Education*, Dublin: Institute of Public Administration.

—— (2002) *Knowledge, Gender and Schooling: The Feminist Thought of Jane Roland Martin*, Boston, MA: Bergin and Garvey.

National Society for the Study of Education (NSSE) (1927) Twenty-Sixth Yearbook Part 1: *Curriculum Making: Past and Present*; Part 2: *Foundations of Curriculum Making*, Bloomington, IL: Public School Publishing Co.

Neill, A.S. (1960) *Summerhill: A Radical Approach to Child-Rearing*, New York: Hart.

Noddings, N. (ed.) (1984) *Caring: A Feminine Approach to Ethics and Moral Education*, Berkeley, CA: University of California Press.

Ornstein, A. and Hunkins, F. (1993) *Curriculum: Foundations, Principles and Theory*, 2nd edn, Boston, MA: Allyn and Bacon.

Ornstein, A.C. and Levine, D.S. (2006) *Foundations of Education*, 9th edn, Boston, MA: Houghton Mifflin.

Pagano, J.A. (1992) "Women and education: in what ways does gender affect the educational process?," in Kincheloe, J. and Steinberg, S. (eds) *Thirteen Questions*, New York: Lang.

Peters, R.S. (1966) *Ethics and Education*, London: Allen and Unwin.

Phenix, P.H. (1964) *Realms of Meaning*, New York: McGraw Hill.

Pinar, W.F. (ed.) (1975) *Curriculum Theorizing: The Reconceptualists*. Berkeley, CA: McCutchan.

—— (1980) "The voyage out: curriculum as the relationship between the knower and the known," *Journal of Curriculum Theorizing*, 2 (1): 7–11.

Popham, W.J. and Baker, E. (1970) *Systematic Instruction*, Englewood Cliffs, NJ: Prentice-Hall.

Pratt, D. (1980) *Curriculum Design and Development*, New York: Harcourt, Brace Jovanovich.

Reid, W.A. (1978) *Thinking about Curriculum*, London: Routledge and Kegan Paul.

—— (1988) "The institutional context of curriculum deliberation," *Journal of Curriculum Supervision*, 4 (1): 3–16.

—— (1994) *Curriculum Planning as Deliberation*, Oslo: University of Oslo.

Rogers, C.R. (1983) *Freedom to Learn for the 80's*, Columbus, OH: Merrill.

Rugg, H.O. (ed.) (1927) *Curriculum Making: Past and Present*. Twenty-Sixth Yearbook of the National Society for the Study of Education, Part 1, Bloomington, IL: Public School Publishing Co.

Schubert, W.H. (1986) *Curriculum: Perspective, Paradigm and Possibility*, New York: Macmillan.

Schwab, J.J. (1969) "The practical 1: a language for curriculum," *School Review*, 78 (1): 1–23.

—— (1971) "The practical 2: arts of the eclectic," *School Review*, 79: 493–542.

—— (1973) "The practical 3: translations into curriculum," *School Review*, 81: 501–22.

—— (1983) "The practical 4: something for curriculum professors to do," *Curriculum Inquiry*, 13 (3): 239–65.

Skilbeck, M. (1976) "School-based curriculum development," in Walton, J. and Welton, J. (eds) *Rational Curriculum Planning: Four Case Studies*, London: Ward Lock.

Snedden, D. (1921) *Sociological Determination of Objectives in Education*, Philadelphia, PA: Lippincott.

Stenhouse, L. (1975) *An Introduction to Curriculum Research and Development*, London: Heinemann.

Taba, H. (1962) *Curriculum Development: Theory and Practice*, New York: Harcourt, Brace and World.

Tanner, D. and Tanner, L. (2007) *Curriculum Development: Theory Into Practice*, 4th edn, Upper Saddle River, NJ: Pearson Education.

Tyler, R. (1949) *Basic Principles of Curriculum and Instruction*, Chicago, IL: University of Chicago Press.

Walker, D.F. (1971) "A naturalistic model of curriculum development," *School Review*, 80 (1): 51–65.

—— (2003) *Fundamentals of Curriculum*, 2nd edn, Mahwah, NJ: Lawrence Erlbaum.

Westbury, I. (1972) "The character of a curriculum for a practical curriculum," *Curriculum Theory Network*, 10 (4): 25–36.

Wheeler, D.K. (1967) *Curriculum Process*, London: University of London Press.

Whitty, G. (1980) "Ideology, politics and curriculum," in Milton Keynes (ed.) *Society, Education and the State, Unit 8*, Milton Keynes: Open University.

Willis, G. (1981) "A reconceptualist perspective on curriculum theorizing," *Journal of Curriculum Theorizing*, 3 (1): 185–92.

4 Some limitations of the objectives model in curriculum

Apple, M.W. (1981) "Social structure, ideology and curriculum," in Lawn, M. and Barton, L. (eds) *Rethinking Curriculum Studies*, London: Croom Helm.

Apple, M. and Christian-Smith, L.K. (eds) (1992) *The Politics of the Textbook*, New York: Routledge.

Bernstein, B. (1971) *Class, Codes and Control. Vol.1 Theoretical Studies towards a Sociology of Language*, London: Routledge and Kegan Paul.

Bloom, B.S. (ed.) (1956) *Taxonomy of Educational Objectives: Cognitive Domain*, New York: David McKay.

Bobbitt, F. (1918) *The Curriculum*, Boston, MA: Houghton Mifflin.

—— (1924) *How to Make a Curriculum*, Boston, MA: Houghton Mifflin.

Dewey, J. (1922) *Human Nature and Conduct*, New York: Random House.

—— (1956) *The Child and the Curriculum*, Chicago, IL: University Press, Phoenix Books.

Eisner, E. (2002) *The Educational Imagination: On the Design and Evaluation of School Programs*, 3rd edn, Upper Saddle River, NJ: Merrill Prentice Hall.

Freire, P. (1970) *Pedagogy of the Oppressed*, trans. M.B. Ramos, New York: Seabury Press.

Giroux, H.A. (1995) "Teachers, public life and curriculum reform," in Ornstein, A.C. and Behar, L.S. (eds) *Contemporary Issues in Curriculum*, Boston, MA: Allyn and Bacon, pp 41–49.

James, W. (1992) *Talks to Teachers on Psychology and to Students on Some of Life's Ideals*, Boston, MA: George Ellis, available online at: http://www.gutenberg.org/etext 16287.

Kliebard, H.M. (1975) "Reapprasial: the Tyler rationale," in Pinar, W. (ed.) *Curriculum Theorizing: The Reconceptualists*, Berkeley, CA: McCutchan, pp. 70–83. Originally published in *School Review*, 1970, 78: 259–72.

McCutcheon, G. (1995) *Developing the Curriculum: Solo and Group Deliberation*, White Plains, NY: Longman.

Macdonald-Ross, M. (1975) "Behavioural objectives: a critical review," in Golby, M., Greenwald, J. and West, R. (eds) *Curriculum Design*, London: Croom Helm, pp. 355–86.

McKernan, J. (1993) "Some limitations of outcome-based education," *Journal of Curriculum and Supervision*, 2 (1): 343–53.

Mager, R.F. (1962) *Preparing Instructional Objectives*, Palo Alto, CA: Fearon.

Marshall, D., Sears, J.T., Allen, L.A., Roberts, P.A. and Schubert, W.H. (2007) *Turning Points in Curriculum: An American Memoir*, 2nd edn, Upper Saddle River, NJ: Pearson Education.

National Commission on Excellence in Education (1983) *A Nation at Risk: The Imperative for Educational Reform*, Washington, D.C.: US Department of Education.

Oakeshott, M. (1962) "Political education," in Oakeshott, M. *Rationalism in Politics*, London: Methuen.

Peters, R.S. (1959) *Authority, Responsibility and Education*, London: Allen and Unwin.
—— (1963) *Education as Initiation*, London: Evans.
—— (1966) *Ethics and Education*, London: Allen and Unwin.
Schubert, W. (1986) *Curriculum: Perspective, Paradigm and Possibility*, New York: Macmillan.
Scriven, M. (1967) "The methodology of evaluation," in Stake, R.E. (ed.) *Perspectives of Evaluation*, American Educational Research Association. Monograph Series on Curriculum Evaluation No. 1, Chicago, IL: Rand McNally, pp. 39–89.
Skilbeck, M. (1976) "School-based curriculum development," in Walton, J. and Welton, J. (eds) *Rational Curriculum Planning: Four Case Studies*, London: Ward Lock.
Sockett, H.T. (1976) *Curriculum Design*, London: Open Books.
Stenhouse, L. (1970) "Some limitations of the use of behavioural objectives in curriculum research and planning," *Paedagogica Europaea*, 6: 73–83.
—— (1975) *An Introduction to Curriculum Research and Development*, London: Heinemann.
Tyler, R.W. (1949) *Basic Principles of Curriculum and Instruction*, Chicago, IL: University of Chicago Press.
Young, M.F.D. (1971) "An approach to the study of curricula as socially organized knowledge," in Young, M.F.D. (ed.) *Knowledge and Control*, London: Collier Macmillan, pp. 19–46.

5 A process-inquiry model for the design of curriculum

Bennett, C. (1993) "Teacher-researchers: all dressed up and no place to go?," *Educational Leadership* 51 (2), October: 69–70.
Bhaskar, R. (1997) *A Realist Theory of Science*, 2nd edn, London: Verso.
Bruner, J. (1966) *Toward a Theory of Instruction*, Cambridge, MA: The Belknap Press of Harvard University Press.
Corey, S. (1953) *Action Research to Improve School Practices*, New York: Columbia University, Teachers College Press.
Dewey, J. (1933) *How We Think*, Lexington, MA: Heath.
—— (1968) *Democracy and Education*, New York: The Free Press.
Elliott, J. (1991) *Action Research for Educational Change*, Philadelphia, PA: Open University Press.
—— (ed.) (1993) *Reconstructing Teacher Education*, London: Falmer.
Freire, P. (1970) *Pedagogy of the Oppressed*, New York: Seabury.
Hanley, J.P., Whitla, D.K., Moo, E.W. and Walter, A.S. (1970) *Curiosity, Competence and Community: Man: A Course of Study – An Evaluation*, 2 Vols, Cambridge, MA: Educational Development Center.
Hare, R.M. (1981) *Moral Thinking*, Oxford: Clarendon Press.
Hirst, P. (1965) "Liberal education and the nature of knowledge," in Archambault, R.D. (ed.) *Philosophical Knowledge and Education*, London: Routledge and Kegan Paul, pp. 113–38.
Hirst, P.H. and Peters, R.S. (1970) *The Logic of Education*, London: Routledge and Kegan Paul.

Jenkins, D. (1975) "Classic and romantic in the curriculum landscape," in Golby, M., Greenwald, J. and West, R. (eds) *Curriculum Design*, London: Croom Helm, pp. 15–26.

Kelly, V. (1989) *Curriculum: Theory and Practice*, 3rd edn, London: Paul Chapman.

McKernan, J. (1993) "Some limitations of outcome-based education," *Journal of Curriculum and Supervision*, 8 (4), Summer: 343–53.

—— (1996) *Curriculum Action Research: A Handbook of Methods and Resources for the Reflective Practitioner*, 2nd edn, London: Kogan Page.

Man: A Course of Study (1970) *Evaluation Strategies*, based on research conducted by Dean Whitla, Janet P. Hanley, Eunice Moo and Arlene Walter at the Educational Development Center, Washington, D.C.: Curriculum Development Associates.

Peters, R.S. (1959) *Authority, Responsibility and Education*, London: Allen and Unwin.

—— (1964) "Education as initiation," in Archambault, R.D. (ed.) *Philosophical Analysis and Education*, New York: Humanities Press.

—— (1966) *Ethics and Education*, London: George Allen and Unwin.

Peters, R.S., Woods, J. and Dray, W.H. (1973) "Aims of education – a conceptual inquiry," in Peters, R.S. (ed.) *The Philosophy of Education*, London: Oxford University Press, pp. 11–57.

Raths, J.D. (1971) "Teaching without specific objectives," *Educational Leadership*, April: 714–20.

Schon, D. (1983) *The Reflective Practitioner: How Professionals Think in Action*, New York: Basic Books.

Spencer, H. (1860) *Education: Intellectual, Moral and Physical*, New York: D. Appleton.

Stenhouse, L. (1975) *An Introduction to Curriculum Research and Development*, London: Heinemann.

—— (1983) *Authority, Education and Emancipation*, London: Heinemann.

6 The teacher as researcher: action research as the basis for teaching and professional development

Altrichter, H., Posch, P. and Somekh, B. (1993) *Teachers Investigate their Work: An Introduction to the Methods of Action Research*, London: Routledge.

Calderhead, J. (1988) *Teachers' Professional Learning*, London: Cassell.

Corey, S. (1953) *Action Research to Improve School Practices*, New York: Columbia University, Teachers' College Press.

Dewey, J. (1929) *The Sources of a Science of Education*, New York: H. Liveright.

Eisner, E. (2002) *The Educational Imagination*, 4th edn, Columbus, OH: Merrill-Pearson.

Elliott, J. (1991) *Action Research for Educational Change*, Milton Keynes: Open University Press.

—— (ed.) (1993) *Reconstructing Teacher Education*, London: Falmer Press.

Fetterman, D. (2001) *Foundations of Empowerment Evaluation*, Thousand Oaks, CA: Sage.

Hoyle, E. (1984) "The professionalization of teachers: a paradox," in Gordon, P. (ed.) *Is Teaching a Profession?*, Bedford Way Papers 15, London: Institute of Education, pp. 44–54.

Lomax, P. (ed.) (1991) *Managing Better Schools and Colleges: An Action Research Way*, British Educational Research Association Dialogues Number 5, Clevedon: Multilingual Matters.

MacDonald, B. and Walker, R. (1976) *Changing the Curriculum*, London: Open Books.

MacIntyre, A. (1988) *Whose Justice? Which Rationality?*, Notre Dame, IN: University of Notre Dame Press.

McKernan, J. (1992) "Varieties of curriculum action research: constraints and typologies in British, Irish and American projects," *Journal of Curriculum Studies*, 25 (5): 445–58.

—— (1996) *Curriculum Action Research: A Handbook of Methods and Resources for the Reflective Practitioner*, 2nd edn, London: Kogan Page.

McNiff, J. (1993) *Teaching as Learning: An Action Research Approach*, London: Routledge.

—— (2000) *Action Research in Organisations*, London: Routledge.

—— (2002) *Action Research: Principles and Practice*, 2nd edn, London: Routledge.

McNiff, J. and Whitehead, J. (2002) *Action Research: Principles and Practice*, 2nd edn, London: Routledge.

McNiff, J., Lomax, P. and Whitehead, J. (1996) *You and Your Action Research Project*, London: Routledge.

O'Hanlon, C. (1997) *Professional Development Through Action Research: International Educational Perspectives*, London: Falmer Press.

Pauly, E. (1991) *The Classroom Crucible*, New York: Basic Books.

Reason, P. and Bradbury, H. (eds) (2000) *Handbook of Action Research: Participative Inquiry and Practice*, Thousand Oaks, CA: Sage.

Revans, R. (1982) *The Origins and Growth of Action Learning*, Bromley: Chartwell-Bratt.

Schaefer, R. (1967) *The School as a Center of Inquiry*, New York: Harper and Row.

Schon, D. (1983) *The Reflective Practitioner: How Professionals Think in Action*, New York: Basic Books.

—— (1987) *Educating the Reflective Practitioner*, San Francisco: Jossey-Bass.

Short, E. (ed.) (1991) *Forms of Curriculum Inquiry*, Albany, NY: State University of New York Press.

Smith, L. and Geoffrey, W. (1968) *The Complexities of an Urban Classroom*, New York: Holt, Rinehart and Winston.

Sockett, H.T. (1983) "Toward a professional code in teaching," in Gordon, P., Perkin, Sockett, H.T. and Hoyle, E. (eds) *Is Teaching a Profession?* Bedford Way Papers 15, London: Institute of Education, pp. 26–43.

Stenhouse, L. (1975) *An Introduction to Curriculum Research and Development*, London: Heinemann.

—— (1981) "What counts as research?," *British Journal of Educational Studies*, 29 (2): 113.

—— (1983) *Authority, Education and Emancipation*, London: Heinemann.

Winter, R. (1989) *Learning from Experience: Principles and Practices in Action Research*, Lewes, Sussex: Falmer Press.

Zeichner, K. and Liston, D. (1987) "Teaching student teachers to reflect," *Harvard Educational Review*, 57 (1), February: 1–22.

7 Action research and philosophy: origins, nature and conduct of inquiry

Altrichter, H., Posch, P. and Somekh, B. (1993) *Teachers Investigate their Work: An Introduction to the Methods of Action Research*, London: Routledge.

Atweh, B., Kemmis, S. and Weeks, P. (eds) (1998) *Action Research in Practice: Partnerships for Social Justice in Education*, London: Routledge.

Barker, R.G. and Wright, H. (1951) *One Boy's Day: A Specimen Record of Behavior*, New York: Harper.

Bhaskar, R. (1986) *Scientific Realism and Human Emancipation*, London: Verso.

—— (1989) *Reclaiming Reality*, London: Verso.

—— (1998) *The Possibility of Naturalism: A Contemporary Critique of the Contemporary Human Sciences*, 3rd edn, London: Routledge.

Carr, W. and Kemmis, S. (1986) *Becoming Critical: Education, Knowledge and Action Research*, Lewes: Sussex Falmer Press.

Carson, T. and Sumara, D. (eds) (1997) *Action Research as a Living Practice*, New York: Peter Lang.

Collier, A. (1994) *Critical Realism: An Introduction to Roy Bhaskar's Philosophy*, London: Verso.

Collier, J. (1945) "United States Indian administration as a laboratory of ethnic relations," *Social Research*, 12, May: 265–303.

Corey, S. (1953) *Action Research to Improve School Practices*, New York: Columbia University, Teachers College Press.

Denzin, N. (1970) *The Research Act in Sociology*, London: Butterworths.

Dewey, J. (1910) *How We Think*, Boston, MA: D.C. Heath.

—— (1929) *The Sources of a Science of Education*, New York: Horace Liveright.

Elliott, J. (1981) "Action research: a framework for self evaluation in schools," Schools Council Programme 2. Teacher Pupil Interaction and the Quality of Learning Project, Cambridge: Cambridge Institute of Education.

—— (1991) *Action Research for Educational Change*, Philadelphia, PA: Open University Press.

Gadamer, H. (1981) *Truth and Method*, New York: Continuum.

Greenwood, D.J. and Levin, M. (1998) *Introduction to Action Research: Social Research for Social Change*, Thousand Oaks, CA: Sage.

—— (2001) "Pragmatic Action Research and the Struggle to Transform Universities into Learning Communities," in Reason, P. and Bradbury, H. (eds) *Handbook of Action Research*, London: Sage.

Habermas, J. (1972) *Knowledge and Human Interest*, London: Heinemann.

Hendricks, C. (2006) *Improving Schools Through Action Research*, Boston, MA: Pearson.

Hodgkinson, H.L. (1957) "Action research: a critique," *Journal of Educational Sociology*, 31 (4), December: 137–53.

Hopkins, D. (1985) *A Teacher's Guide to Classroom Research*, Philadelphia, PA: Open University Press.

Hustler, D., Cassidy, A. and Cuff, E. (eds) (1986) *Action Research in Classrooms and Schools*, London: Allen and Unwin.

Kaboub, F. (2001) "Roy Bhaskar's Critical Realism: a brief overview and critical evaluation," available online at: http://f.students.umkc.edu.fkfc8/bhaskarcr.htm.

Levin, B. and Rock, T. (2003) "The effects of collaborative action research on pre-service and experienced teacher partners in professional development schools," *Journal of Teacher Education*, 54 (2): 135–49.

Lewin, K. (1946) "Action research and minority problems," *Journal of Social Issues*, 2: 34–46.

—— (1948) *Resolving Social Conflicts*, New York: Harper.

—— (1951) *Field Theory in Social Science*, New York: Harper.

McKernan, J. (1991) "Action inquiry: studied enactment," in Short, Edmund C. (ed.) *Forms of Curriculum Inquiry*, Albany, NY: State University of New York Press, pp. 309–26.

—— (1996) *Curriculum Action Research: A Handbook of Methods and Resources for the Reflective Practitioner*, 2nd edn, London: Kogan Page.

—— (2004) "George Bernard Shaw, the Fabian Society and Reconstructionist Education Policy: the London School of Economics and Political Science," *Journal for Critical Education Policy Studies*, 2 (2), September: 1–18, available online at: www.jceps.com.

Mayo, E. (1949) *Social Problems of an Industrial Civilisation*, London: Routledge and Kegan Paul.

Mills, G.E. (2003) *Action Research: A Guide for the Teacher Researcher*, New York: Merrill-Prentice Hall.

Moreno, J.L. (1934) "Who shall survive?," Nervous mental disease monograph, No. 58, Washington, D.C.

Noffke, S. (1995) *Educational Action Research: Becoming Practically Critical*, New York: Teachers College Press.

Rorty, R. (1979) *Philosophy and the Mirror of Nature*, Princeton, NJ: Princeton University Press.

—— (1989) *Contingency, Irony, and Solidarity*, Cambridge: Cambridge University Press.

—— (1999) *Philosophy and Social Hope*, London: Penguin.

Sagor, R. (2000) *Guiding School Improvement with Action Research*, Alexandria, VA: Association for Curriculum Supervision and Development.

Sanford, N. (1970) "Whatever happened to action research?," *Journal of Social Issues*, 26 (4): 3–23.

Schaefer, R. (1967) *The School as a Center of Inquiry*, New York: Harper and Row.

Short, E.C. (ed.) (1991) *Forms of Curriculum Inquiry*, Albany, NY: State University of New York Press.

Spradley, J.P. (1980) *Participant Observation*, New York: Holt, Rinehart and Winston.

Stenhouse, L. (1975) *An Introduction to Curriculum Research and Development*, London: Heinemann.

—— (1981) "What counts as research?," *British Journal of Educational Studies*, 29 (2), June: 113.

—— (1983) *Authority, Education and Emancipation*, London: Heinemann.

Taba, H. and Noel, E. (1957) *Action Research: A Case Study*, Washington, D.C.: Association for Supervision and Curriculum Development, National Education Association.

Wallace, M. (1987) "A historical review of action research: some implications for the education of teachers in their managerial role," *Journal of Education for Teaching*, 13 (2): 97–115.

Winter, R. (2001) "Action research, relativism and critical realism: a theoretical justification for action research," available online at: www.did.stu.mmu.ac/uk/cam/members_papers/Richard_winter.html.

8 The action research seminar and democratic pedagogy

Altrichter, H. (1991) "Towards a theory of teaching action research," in Collins, C. and Chippendale, P. (eds) *Proceedings of the First World Congress on Action Research and Process Management*, Vol. 1, Brisbane, Queensland: Acorn Press, pp. 21–32.

Carr, W. and Kemmis, S. (1986) *Becoming Critical: Education, Knowledge and Action Research*, Lewes, Sussex: Falmer.

Dewey, J. (1933) *How We Think*, Chicago, IL: Henry Regnery.

—— (1969) *Experience and Education*, London: Collier-Macmillan.

Elliott, J. (1991) *Action Research for Educational Change*, Milton Keynes: Open University Press.

Elliott, J. and Sarland, C. (1995) "A study of teachers as researchers in the context of award-bearing courses and research degrees," *British Educational Research Journal*, 21 (3): 371–86.

Freire, P. (1972) *Pedagogy of the Oppressed*, London: Penguin Books.

Giroux, H. (1985) "Teachers as transformative intellectuals," *Social Education*, 49: 376–79.

—— (1988) *Teachers as Intellectuals*, Granby, MA: Bergin and Garvey.

Lewin, K. (1951) *Field Theory in Social Science*, New York: Harper.

Liston, D. and Zeichner, K. (1990) "Action research and reflective teaching in preservice teacher education," *Journal of Education for Teaching*, 16 (3): 235–54.

Lomax, P. (1994) "Standards, criteria and the problematic of action research within award-bearing courses," *Educational Action Research*, 2 (1): 113–26.

McKernan, J. (1988) "The countenance of curriculum action research: traditional, collaborative and critical-emancipatory conceptions," *Journal of Curriculum and Supervision*, 3 (3): 173–200.

—— (1994) "Teaching educational action research: a tale of three cities," *Educational Action Research*, 2 (1): 95–112.

—— (1996) *Curriculum Action Research: A Handbook of Methods and Resources for the Reflective Practitioner*, 2nd edn, London: Kogan Page.

McKernan, J. et al. (1985) *Learning for Life: Tutor's Guide*, Dublin: Gill and Macmillan.

Noddings, N. (1984) *Caring: A Feminine Approach to Ethics and Moral Education*, Berkeley, CA: University of California Press.

—— (1992) *The Challenge to Care in Schools*, New York: Teachers College Press.

Noffke, S. (1995) "Action research and democratic schooling: problematics and potentials," in Noffke, S. and Stevenson, R. (eds) *Educational Action Research: Becoming Practically Critical*, New York: Teachers College Press, pp. 1–10.

Noffke, S. and Stevenson, R. (eds) (1995) *Educational Action Research: Becoming Practically Critical*, New York: Teachers College Press.

Peters, R.S. (1966) *Ethics and Education*, London: Allen and Unwin.

Revans, R. (1982) *The Origins and Growth of Action Learning*, Bromley: Chartwell-Bratt.

Shumsky, A. (1958) *The Action Research Way of Learning: An Approach to In-service Education*, New York: Bureau of Publications, Columbia University, Teachers College.

Stenhouse, L. (1975) *An Introduction to Curriculum Research and Development*, London: Heinemann.

—— (1983) *Authority, Education and Emancipation*, London: Heinemann.

Stevenson, R., Noffke, S., Flores, E. and Granger, S. (1995) "Teaching action research: a case study," in Noffke, S. and Stevenson, R. (eds) *Educational Action Research: Becoming Practically Critical*, New York: Teachers College Press, pp. 60–73.

Taba, H. and Noel, N. (1957) *Action Research: A Case Study*, Washington, DC: Association for Supervision and Curriculum Development, NEA.

Zeichner, K. and Gore, J. (1995) "Using action research as a vehicle for student teacher reflection: a social reconstructionist approach," in Noffke, S. and Stevenson, R. (eds) *Educational Action Research: Becoming Practically Critical*, New York: Teachers College Press, pp. 13–30.

9 Controversial issues, evidence and pedagogy

Fraser, D.M. (1963) *Deciding What to Teach*, Washington, D.C.: National Education Association.

Lewin, K. (1946) "Action research and minority problems," *Journal of Social Issues*, 2: 44–46.

Peters, R.S. (1966) *Ethics and Education*, London: Allen and Unwin.

Rokeach, M. (1973) *The Nature of Human Values*, New York: Free Press.

Simon, S.B., Howe, H. and Kirschenbaum, H. (1972) *Values Clarification: A Handbook of Practical Strategies for Teachers and Students*, New York: Hart.

Stenhouse, L. (1975) *An Introduction to Curriculum Research and Development*, London: Heinemann.

—— (1983) *Authority, Education and Emancipation*, London: Heinemann.

10 Ethics, inquiry and practical reason: towards an improved pedagogy

Abelard, P. (1904) *Sic et Non*, trans. and ed. James Harvey Robinson, *Readings in European History*, 2 Vols. Boston, MA: Ginn & Co., 1904–06, Vol. I: *From the Breaking up of the Roman Empire to the Protestant Revolt*, pp. 450–51.

Aristotle (1998) *Nichomachean Ethics*, trans. J.L. Ackrill, J.O. Urmson and D. Ross, Oxford: Oxford University Press.

Carr, W. and Kemmis, S. (1986) *Becoming Critical: Education, Knowledge and Action Research*, Lewes, Sussex: Falmer Press.

Dewey, J. (1910) *How We Think*, Boston, MA: D.C. Heath.

—— (1938) *Logic: The Theory of Inquiry*, New York: Henry Holt.

Donohue, J.W. (1968) *St. Thomas Aquinas and Education*, New York: Random House.

Dunne, J. (1997) *Back to the Rough Ground: Phronesis and Techne in Modern Philosophy and Aristotle*, South Bend, IN: University of Notre Dame Press.

Egan, K. (1990) *Romantic Understanding: The Development of Rationality and Imagination*, New York: Routledge.

—— (1992) *Imagination in Teaching and Learning*, London: Routledge.

—— (2005) *An Imaginative Approach to Teaching*, San Francisco, CA: Jossey Bass.

Elliott, J. (ed.) (1993) *Reconstructing Teacher Education*, London: Falmer Press.

Hare, R.M. (1981) *Moral Thinking*, Oxford: Clarendon Press.

Kant, I. (1960) *Education*, Ann Arbor, MI: University of Michigan Press.

Marenbon, J. (1997) *The Philosophy of Peter Abelard*, Cambridge: Cambridge University Press.

National Education Association Code of Conduct, available online at: www.nea.org.

Oakeshott, M. (1933) *Experience and its Modes*, Cambridge: Cambridge University Press.

Ornstein, A.C. and Levine, D.U. (2005) *Foundations of Education*, 9th edn, Boston, MA: Houghton Mifflin (see Chapter 2, "The Teaching Profession").

Plato, *Republic*, available online at: http://classics.mit.edu//Plato/republic.html.

Postman, N. and Weingartner, C. (1969) *Teaching as a Subversive Activity*, New York: Delacorte Press.

Schubert, W.H. (1986) *Curriculum: Perspective, Paradigm and Possibility*, New York: Macmillan.

Sikes, J. (1961) *Peter Abelard*, New York: Russell and Russell.

Stenhouse, L. (1975) *An Introduction to Curriculum Research and Development*, London: Heinemann Education.

—— (1983) *Authority, Education and Emancipation*, London: Heinemann.

Warnock, M. (1976) *Imagination*, London: Faber.

11 Teachers' human values and ideologies

Allport, G.W., Vernon, P.E. and Lindzey, G. (1960) *A Study of Value*, Boston, MA: Houghton Mifflin.

Dewey, John (1938) *Logic: The Theory of Inquiry*, New York: Henry Holt.

Feather, N.T. (1971) "Test–retest reliability of individual values and value systems," *Australian Psychologist*, 6: 181–88.

Lynch, K. (1989) *The Hidden Curriculum, Reproduction in Education: An Appraisal*, London: Falmer.

McKernan, J. (1996) *Curriculum Action Research*, 2nd edn, London: Kogan Page.

McKernan, J. and Russell, J. (1980) "Differences of religion and sex in the value systems of Northern Ireland adolescents," *British Journal of Social and Clinical Psychology*, 19: 115–18.

Peters, R.S. (1966) *Ethics and Education*, London: Allen and Unwin.

Rokeach, M. (1973) *The Nature of Human Value*, New York: Free Press.

Stenhouse, L. (1975) *An Introduction to Curriculum Research and Development*, London: Heinemann.

12 The countenance of evaluation and the special place of action research

Bennett, C. (1993) "Teacher-researchers: all dressed up and no place to go?," *Educational Leadership*, 51 (2), October: 69–70.

Bobbitt, F. (1918) *The Curriculum*, Boston, MA: Houghton Mifflin.

Corey, S. (1953) *Action Research to Improve School Practices*, New York: Teachers College Press, Columbia University.

Denzin, N. (1970) *The Research Act in Sociology*, London: Butterworths.

Dewey, J. (1929) *The Sources of a Science of Education*, New York: Horace Liveright.

—— (1966) *Democracy and Education*, New York: The Free Press.

Eisner, E. (2002) *The Educational Imagination*, 3rd edn, Columbus, OH: Merrill Prentice Hall.

Elliott, J. (1981) Action research: a framework for self evaluation in schools. Working Paper No. 1, Schools Council Program 2, Teacher–Pupil Interaction and the Quality of Learning Project, Cambridge: Cambridge Institute of Education.

—— (ed.) (1993) *Reconstructing Teacher Education: Teacher Development*, London: Falmer Press.

Fetterman, David (2001) *Foundations of Empowerment Evaluation*, Thousand Oaks, CA: Sage.

Fetterman, D.M., Kaftarian, S. and Wandersman, A. (eds) (1996) *Empowerment Evaluation: Knowledge and Tools for Self-assessment and Accountability*, Newbury Park, CA: Sage.

Hamilton, D. (1976) *Curriculum Evaluation*, London: Open Books.

Kelly, A.V. (1989) *The Curriculum: Theory and Practice*, 3rd edn, London: Paul Chapman.

MacDonald, B. (1973) "Educational evaluation of the National Development Programme in Computer Assisted Learning. A Programme Proposal prepared for consideration by Programme Committee of the National Programme," unpublished paper.

—— (1975) "Evaluation and the control of education," in Tawney, D. (ed.) *Curriculum Evaluation Today: Trends and Implications*, London: Macmillan, pp. 125–36.

McKernan, J. (1991) "Action inquiry: studied enactment," in Short, E. (ed.) *Forms of Curriculum Inquiry*, Albany, NY: State University of New York Press, pp. 309–26.

—— (1996) *Curriculum Action Research: A Handbook of Methods and Resources for the Reflective Practitioner*, 2nd edn, London: Kogan Page.

Parlett, M. and Hamilton, D. (1972) "Evaluation as illumination: a new approach to the study of educational programmes," Occasional Paper No. 9, Edinburgh: Centre for Research in the Educational Sciences, Edinburgh University.

Revans, R. (1982) *The Origins and Growth of Action Learning*, Bromwell: Chartwell-Bratt.

Schon, D. (1983) *The Reflective Practitioner: How Professionals Think in Action*, New York: Basic Books.

—— (1987) *Educating the Reflective Practitioner*, San Francisco, CA: Jossey Bass.

Scriven, M. (1967) "The methodology of evaluation," in Stake, R. (ed.) *Perspectives of Educational Evaluation*, Chicago, IL: Rand McNally, pp. 39–89.

Sockett, H. (1976) "Teacher accountability," *Proceedings of the Philosophy of Education Society*, Summer: 34–57.

Stake, R. (1967) "The countenance of educational evaluation," *Teachers College Record*, 68, April: 523–40.

Stenhouse, L. (1975) *An Introduction to Curriculum Research and Development*, London: Heinemann.

—— (1981) "What counts as research?," *British Journal of Educational Studies*, 29 (2), June: 113.

—— (1983) *Authority, Education and Emancipation*, London: Heinemann.

Stufflebeam, D. (1971) *Educational Evaluation and Decision-making*, Ithaca, IL: Peacock.

Trow, M. (1957) "Comment on participant observation and interviewing: a comparison," *Human Organization*, 16: 33–35.

Tyler, R.W. (1949) *Basic Principles of Curriculum and Instruction*, Chicago, IL: University of Chicago Press.

Index